CONSTITUTIONAL ISSUES

ABORTION

CONSTITUTIONAL ISSUES

ABORTION

Mark Tushnet

A HAROLD STEINBERG BOOK

Facts On File, Inc.

AN INFOBASE HOLDINGS COMPANY

Abortion

Facts On File, Inc.
11 Penn Plaza
New York, NY 10001

Library of Congress Cataloging-in-Publication Data
Tushnet, Mark V., 1945–
    Abortion / Mark Tushnet.
    p. cm. (Constitutional issues)
    "A Harold Steinberg book."
    Includes bibliographical references and index.
    ISBN 0-8160-2503-7 (alk. paper)
    1. Abortion—Law and legislation—United States. 2. Civil
rights—United States. I. Title. II. Series
KF3771.T87 1996
344.73'04192—dc 20   95-47284
[347.3044192]

Contents

Publisher's Preface

According to many political observers, the enduring legacy of the Reagan-Bush presidencies may not be any legislation or program; rather, it may be their appointment, between them, of five United States Supreme Court justices (O'Connor, Scalia, Kennedy, Souter and Thomas)—and Justice Rehnquist as chief justice—who will influence the course of constitutional law for decades.

This observation is a reflection of the Supreme Court's prominence in the political, social and economic life of the country—an influence that has never been greater than in the past fifty years. In recent decades, for example, our entire political structure has been changed by reapportionment cases that have altered the manner in which elected representatives are chosen. Further, the Court's decision in *Brown v. Board of Education* in 1954 ushered in the civil rights revolution.

The Court's decisions on other social issues have wrought even greater changes. Specifically, its decision on abortion in *Roe v. Wade* in 1973 attracted controversy from the moment it was handed down and has remained at the center of one of the most volatile issues of our day. This latest book in the *Constitutional Issues* series examines abortion as a constitutional issue. Prior to *Roe v. Wade*, going back to the mid-1800s, performing an abortion was in most places a criminal act, covered by state laws intended to protect women from unqualified practitioners. As the twentieth century advanced, progress in medicine reduced the dangers of the procedure, while increased frankness in the public sphere allowed a more open discussion of sexuality. Abortion came to be viewed as a fundamental individual freedom—a constitutionally protected right. It is the conflict between individual freedoms as guaranteed in the Constitution and competing states' rights that has fueled the debate in the Court.

Professor Mark Tushnet, a recognized authority on the Supreme Court, explores in depth the Court's rulings on abortion, as well as the processes through which these decisions were reached. Professor Tushnet is associate dean of the Georgetown Law Center. He is a graduate of Yale Law School and served as law clerk to Supreme Court Justice Thurgood Marshall.

The previous books in the *Constitutional Issues* series are *Freedom of the Press* by Professor Bernard Schwartz and *The Death Penalty*, also by Professor Tushnet.

Harold Steinberg
Series Publisher

Author's Preface

The Supreme Court's decisions on abortion have been among its most controversial. This book attempts to provide readers with an explanation of how the Court has dealt with the constitutional issues associated with abortion. It avoids discussions of the merits of different policies regarding abortion, and deals with the politics of abortion only when political matters have had some impact on the development of the Court's constitutional jurisprudence. As Chapter 1 stresses, however, the case for treating abortion as a constitutional issue is more difficult than the case against doing so. As a result, Chapter 1 spends substantially more space on "defending"—really, explaining—the arguments for treating abortion as a constitutional issue than it does on challenging those arguments.

Readers should know that as a law clerk for Justice Thurgood Marshall when *Roe v. Wade* was decided, I drafted the letter reprinted in Appendix C. My recollection, which may be imperfect, is that Justice Marshall, after learning that Justices William Brennan and Potter Stewart had been expressing some concern about Justice Harry Blackmun's proposed opinion, decided to send Blackmun a letter saying that he agreed with what he understood to be their concerns.

1

Abortion as a Constitutional Issue

Abortions have been performed since before the United States became a nation. Most were illegal under the common law. In the late nineteenth century legislatures enacted statutes defining more precisely the circumstances under which performing an abortion would be illegal. By the 1960s a strong current of opinion had developed criticizing the severity of existing antiabortion statutes. Reformers had achieved some legislative successes: Prominent legal reform groups urged that abortion laws be made less restrictive, and some state legislatures had agreed. These reform successes themselves generated opposition, and antiabortion groups had begun to mobilize against reforms in the early 1970s.

Efforts to persuade legislatures to modify restrictive abortion laws went hand in hand with challenges to the constitutionality of such laws. In 1973 the Supreme Court's decisions in *Roe v. Wade* (involving a traditional restrictive abortion law) and *Doe v. Bolton* (involving a more modern, somewhat less restrictive one) found that restrictive abortion laws violated the Constitution.[1]

Those decisions made abortion law even more contentious, as antiabortion advocates sought legislation that would somehow reduce the number of abortions while still surviving judicial review. By the early 1990s it seemed possible that the Supreme Court would abandon its two-decade effort to deal with abortion as a constitutional issue. Instead, in *Planned Parenthood of Southeastern Pennsylvania v. Casey* (1992), the Supreme Court endorsed what it called the central holding of *Roe* and *Doe*, reaffirming that the Constitution barred states from enacting abortion laws that placed what the prevailing opinion by Justices Sandra Day O'Connor, Anthony Kennedy, and David Souter called *undue burdens* on a woman's right to choose to have an abortion.

Why should abortion be a *constitutional* issue? Of course, people in any society have differing views about whether their laws should allow abortion at all, and about the extent to which the law should regulate abortions. In our constitutional system, most disagreements about public policy are decided by majority vote. State governments invoke what lawyers call their *police powers* to regulate health and safety, and even to adopt regulations designed to enforce the purely moral views held by a majority of the voters (to ban gambling, for example).

(The national government, acting through Congress and the President, has more limited powers. The Constitution lists some powers Congress has—it can regulate interstate commerce and develop rules for the District of Columbia, for example—and, ordinarily, Congress can legislate only if it ties what it does to one of these so-called *enumerated powers*. Most abortion regulations are adopted at the state level, but there is one important exception: Congress has the power to spend money for the public welfare. When it enacts a spending program, Congress can impose some conditions on the use of its money. As a result, Congress has limited the use of federal money to pay for abortions in the general Medicaid health program.)

Sometimes the Constitution limits what state governments can do. Even in attempting to enforce health and safety, they cannot violate these limits. It might make it easier to enforce regulations about what sorts of chemicals are used in factories, for example, if health inspectors could simply walk in whenever they wanted. However, the Fourth Amendment, which prohibits unreasonable searches, may be interpreted to mean that safety inspectors have to go to a judge in order to have a workplace safety inspection approved.

State laws limiting abortions clearly fall within the general scope of a state government's police powers. If abortions are not completely prohibited, regulations might be designed to ensure that abortions occur under safe conditions—an exercise of the police power to regulate health. More controversially, limits on abortion can protect the life—or, as the Supreme Court has put it, the potential life—of the fetus. The fetus need not be considered a human being because states can use their police powers to protect nonhuman entities. Laws against abuse of animals or against destroying historic buildings, for example, are clearly within the states' police powers. Perhaps most controversially, limits on abortion can express a majority's view that abortions are simply wrong.

To make abortion a constitutional issue, then, we have to find some limit in the Constitution on a government's police powers. Public discussion of abortion has tended to use the word *privacy* to describe that limit. However, there is no "privacy amendment" to the Constitution: no constitutional provision specifically mentions a right to privacy, as the First Amendment mentions a right to free speech. The constitutional case against state regulation of abortion has had to be constructed out of different materials. How sturdy—or flimsy—is it?

The materials that follow systematically present the case *for* treating abortion as a constitutional issue. The reason for that approach is straightforward. The case *against* doing so is almost entirely negative: the Constitution does not mention abortion, privacy, or the right to choose, and none of the arguments for treating abortion as a constitutional issue is enough to overcome that silence. To assess the case against treating abortion as a constitutional issue, we therefore have to examine in some detail the case in favor.

The Constitution and Unenumerated Rights: The Ninth Amendment

When the Constitution was first proposed, its opponents, motivated by a wide range of concerns, discovered that many people were concerned that the Constitution gave power to the new national government but included few explicit restrictions on the new government's power. Taking advantage of that, the Constitution's opponents mounted a sustained campaign against the Constitution's failure to include a bill of rights. James Madison, leading the Constitution's supporters in Virginia, and his colleagues in other states promised that their first act, once the new government went into operation, would be to propose a set of amendments that would expressly limit the national government's powers.

Madison was not enthusiastic about the Bill of Rights he did introduce. He thought that the unamended Constitution actually did limit the government's power appropriately, by its system of checks and balances and by some specific limits such as a ban on retroactive criminal laws. He was also concerned, though, that if the Constitution listed specific constitutional rights, such as a right to free expression, it might be interpreted to mean that *no other* rights existed. This distinction between constitutionally enumerated rights and unenumerated rights lies at the heart of the constitutional controversy over abortion.

The first Congress, which proposed the Bill of Rights, attempted to deal with Madison's concern by adopting the Ninth Amendment. The first eight amendments are what we usually call the Bill of Rights. They list a set of rather specific constitutional rights—to free speech (First Amendment), to keep and bear arms (Second Amendment), to confront witnesses against defendants in criminal trials (Sixth Amendment). Of course, interpreting *these*

ABORTION

provisions is not always easy, but the Constitution's words do provide some guidance.

The Ninth Amendment is different. It states, "The enumeration in the Constitution, of certain rights, shall not be construed to deny or disparage others retained by the people." What does this mean? Most obviously, it tries to rule out a certain kind of argument. Suppose someone says that the Constitution protects a right to privacy. An opponent responds, "Because the right to privacy is not listed in the first eight amendments or anywhere else, the Constitution does not protect such a right." This response takes the enumeration of rights in the first eight amendments and elsewhere in the Constitution as an argument against the existence of a right to privacy, or as an argument that courts should not enforce a right to privacy as vigorously as they enforce free speech rights. The Ninth Amendment says that such a response is inadequate: The response quite literally construes the enumeration to deny or disparage other rights.

The Ninth Amendment seems to do more than that, however. At the very least, it acknowledges that there *are* some unenumerated rights retained by the people, although it does not tell us what those rights are, or how to identify them. Further, the Ninth Amendment was rarely cited in cases prior to those leading to the Supreme Court's abortion decisions, and, as a result, clearly defining the limits and rights granted by the amendment has been made that much more difficult.[2] Judge Robert Bork said that, as far as he could tell, it was as if a giant inkblot covered the words that would tell us what the Ninth Amendment meant.

The first step in understanding the Ninth Amendment is to figure out *which government* it addresses. The First Amendment is explicitly directed at Congress: "Congress shall make no law respecting an establishment of religion . . ." Most of the other provisions of the Bill of Rights are stated more generally, and might have been interpreted to acknowledge rights that both the national and state governments had to respect. For example, the Fifth Amendment's statement that no one shall "be deprived of life, liberty, or property, without due process of law" does not refer explicitly to Congress or the national government.

In 1833 the Supreme Court held that the Fifth Amendment restricted only the national government (*Barron v. Baltimore*).[3] That decision was not controversial at the time. A few years later, though, some constitutional thinkers associated with the movement to abolish slavery began to rethink the decision. They believed that slavery deprived slaves of their liberty without due process. Slavery, though,

4

was created by state law, and these abolitionists therefore had to argue that the Fifth Amendment restricted state governments as well. Although these arguments were not successful before the Civil War, they played a role, as we will see, in the framing of the Fourteenth Amendment, enacted after the war. Their legacy, then, affects the contemporary debate about unenumerated rights.

If the Bill of Rights restricts only the national government, the Ninth Amendment becomes a real puzzle. Scholars have identified two sources of unenumerated rights: in state law or in what has been called a *higher law,* a natural law of fundamental rights.

If unenumerated rights are founded in the laws of each individual state, states could deny them. Unenumerated rights could not be invoked against state governments: States could use their ordinary police powers to regulate abortions or any other aspect of privacy. The concern here is that it then becomes difficult to understand the Ninth Amendment's legal effect: What restrictions does it place on the national government?

Suppose a state constitution protected the right of its residents to engage in gambling. No one would contend that such a state constitutional right had any effect on Congress's power to regulate interstate commerce by prohibiting gambling because Congress can use its powers to override state law, even if the state law is described as a state-based constitutional right. Unenumerated rights based only on state law, then, really cannot restrict national power.

The alternative is to say that unenumerated rights are founded on some higher law. Historians and legal scholars have described that higher law by a number of terms: natural rights, God-given rights, background rights, fundamental rights. The terms signal different ways of identifying what these unenumerated rights are, a topic which is discussed later. For now, the primary point is that once we recognize unenumerated rights based on a higher law, it is hard to understand why *only* the national government has to respect those rights. If you have a natural or God-given or fundamental right to engage in your chosen profession, for example, it is hard to see why it is wrong for the national government to restrict that right but permissible for a state government to do so.

Constitutional scholars remain divided over the source of the unenumerated rights recognized in the Ninth Amendment. Until about a generation ago, there was a substantial consensus that those rights were based on state law. Today, opinion is much more divided; probably only a slight majority of those who have studied the question believe that the Ninth Amendment recognizes rights based on a higher law, and that it therefore restricts state governments as well as the national government.

It has sometimes been suggested that the Ninth Amendment is a moral and political statement rather than a legal one. That is, it is aimed at legislators, cautioning them against enacting laws that infringe on important though unenumerated rights. According to this view, the Ninth Amendment makes it clear that arguments like the following have a basis in the Constitution: "The proposal you are considering does restrict important rights, and you shouldn't think that it is enough for you to point out that those rights are not listed in the Constitution; you have to have a pretty good reason for enacting the proposal."

This suggestion runs against the words of the amendment itself. There may be constitutional provisions that are moral or political directions to legislators rather than legal restrictions on government power, but the Ninth Amendment's words seem to mean that it is not one of them. Consider what happens under this suggestion if a litigant petitions the courts to enforce an unenumerated right to restrict government power. The court responds that it enforces only legal restrictions on government power, and that the Ninth Amendment is a moral or political command, which the courts do not enforce. That treats enumerated rights as legal rights, enforceable by the courts, and unenumerated rights as something else, not enforceable by the courts. That, in turn, seems to be taking (or construing) the enumeration of certain rights as a reason for denying or disparaging unenumerated rights.

The arguments for treating the Ninth Amendment as justifying the courts in enforcing unenumerated rights are not so overwhelming as to make such judicial action uncontroversial. They are, however, good enough to support the conclusion that judicial enforcement of unenumerated rights is not without *some* support in the Constitution's text.

Fundamental Rights and Other Constitutional Provisions

The Ninth Amendment is not the only textual basis for protecting unenumerated rights. Courts, scholars, and litigants have relied on several other provisions:

The privileges and immunities clause Section 2 of Article IV of the Constitution says that "The citizens of each state shall be entitled to all privileges and immunities of citizens in the several states." Drawn from the Articles of Confederation, Article IV's *privileges and immunities* clause guarantees equal treatment within each state, no matter where a person comes from. It was one of the main provisions demonstrating that the Constitution created a single nation.

At the same time, though, everyone knew that states should be allowed to treat their residents differently from people who were just passing through. Citizens of other states had to be given local "privileges and immunities," but that category did not cover everything a state government offered. So, what were privileges and immunities?

In 1823, Justice Bushrod Washington (President George Washington's favorite nephew) decided a case about the clause while sitting as a lower-court judge in Pennsylvania. New Jersey barred nonresidents from gathering oysters in the state's waters, and a Pennsylvanian challenged the statute as a violation of the privileges and immunities clause. Justice Washington provided later generations with the standard definition of privileges and immunities: They were *"fundamental*; which belong of right to the citizens of all free governments . . . What these fundamental principles are, it would be more tedious than difficult to enumerate. They may all, however, be comprehended under the following general heads: protection by the government, with the right to acquire and possess property of every kind, and to pursue and obtain happiness and safety . . ." *(Corfield v. Coryell*, 1823).[4] The right to take oysters, though, was not fundamental, so the New Jersey statute was constitutional.

The idea that the legal term *privileges and immunities* referred to fundamental rights was taken up by abolitionists who frequently referred to *Corfield v. Coryell* as they challenged slavery. A few abolitionist theorists argued that slavery violated the existing Constitution precisely because it denied slaves the fundamental rights Washington's opinion recognized.

After the Civil War the Fourteenth Amendment used the language of the privileges and immunities clause. Its first sentence states, "All persons born or naturalized in the United States . . . are citizens of the United States and of the State wherein they reside." The next sentence is, "No State shall make or enforce any law which shall abridge the privileges and immunities of citizens of the United States." Most proponents of the Amendment believed that it carried into the Constitution Justice Washington's definition of protected privileges and immunities. Article IV's clause guaranteed equality: Whatever fundamental rights states gave their own citizens had to be given to nonresidents. The Fourteenth Amendment, in contrast,

7

had substantive content: States could not deny fundamental rights even to their own citizens.

The Fourteenth Amendment was adopted in 1868. Five years later the Supreme Court construed it for the first time (*Slaughterhouse Cases*, 1873).[5] The setting did not encourage an expansive interpretation of the amendment. Although, as the Court put it, the main aim of the amendment was to ensure "the freedom of the slave race, the secure and firm establishment of that freedom, and the protection of the newly-made freeman and citizen from the oppressions of those who had formerly exercised unlimited domain over him," the case before the Court involved a simple commercial regulation. Responding to concerns about pollution and illness associated with the slaughterhouses where cattle were butchered, the Louisiana legislature had passed a statute giving a single company a monopoly over slaughtering in New Orleans. (Although there have been suggestions that the monopolists bribed legislators to get the statute enacted, recent scholarship indicates that, bribery or not, there were serious health problems associated with butchering in New Orleans, and requiring all butchering to be done at one location made sense.)[6] Butchers who could no longer practice their trade challenged the monopoly as a violation of the Fourteenth Amendment.

A five-justice majority of the Supreme Court read the privileges and immunities clause narrowly and upheld Louisiana's law. The Court agreed that it barred states from violating *certain* substantive rights. But, it said, the amendment did not incorporate Justice Washington's full set of "fundamental" rights. Focusing on the clause's language, Justice Samuel Miller pointed out that the clause protected the privileges and immunities of citizens of the United States, rather than, as Article IV said, citizens of the several states. For Miller, this showed that the Fourteenth Amendment created a special category of rights fundamental to citizenship *of the United States*, that is, rights that were specially associated with the nation. For example, Miller said that every citizen had a right to travel to the nation's capital unimpeded by any state regulation, and to the protection of the national government while on the high seas.

Obviously, this was a far more restrictive conception of privileges and immunities than Justice Washington had offered. Justice Stephen Field, writing for the four dissenters, thought that the Fourteenth Amendment would have been "a vain and idle enactment" unless it protected a broader list of fundamental rights. For Field, Justice Washington's notion was correct: The Fourteenth Amendment barred states from abridging those fundamental rights "which of right belong to the citizens of all free governments." Among them,

Field wrote, was "the right to pursue a lawful employment in a lawful manner." The butchering monopoly violated that right.

The Supreme Court's narrow definition of Fourteenth Amendment privileges and immunities has prevailed to this day. The idea that the Constitution *must* protect fundamental rights, even if not enumerated, has nonetheless persisted. Indeed, two decades after the *Slaughterhouse Cases* the Supreme Court began to use the Fourteenth Amendment's due process clause as a sword to strike down state laws it believed violated the fundamental right to contract as one pleased. Justice Field's vision of the Constitution prevailed, even though the later Court relied on a provision whose words were less suitable than the privileges and immunities clause.

The due process clause The Constitution twice says that government may not deprive people of liberty without due process of law. Although the *Barron v. Baltimore* decision in 1833 held that the Fifth Amendment's due process clause restricted only the national government, after the Civil War a due process provision was written into the Fourteenth Amendment, where it expressly restricts state governments.

The words of the due process clause seem to give it only a procedural meaning: If a state is going to take my liberty or property, it has to use fair procedures. Understood in that way, the due process clause would not limit the substance of what government could do, but would simply regulate the way it went about doing what it wanted.

A purely procedural interpretation of the due process clause is particularly well suited to the Fourteenth Amendment. That Amendment has three clauses: the privileges and immunities clause, the due process clause, and a ban on state actions that deny the equal protection of the laws. These could be understood to deal with the three ways a government could try to oppress its citizens. It could adopt oppressive substantive laws, but the privileges and immunities clause bans that. Or it could use unfair procedures to take people's liberty or property, but the due process clause bans that. Or, finally, it could administer the law unevenly, oppressing a portion of the population, but the equal protection clause bans that.

The Supreme Court's narrow interpretation of the privileges and immunities clause in the *Slaughterhouse Cases* meant that clause could not check oppressive substantive laws. The pressure to have some constitutional barrier to such laws, though, persisted. Within a generation of the *Slaughterhouse Cases* the Supreme Court began to invoke the due process clause to protect unenumerated fundamental rights. These so-called "substantive due process" cases became the foundation for the Court's protection of an unenumerated right of privacy—even though, as one scholar has said, the term "substantive due process" is "a contradiction in terms—sort of like 'green pastel redness.' "[7]

In fact, however, the notion of substantive due process has rather deep roots in Anglo-American law. The term usually is traced to the Magna Carta of 1215, which barred the king from acting without "process of law." Over the centuries the term *due process* began to refer to a requirement that governments avoid arbitrary actions. Before the Civil War, one state court had held government regulation of business—a ban on use or possession of liquor, for example—to violate the state's due process clause.[8] In the notorious *Dred Scott* case, the United States Supreme Court said that a congressional statute banning slavery in federal territories would violate the Fifth Amendment's due process clause.[9]

By 1868, when the Fourteenth Amendment was adopted, the notion that governments could not act arbitrarily was universally accepted, and it was not a distortion of the era's legal language to say that the due process clause banned arbitrary action. Of course, saying that the due process clause bans arbitrary action does not tell us what actions are arbitrary and therefore unconstitutional. It does, however, provide additional textual support for the proposition that the Constitution protects unenumerated rights.

The establishment clause The First Amendment provides that "Congress shall make no law respecting an establishment of religion." Interpreting the establishment clause, the Supreme Court has indicated that laws whose "primary purpose" is advancing religion are unconstitutional. Occasionally people argue that this means that laws *motivated* by religious concerns should be unconstitutional.

Even scholars initially attracted to that argument have generally ended up rejecting it.[10] The difficulty arises in that many different laws may have religious motivations without becoming establishments of religion: Support for civil rights laws or for expansive public assistance to the poor may be based on religious grounds, and yet no one would seriously contend that they are therefore unconstitutional.

Many scholars reject the proposition that we can tell whether we have an establishment of religion by looking at the legislature's motives. However, even if impermissible motives have something to do with the establishment clause, the strongest argument likely is that laws motivated *only* by religious reasons—and by nothing else—are impermissible. The legal philosopher Ronald Dworkin has developed an elaborate argument that restrictive abortion laws necessarily rest on a view of the sanctity of human life that can only be characterized as religious.[11] If Dworkin's argument were persuasive, it might show that restrictive abortion laws were establishments of religion. Dworkin does draw that conclusion, but most of the commentary on Dworkin's work is quite skeptical. His critics believe that there are many nonreligious reasons for supporting restrictive abortion laws, not all of which are closely connected to the idea that human life is sacred. Dworkin's argument addresses these criticisms by adopting a broad definition of sacredness, which itself indicates to his critics that his argument is weak.

Relying on Fundamental Rights in Constitutional Law: The Early Years

Except for the period between 1937 and 1965, the Supreme Court has consistently stated that there are unenumerated constitutional rights, and it sometimes enforced them. (As we will see, even during that period the concept of unenumerated rights remained part of constitutional law.)

In 1798, within a decade of the Constitution's adoption, one Supreme Court justice explicitly stated that the Court should invalidate laws that violate "certain vital principles in our free republican governments" (Justice Samuel Chase, in *Calder v. Bull*, 1798).[12] For Chase, those principles limited legislative power, whether or not they were stated in the Constitution. His examples were statutes that punished citizens for innocent actions, made a person a judge in his own cause, or took property from one person and gave it to another. "It is against all reason and justice," according to Chase, "for a people to entrust a legislature with such powers; and therefore, it cannot be presumed that they have done it."

A little more than a decade later, Chief Justice John Marshall justified a Court decision invalidating a state legislature's attempt to rescind land grants by invoking "general principles which are common to our free institutions" (*Fletcher v. Peck*, 1810).[13] (A corrupt state legislature had given the land to people who had bribed the legislators; the bribers then sold it to purchasers who were not aware of the bribery; a reform legislature tried to get the land back from the innocent purchasers.)

These early hints of a natural law Constitution with judicially enforceable unenumerated rights show that early justices were not averse to invoking unenumerated rights. However, they are not

11

strong precedents. Justice Chase actually voted to uphold the challenged statute in *Calder*. Most of his examples could be unconstitutional because they violated enumerated rights: procedural due process for the "judge in his own case" statute, the clause prohibiting a legislature from taking property for public use without just compensation in the "take from A to give to B" statute. Chief Justice Marshall found the land grant statute unconstitutional because it violated the provision barring statutes from impairing the obligation of contracts (the contract between the purchasers and the bribers).

The invocation of unenumerated rights can be bolstered against these criticisms. For example, Chase might point out that when a legislature took A's property to give it to B, it was not attempting to pursue some *public* use, only a private one, and it therefore was not covered by the takings clause. More dramatically, no specific constitutional provision appears to bar the government from making an innocent act unlawful. Consider a law banning earpiercing (with no pretense that the practice is medically unsafe), or banning people from wearing hats in public, or from wearing their hair in braids. *Something* seems to be wrong with those statutes—unless there is a decent police power justification for them—but nothing in the Constitution seems to acknowledge rights the statutes violate.

Relying on Fundamental Rights in Constitutional Law: The Discrediting and Revival of Substantive Due Process

Near the end of the nineteenth century the Supreme Court began to impose new limits on governmental regulation. Relying primarily on the due process clause as the source of an unenumerated "right to contract," the Court invalidated significant aspects of the reforms supported by labor unions and the Progressive political movement.

The Court's most famous—or notorious—decision gave the period its name. In *Lochner v. New York* (1905), the Court held unconstitutional a state statute imposing a maximum sixty-hour workweek for bakers.[14] The Court's majority rejected the argument that bakers who worked long hours somehow endangered the public, and it was not convinced that bakers who worked long hours were any more likely to fall ill from overwork than other workers, whose hours were not limited by law. No one contended, the Court said, that bakers were somehow unable to negotiate contracts freely with their employers, and if some bakers wanted to make more money for long hours of work, they had a constitutional right to do so.

Over the next three decades the Supreme Court adhered to the *Lochner* philosophy. The Court did uphold laws restricting the hours women and miners could work, believing that, unlike bakers, they needed protection from their own contracts (women for traditionalist reasons, miners because they worked in such isolation from the rest of the society that they could easily be exploited).[15] But it routinely rejected what the *Lochner* Court called "labor laws pure and simple"—Progressive Era reforms that aimed at alleviating what the reformers believed were conditions under which workers were exploited. States could not enact laws barring employers from insisting that their workers refrain from joining unions;[16] they could not set minimum wage requirements or regulate prices;[17] and, in one celebrated case, a lower court following the *Lochner* philosophy held unconstitutional New York's effort to create a worker's compensation system.[18]

From today's vantage point, many of the Court's decisions during the *Lochner* era seem misguided, though not all. During World War I a wave of anti-German and nativist sentiment swept the country. Nebraska's legislature enacted a statute barring *any* school from teaching modern languages, including German, to elementary school children. A teacher was convicted for using a book written in German as a reading text. The Supreme Court held the statute unconstitutional because it violated the rights of individuals to "contract, to engage in . . . common occupations of life to acquire useful knowledge, to marry, to establish a home and bring up children, . . . and generally to enjoy those privileges . . . essential to the orderly pursuit of happiness by free men" (*Meyer v. Nebraska*, 1923).[19] Two years later the Court invoked the same set of unenumerated rights to invalidate an Oregon law requiring that all children be sent to public schools (*Pierce v. Society of Sisters*, 1925).[20]

Labor unions and Progressive reformers assailed the *Lochner* philosophy from the start. They were assisted by an eloquent dissent in *Lochner* itself, written by Justice Oliver Wendell Holmes. Justice Holmes criticized the majority for relying on "an economic theory which a large part of the country does not entertain." According to Holmes, "a constitution is not intended to embody a particular economic theory, whether of paternalism . . . or of laissez faire." Instead, unless a legislature "infringe[d] fundamental principles as they have been understood by the traditions of our people and our law," the majority was entitled to have its way. (Holmes dissented in the Nebraska language case, but not in the Oregon public schools one.)

13

When the Great Depression of the 1930s provoked another round of aggressive legislation seeking to address the economic crisis, the Court's stance against that legislation provoked a constitutional crisis. The *Lochner* philosophy finally crumbled under an attack that had been going on since the *Lochner* era's onset. What was to replace it?

Lochner's critics were motivated by their disagreement with the Court's results and had a choice about how to express that disagreement. They could have said that the Court *could* enforce unenumerated rights but rejected the Court's identification of the liberty of contract as such a right. Instead, they argued that the Court had no business enforcing unenumerated rights. A stance of judicial restraint, they said, should replace the judicial activism that characterized the *Lochner* era.

At least in form, the critics who urged judicial restraint prevailed for a few decades. The urge to allow the courts to protect fundamental rights persisted, though. Judicial practice was less consistent with the philosophy of judicial restraint than the Court's official pronouncements suggested.

Only a few years after the Court apparently repudiated the effort to protect fundamental rights, the language of fundamental rights cropped up again. In 1942 the Supreme Court considered the constitutionality of an Oklahoma statute permitting the state to sterilize "habitual criminals," which the statute defined as those who had committed three "felonies involving moral turpitude" (*Skinner v. Oklahoma*, 1942).[21] Justice William O. Douglas wrote the Court's opinion invalidating the statute. He wrote that the statute dealt with "one of the basic civil rights of man. Marriage and procreation are fundamental to the very existence and survival of the race." Instead of finding the statute unconstitutional because it restricted fundamental rights, the Court relied on the Fourteenth Amendment's equal protection clause. The Oklahoma statute excluded violations of the prohibition laws and embezzlement from the definition of "felonies involving moral turpitude." According to Justice Douglas, "strict scrutiny of the classification which a state makes in a sterilization law is essential, lest unwittingly, or otherwise, invidious discriminations are made against groups . . ."

Justice Douglas's opinion in *Skinner* had two elements. First, it once again showed the Court willing to identify certain rights as fundamental. Second, legislation that treated people differently in connection with such rights had to satisfy the so-called "strict scrutiny" requirement. (As the strict scrutiny test evolved, it came to mean, as one scholar famously put it, that the scrutiny was "strict in theory, fatal in fact.")[22] The idea of strict scrutiny resurfaced in the later abortion decisions.

Before that, however, the Court continued to identify fundamental rights. In a series of decisions in the 1950s, for example, the Court held that people had a fundamental right of access to the courts.[23] As a result, statutes that made it impossible for poor people to exercise that right—by imposing a fee they could not afford—could not survive the strict scrutiny given to statutes that provided access to the courts to one group—those who could afford it—and denied it to the poor.

Even as the Court's official theory rejected any claim that it could directly enforce fundamental rights, the Court continued to do so indirectly. The tension between the official theory and the Court's practice was widely noted and scholars of the period tended to argue that the Court should more consistently adhere to the theory of judicial restraint. Often, when the Court invoked fundamental rights in the course of applying the equal protection clause, other critics thought that it would have been more honest to rely directly on the fundamental rights. The real problem in the Oklahoma sterilization case, to these critics, was not that the state treated embezzlers and chicken thieves differently, but that it imposed such a severe penalty on habitual felons: The Court's equal protection theory meant that the sterilization penalty could be imposed only if Oklahoma eliminated the exclusion of embezzlers from the category eligible for the penalty, but that, these critics thought, seemed to miss the basic point.

Even after the New Deal constitutional crisis and the official repudiation of the *Lochner* philosophy, the Court continued to act as if unenumerated fundamental rights played an important role in constitutional adjudication. For a few decades, that role was secondary—supporting equal protection decisions but not directly justifying the Court's invalidation of statutes. It took the emergence of a jurisprudence of privacy for fundamental rights to take the stage in a leading role.

Identifying Unenumerated Rights: Tradition

Running beneath Supreme Court decisions invalidating statutes because they violate enumerated constitutional rights has been a subterranean stream acknowledging that the courts could, and sometimes would, invalidate statutes because they violate unenumerated rights. What, though, are those rights?

Courts and scholars have relied on three general sources for identifying unenumerated or fundamental rights: tradition, precedent, and natural law (or philosophy, or human reason).

Even Justice Holmes, dissenting in *Lochner*, seemed to agree that legislatures could not "infringe fundamental rights as they have been understood by the traditions of our people." The argument for relying on tradition to identify fundamental rights is straightforward: The fact that for a long time we as a people have not let our government regulate some activity indicates that we believe we have a fundamental right to engage in it. That simple statement conceals some enormous difficulties.

One problem is that relying on tradition-based fundamental rights to invalidate new laws may obstruct legislatures in their efforts to adapt to new circumstances. Legislatures may agree that they properly did not try to regulate some activity in the past, but that new circumstances have made the problem more pressing than it used to be; the people of the state, acting through their legislature, should not be barred from addressing this newly important problem.

For example, legislatures in the past did not enact laws penalizing people for living in extended families rather than in nuclear (father-mother-children) families. Today, some legislatures may believe that some modest restrictions should be placed on extended families to encourage people to stay in nuclear families, which—legislatures may believe—contribute more than extended families do to social stability, productivity, and education. So, for example, a legislature might zone an area for single-family housing, and define the term to allow only nuclear families to live in the area. Relying on a tradition-based theory of fundamental rights, the Supreme Court invalidated such a zoning regulation (*Moore v. East Cleveland*, 1977), which had the effect of barring a grandmother from taking care of her grandchildren.[24]

The problem that tradition-based rights may inhibit appropriate adaptation to new circumstances does not arise in the abortion context. A more important problem does. A tradition-based argument could not possibly justify the courts in striking down legislation, like laws restricting the availability of abortions, that have been on the statute books for a long time. At most, the argument justifies invalidating new laws, or laws that only one or two cities or states have adopted. In *Roe v. Wade*, the dissents by Justices Rehnquist and White pointed out how widespread and long-standing abortion laws were. They believed that this was enough to show that the Court's decision could not be justified by invoking a fundamental right founded in tradition.

As judges and scholars have worked out the argument for identifying fundamental rights through tradition, the response offered by Justices Rehnquist and White has turned out to be weaker than they thought. The difficulty lies in what has come to be called the *level of generality* problem. Everything turns on how specifically or abstractly we define the right claimed to be fundamental. If the right is "the right to choose to have an abortion"—a relatively specific right—then a tradition-based analysis will lead to the conclusion that the right is not fundamental. But, if the right is "privacy" or "the right to make basic decisions central to a woman's life"—more general rights—perhaps a tradition-based analysis will lead to the conclusion that the right *is* fundamental. How, then, do we decide on what level of generality to specify the claimed right?

Justice Scalia suggested one answer: Choose "the most specific level at which a relevant tradition protecting, or denying protection to, the asserted right can be identified" (*Michael H. v. Gerald D.*, 1989).[25] This solves the problem where the person asserting the right is challenging widely adopted laws on the ground that they violate tradition, as in the abortion context.

The so-called "right to die" controversy helps identify one problem with Justice Scalia's proposal. Suppose we know that someone who has been fully informed about her medical condition decides that, all things considered, she would prefer to end her life now rather than endure what she expects to be an excruciating period of decline and dying. She therefore directs that, when she loses consciousness, she wants to be denied the nutrition that would keep her "alive." If the hospital asks a state court what it is legally allowed to do, what is the answer? The state might take the position that denying the patient nutrition amounts to allowing her to commit suicide, contrary to state law. The patient claims that she has a constitutionally protected right based on tradition to determine the course of her own medical treatment where matters of life and death are at stake. The state responds that she has no constitutionally protected right to commit suicide. Which tradition is more specific, the one denying protection to all forms of suicide, the one protecting patient choice in all matters of medical care, or the one protecting patient choice in the narrow circumstances presented here? It is not at all clear how to answer that question within Justice Scalia's framework.

Consider even more, the person challenging a novel form of regulation, such as a ban on extended families in areas zoned for single families. The challenger might say that, because there is no tradition *denying* protection to the underlying activity of living in an extended family, we must move to a higher level of abstraction, such as the right to live with your family as *you* define it. That right is protected by tradition, and so the zoning ordinance should be unconstitutional.

Those who defend the ordinance will reply, however, that the challenger has wrongly identified the underlying activity. It is not "living in an extended family," but "having living arrangements that cause the kinds of social problems to which the zoning ordinance responds." That activity includes vagrancy and other activities that governments have traditionally regulated. As a result, there *is* a tradition of denying protection to the activity.

As two critics have put it, "there is no universal metric of specificity against which to measure an asserted right."[26] The difficulty with Justice Scalia's suggested solution to the level of generality problem is that it shifts the focus of concern, and does so in a one-sided way. Instead of worrying about specifying the *right* at the proper level of generality, we now have to worry about specifying the underlying *activity* at the proper level of generality. No matter what the activity, there will always be a way of specifying it so that we can locate a tradition denying protection to it. Justice Scalia's solution to the level of generality problem is therefore a prescription for affirming all government regulations against claims that they violate tradition-based fundamental rights. As such, it moves outside the boundary of the effort to determine a method of identifying unenumerated fundamental rights protected against government regulation.

At present, there appears to be no solution to the level of generality problem in sight. If judges are to rely on tradition as a basis for invalidating widely adopted laws, they will have to defend their specification of the relevant tradition by referring to some other sources, such as precedent, or natural-law reasoning.

Identifying Unenumerated Rights: The Court's Decisions

One solution to the problem of identifying "the traditions of the people" lies in looking to the decisions governments have actually made. Statutes endorsed by the people's representatives are only one set of such decisions. Another are the decisions by the courts themselves. Perhaps, by examining the limits the courts have placed on government, we can identify fundamental rights that underlie or justify the courts' decisions.

Justice William O. Douglas provided the best example of this approach in his opinion for the Court in *Griswold v. Connecticut*

(1965).[27] The Court held unconstitutional a state statute making it a crime to use contraceptives. Examining the Court's prior decisions, Justice Douglas identified several in which the Court had protected rights that were not specifically enumerated. He relied on *Meyer* and *Pierce*, from the era of substantive due process. He also noted that the Court had given constitutional protection to a right of association, barring a state from forcing the National Association for the Advancement of Colored People to disclose its membership lists. The right of association may be related to rights of free expression, but it is not specifically enumerated.

According to Douglas, these opinions showed that the Court was willing to protect unenumerated rights that were somehow related to enumerated ones. He used the widely criticized metaphor that "specific guarantees in the Bill of Rights have penumbras, formed by emanations from those guarantees that help give them life and substance." Probably a better way to understand Douglas's argument is that specific guarantees were inserted into the Constitution because of the framers' concerns about particular kinds of government oppression. When the same concerns were triggered by government acts not specifically covered by the guarantees, the courts should still be ready to hold them unconstitutional.

What, then, were the concerns underlying the specific constitutional guarantees? Douglas argued that the concerns could be described as an interest in privacy. As he stated, "Would we allow the police to search the sacred precincts of marital bedrooms for telltale signs of the use of contraceptives? The very idea is repulsive to the notions of privacy surrounding the marriage relationship." (If the police have probable cause to believe that someone has committed a crime, such as using contraceptives, they can get a search warrant to look for physical evidence that the crime was committed.)

The idea of privacy in *Griswold* might have been confined to a concept of secrecy or informational privacy. In a separate opinion in *Doe v. Bolton*, Justice Douglas extended the argument by drawing on additional cases. He relied on classic free speech cases to support the proposition that "liberty" included "the autonomous control over the development and expression of one's intellect, interests, tastes, and personality." He relied on *Meyer* and *Griswold* to show that it included "freedom of choice in the basic decisions of one's life respecting marriage, divorce, procreation, contraception, and the education and upbringing of children." And, finally, he relied on *Skinner* and cases striking laws aimed at vagrants to show that it included "the freedom to care for one's health and person, freedom from bodily restraint or compulsion, freedom to walk, stroll, or loaf."

These interests might be described as interests in *decisional autonomy*—the right of each person to make decisions important to his or her life—rather than informational privacy. The Court's decisions, Douglas argued, established that the Constitution barred states from infringing on decisional autonomy. He agreed with the majority in *Roe v. Wade* that the interest in decisional autonomy was "broad enough to encompass a woman's decision whether or not to terminate her pregnancy."

Douglas's approach is vulnerable to several criticisms. First, the Constitution's specific guarantees may not have "penumbras" that protect unenumerated rights. The guarantees protect what they protect and nothing more. The cases Justice Douglas relied on should be understood, according to this criticism, as protecting specifically enumerated rights. So, for example, compulsory disclosure of membership lists should be treated as violating free speech rights, period.

Second, describing the interests protected by either specific constitutional provisions or their penumbras as interests in informational privacy *or* decisional autonomy is too broad. Perhaps the Constitution protects some unenumerated rights, but not a right that covers choice in matters of abortion.

The first criticism aims at the use of precedents to identify fundamental rights, and probably is best understood as a challenge to the idea that courts can enforce unenumerated fundamental rights. The second is more specific: It challenges the idea that we can read the precedents to support the broad right of privacy in abortion matters that Justice Douglas found.

Identifying Unenumerated Rights: The Idea of Natural Law

Another possible source of unenumerated rights is natural law. There is a long philosophical tradition of natural law reasoning. Although much natural law reasoning is founded on religious grounds, many philosophers believe that people can use purely secular premises to deduce particular conclusions about what governments can properly do. Philosophers have developed their arguments about abortion with great sophistication, and the best arguments have many details and qualifications that cannot be presented in this format. What follows is a sketch of the philosophical or natural law argument supporting a right to choose with respect to abortion. (Traditional natural law reasoning has deep religious roots, particularly in Roman Catholic moral theology. As a result, there is a substantial literature arguing against abortion rights on natural law grounds. Again, because the aim of this chapter is to explain how abortion can become a constitutional rather than a legislative issue, it does not discuss those arguments.)

The starting point for a natural law or fundamental rights argument for choice in matters of pregnancy and abortion is that pregnancy is burdensome, and an unwanted pregnancy is especially burdensome. The sheer physical aspects of an ordinary pregnancy include an increase in the woman's weight, water retention, fatigue, nausea (familiarly called morning sickness), back pain, and more. Indeed, one legal commentator suggests that if you read a description of the physical aspects of pregnancy without knowing what was being described, you would probably think that the person involved was quite ill.[28] And, of course, not all pregnancies are simple: Complications include strokes and heart attacks.

Women who choose not to have abortions typically find these burdens worth bearing, because they want to have and (usually) raise the child who will be born. What of women whose pregnancies are unwanted? If they find abortions unavailable, they may, in the end, be happy anyway. The course of their lives, though, will almost certainly be diverted. For some, bearing an unwanted child may mean abandoning career plans; for others, it may mean maintaining relationships with men with whom they would rather not be involved; for still others, it may mean confronting extremely straitened economic circumstances. Again, not every woman who bears an unwanted child will face these consequences and not every woman who does will end up thinking that her life was changed for the worse by the pregnancy. For those who do, however, the fact that the pregnancy is unwanted exacerbates the burdens of pregnancy.

The fact that pregnancy is burdensome shows why it is important, in developing a fundamental rights–based argument for abortion, to consider whether a fetus is a person in some relevant sense. No one denies that fetuses are members of the human species; the argument is about whether membership in the species—in itself and without any other characteristics—is morally significant.

Why should it matter that, on some arguments, fetuses are not persons? After all, the government can make it illegal to kill bald eagles even though bald eagles are not people. Why, then, can't the government make it illegal to kill a fetus even if the fetus is not a person? For those who believe that the right to choose is fundamental, the answer is that denying women the right to choose to have abortions imposes far more severe burdens on them than a ban on killing bald eagles imposes on hunters.

The claim that a fetus is not a person in a morally relevant sense is quite controversial. Philosophers have developed elaborate arguments about what might qualify a being as a person in that sense. The problem for them is how to distinguish, for example, a fetus from a new–born baby or from a person near the end of life who is in an apparently irreversible coma. No consensus among philosophers exists on this. For example, it cannot be that what qualifies something as a person is the potential to become a full-fledged person whose rights are uncontroversially entitled to respect: The person in a coma has no potential for such development, yet most philosophers think that that fact is quite irrelevant to questions about how we should treat people in comas.

To the extent that philosophers have narrowed the possibilities for defining *person* in a morally relevant sense, their definitions center on two features of personhood:

- a capacity to develop a plan of life, and to execute that plan, even if the assistance of others is required, or
- being part of a fairly dense network of social relations, which includes people with whom you have interacted in the past and who have developed ties of affection and respect for you.

Even these features cause some problems: Newborn babies do not have the capacity to develop a life plan and it is not clear that they are part of the kind of social network at stake.

However, proponents of these definitions suggest, whatever difficulties the definitions pose in other circumstances, they show that fetuses are not persons in a morally relevant sense. If so, they are just like bald eagles, and it is wrong to impose substantial burdens on women simply to avoid destroying fetuses.

Suppose that we concluded, though, that mere membership in the species was enough to make an entity a person, or that we found the arguments supporting the conclusion that a fetus is not a person so troublesome—because of their implications for newborn babies, for example—that we could not accept a natural rights argument for choice with respect to abortion if it required us to treat the fetus as anything other than a person. If the fetus is a person, does that necessarily imply that choice in abortion cannot be a fundamental right?

Here the answer is reasonably clear: The mere fact that a fetus is a person does not in itself rule out treating choice as a fundamental right. Sometimes, that is, people have a right to kill other people. The most dramatic example is the right of self-defense.

Both legally and, most people think, morally, a person can justifiably kill a person who is actively threatening his or her life.

The analogy between abortion and self-defense might support a fundamental right to choose to have an abortion when the woman's life is threatened by the pregnancy. Here much turns on how broadly we define *threat*. If we follow the analogy to self-defense in the law, the risk that the pregnant woman would die soon would have to be rather high, and there would have to be no other reasonable ways of reducing the threat. The direct analogy to self-defense, then, might support a right to choose only in rather narrow circumstances.

The self-defense analogy is not perfect. The core image of justifiable self-defense involves a person responding to someone who is wrongly attacking her. Some have argued that killing in self-defense is justified not by the threat to life alone but by the wrongfulness of the threat. The case is different, then, if the threat arises innocently. They have in mind cases like these: Someone is walking down a path, and is about to break a trip-wire that will fire a gun at your head; you have no time to shout a warning or even move (perhaps you have been tied to a chair), but you can shoot your own gun to kill the innocent hiker. Of the two innocent people, one must die, but which one?

Typically, philosophers and citizens alike find these kinds of questions quite difficult. Probably the most elaborate set of arguments about them involve what philosophers, drawing on Catholic natural law teaching, call "the principle of double effect." According to that principle, sometimes you can justifiably do something that has the effect of killing another person, but you cannot make the killing your direct purpose. Consider a nation at war. The president directs airplanes to drop bombs on a crucial arms plant, knowing that some innocent civilians who live in the area will die from the bombs. This may be justifiable. In contrast, the president should not direct the planes to drop bombs on innocent civilians to terrorize the survivors into rebelling against their government to end the war. In the first case the killing is an indirect effect of the attack on the arms plant, while in the second it is the very purpose of the bombing.

Applied to the abortion issue, the principle of double effect implies that it is not wrong to perform a hysterectomy on a pregnant woman with cancer of the uterus. The operation kills the fetus, but that is an undesired but inevitable effect of a procedure performed to save the woman's life. Proponents of the principle of double effect limit its application, however. Not all abortions done to save the woman's life fall within the principle. Sometimes the woman's life is saved by means of killing the fetus, as when the woman's life is endangered by the stresses the pregnancy places on her heart. An abortion done to save the woman's life under these circumstances is not within the principle of double effect, because killing the fetus is precisely what the procedure is designed to do.

The principle of double effect is itself controversial, in large part because it has proven difficult to work out distinctions between permissible indirect effects and impermissible direct ones. Most proponents of the principle of double effect argue that it makes abortions impermissible (even, for many, to preserve the life of the woman). For them, abortion simply is killing the fetus, nothing more; the woman, however, seeks to accomplish some other goal—saving her life—but she does so by directly killing an innocent person.

Critics, in contrast, argue that killing the fetus is *not* the very purpose of having an abortion. Many women who have abortions, they argue, would be happy to discover a technique by which the fetus could be removed from their bodies and sustained without their assistance. For these critics, the fact that abortions today necessarily lead to the fetus's death is an unfortunate, but wholly contingent, aspect of the procedure, just as the presence of innocent civilians near the arms plant is contingent.

If principles of natural law support applying the principle of double effect to abortion, there might be no fundamental right to choose with respect to abortion. There is an alternative philosophical analysis of the right to choose that has been enormously influential. This alternative develops the analogy to self-defense in a way that many have found compelling. Judith Jarvis Thompson, a philosopher at the Massachusetts Institute of Technology, developed this alternative in her article "A Defense of Abortion," published shortly before the Supreme Court decided *Roe v. Wade*.[29]

Thompson begins by asking readers to imagine a scenario: You have been kidnapped during the night by a society of music lovers and then connected to a world-famous violinist, who will die of kidney failure unless he remains connected to you for nine months. Without elaborating on the burdens that remaining connected impose, Thompson argues that you would commit no wrong in disconnecting yourself from the violinist even if you knew that he would die as a result—and even if remaining connected posed no threat to your life in the sense used when we talk about self-defense. And, she suggests, it should not matter if you ask someone else to help you if you cannot reach the tubes connecting you to the violinist; that suggestion deals with the fact that, in general, women can obtain abortions only with the assistance of someone else. Thompson concludes that you have a fundamental right to choose here, even if your choice results in the death of another person.

One element of the dying-violinist story is *coercion:* You did not consent to being connected to the violinist, and indeed were forced into the connection without your knowledge. To that extent Thompson's argument might show that the right to choose is fundamental where the pregnancy results from rape (and, of course, where the woman's life is endangered). Even this conclusion is worth emphasizing. Many people believe that abortions in cases of pregnancies resulting from rape should not be outlawed. Those who oppose choice on the ground that the fetus, a person, has a right to life equal to that of the woman have difficulty explaining why there should be a "rape" exception. After all, the fetus is hardly responsible for the initial coercion; it is as innocent as any other fetus, and killing it would be killing an innocent person.

Once again the scope of Thompson's argument, even to this point, might be controversial. The problem lies in defining coercion. The classic rape is clearly coercive. What, though, of a pregnancy resulting from sexual intercourse in a relationship where the man regularly beats the woman? Does her fear of being beaten if she refuses to have intercourse mean that she is raped? And, what of the case where the man threatens to leave the relationship and throw the woman into dire economic circumstances?

Thompson herself did not address these controversial aspects of the concept of coercion. Instead, she shifted the focus to what we might call "ordinary" sexual intercourse. Thompson asked readers to consider a woman who did not want to become pregnant and then had intercourse after taking appropriate precautions. She used the image of "people-seeds drift[ing] in the air like pollen." You can put screens on your windows, but even the best screens occasionally are defective, and a people-seed can drift in and take root. Because you took appropriate precautions, Thompson argues, you have not consented to having the developing "person-plant" in your house, and you can as justifiably remove it as you could disconnect yourself from the violinist.

Thompson completes her argument by pointing out that there are *always* additional precautions a person can take against the people-seeds: Seal the house even more tightly, for example. That, however, requires a person to submit to unreasonably restrictive burdens: A woman can substantially reduce the risk that she will not have an unwanted pregnancy if she never leaves her house and never engages in sexual intercourse. But, Thompson argues, avoiding the risk of getting into a situation in which you will think it appropriate to kill another person by imposing such severe restraints on your life is quite unreasonable.

Thompson's argument may not conclusively establish a broad fundamental right to choose. For example, what of pregnancies that result when voluntary intercourse occurs and the participants do not take reasonable precautions against pregnancy? Perhaps here the answer, from a fundamental rights perspective, is that the very inquiry into whether people took precautions when engaging in intercourse violates a different fundamental right—not the right to choose, but the right to keep intimate details about one's sexual life private.

Some opponents of the right to choose have tried to take on Thompson's argument directly. Judge John Noonan, for example, challenges the relatively antiseptic image of simply disconnecting yourself from the violinist and walking away, by describing in detail the way in which abortions kill fetuses.[30] His suggestion is that you would be less convinced about your right to disconnect yourself from the violinist if you knew that you were going to have to sit there and watch the violinist writhe in pain while dying.

There is one last point that might bolster the fundamental-rights argument for a right to choose. Thompson noted that she was not arguing that a person who chose to disconnect himself from the violinist was doing the *right* thing; indeed, she suggested, in many situations we would praise the person who chose to remain connected as a Good Samaritan.

Situations of Good Samaritanism analogous to abortion sometimes do arise. For example, some people suffering from kidney disease might benefit from a kidney transplant, and sometimes there are a fair number of people who *could* donate a kidney for the transplant. Our society, though, does not require anyone to do so; there are even cases where courts have refused to order close relatives of a person in need to donate an organ to save the relative's life. Proponents of the right to choose ask why, then, should only those women who become pregnant be forced to be Good Samaritans?

The natural rights–based arguments for a right to choose, like the text-based ones, are hardly conclusive. Each rests on controversial moral theories (as do arguments that fetuses have a right to life). But, like the text-based arguments, the natural-rights arguments are strong enough to help explain why abortion has become a constitutional issue.

Equality and Abortion

The "selective Good Samaritan" argument suggests a final constitutional approach to the question of abortion. Legal scholars relying on arguments like Thompson's have pointed out that, without a right to choose, burdens are imposed on *women*, but in our society we almost never impose similar burdens on men. Since the early 1970s the Supreme Court has been developing a constitutional law of gender equality. Under that law, states must apply the same rules to men and women unless they can show that different rules "serve important governmental objectives and [are] . . . substantially related to achievement of those objectives."[31] (In the jargon of constitutional law, laws classifying on the basis of gender must survive *intermediate scrutiny*.)

If laws restricting the availability of abortions are treated as forms of gender discrimination, would they satisfy the Court's requirements? Of course, no one questions that preserving human life is an important government purpose. The "Good Samaritan" argument points out, however, that that really is not the question. Rather, the question is whether there is an important government purpose in imposing burdens associated with restrictive abortion laws but not imposing burdens on men in similar situations. In particular, is there an important government purpose in restricting the availability of abortions—described for these purposes as "coerced continuation of pregnancy"—but not coercing men (and women) to donate their organs when that would save another person's life?

The argument for treating abortion as a constitutional issue takes the answer to be "No." Most scholars who have addressed the question agree, but some argue that the law in fact does treat men and women equally. First, they note, traditionally American draft laws have coerced men into serving in the military while exempting women. The draft thus serves as an example for the proposition that men as well as women are coerced into risking their lives in the service of some public goal.

Second, they suggest, pregnant women are not truly comparable to those asked to contribute an organ to save a life. Depending on the procedure involved, organ donations may be more (or less) risky than continuing a pregnancy through a full nine months. Perhaps more important, abortions are guaranteed to end the life of the fetus, while organ donations merely improve the recipient's chances of surviving. Because coerced organ donations are not the same as restrictive abortion laws (perhaps being more burdensome and less effective), the law does not treat women differently from men in similar circumstances—there really are no men in circumstances similar to pregnancy.

Cass Sunstein has responded to these arguments, in support of the equality argument against restrictive abortion laws.[32] For

Sunstein, the courts give intermediate scrutiny to laws discriminating against women to ensure that the laws do not perpetuate what the Court has called "archaic and overbroad generalizations" about women and men. But, Sunstein argues, when we look at the gender-discriminatory draft law together with restrictive abortion laws, we see the law being used precisely to reaffirm traditional, stereotypical views about the appropriate roles of women—as mothers—and men—as fighters.

Further, Sunstein argues, the argument comparing restrictive abortion laws and coerced organ donations is more complex. The Supreme Court's intermediate scrutiny not only requires that a law's distinctions between men and women serve an important government goal, but also that the distinctions are "substantially related to achievement of those goals." Taking the goal to be preserving human life, Sunstein argues that restrictive abortion laws in fact do rather little to "achieve" or promote that goal. True, restrictive abortion laws may reduce the number of legal abortions performed, but they may have relatively little effect on the total number of abortions performed. And, because illegal abortions are performed under circumstances that pose greater risks to women, the total number of lives lost (counting fetuses as human) may be *greater* if the abortion laws are restrictive than if they are not. Sunstein concedes that the facts on which this last argument relies are not solidly established, in part because (for understandable reasons) it is quite difficult to get accurate information about the number of illegal abortions.

Another group critical of equality arguments believes that such arguments do not go far enough. They believe that the problems with restrictive abortion laws would persist even if, for example, the law came to require coerced organ transplants from men. To these critics, the "privacy"-based arguments for choice with respect to abortion are forceful completely independent of the question of gender equality.

Again, the point here is not to show that the arguments for making abortion a constitutional issue decisively settle the controversy in favor of the Supreme Court's position, but only to show that those arguments are strong enough to make it legally sensible to treat abortion as a constitutional issue even though the Constitution itself does not specifically address abortion or privacy as such.

2

The Supreme Court on Abortion: The Legal Background

The abortion issue has been as controversial inside the Court as it has been outside. Starting with a decision finding unconstitutional what even the dissenters called an "uncommonly silly law," the Court first articulated a right of privacy and then held in 1973 that the right was "broad enough" to cover a woman's decision to have an abortion. Within the Court, the initial abortion decisions were a matter of some controversy, though nothing like what would happen over the next decades. Three of President Richard Nixon's appointees to the Supreme Court supported the Court's initial abortion decisions: Harry A. Blackmun, who wrote the opinions, Lewis F. Powell, and Chief Justice Warren E. Burger. Burger's support for the decisions was weak from the start. As more cases came to the Court, Burger gradually started voting to uphold restrictions on the availability of abortions.

The real challenges to the 1973 decisions came, though, as Presidents Ronald Reagan and George Bush appointed new justices. Although none was subjected to an explicit "litmus test" in the sense that they were not asked explicitly whether they would vote to overturn *Roe v. Wade*, the new appointees all adhered to what they described as a philosophy of judicial restraint, and many people—supporters and opponents of *Roe* alike—believed that "judicial restraint" was a code phrase used to criticize *Roe*. When Justice Powell retired in 1986, President Reagan first nominated appeals court judge Robert Bork, an aggressive critic of *Roe*. The controversy over the nomination, which eventually failed, was intense in part because as people counted the votes on the Supreme Court, they believed that with Bork's appointment there would be five justices who would reverse *Roe*. Why that did not happen is part of the story that follows.

The Court's 1973 decisions involved two statutes. The first was Texas's traditional abortion statute, which banned abortions except to save the woman's life. The second was a Georgia statute modeled on proposals made by legal and medical reformers. This more modern statute allowed abortions when approved by a panel of three doctors and a hospital's review committee. (It also had a number of other restrictions, such as a requirement that, if an abortion was sought on the basis that the pregnancy resulted from rape, a local prosecutor had to certify that the rape probably had occurred.) The Supreme Court's decision finding these statutes unconstitutional rested on challenges to state laws regulating sexual activity that went back nearly forty years.

The Background: Tileston v. Ullman and Poe v. Ullman

Historian David Garrow traces the abortion decisions to efforts by the Connecticut Birth Control League to open family planning clinics in the late 1930s.[1] The Birth Control League was an affiliate of a broader birth control movement, which had become prominent nationally through the activities of Margaret Sanger, an outspoken advocate of women's rights who believed that birth control was an essential part of women's rights. Katharine Hepburn, the famous actress's mother, was one of the Connecticut League's founders.

Connecticut had a law, dating to 1879, that banned the use of birth control devices. The Birth Control League was concerned that its clinics would be charged with aiding people who violated the anti-contraceptive law. For about a decade starting in 1923 the League petitioned the Connecticut legislature to repeal the 1879 law, but the legislature was not interested. The legislature had a large number of Roman Catholics, and Connecticut's bishops strongly opposed repeal. After several unsuccessful efforts to get the legislature to debate the law's repeal, a repeal proposal came to the floor in 1929, and it was defeated by the huge margin of 226 votes to 18. Two years later repeal had gained additional support, but it still lost, 172 votes to 76. Even when advocates of repeal managed to get the legislature's lower house to approve an amendment that would have allowed doctors to provide contraceptive advice and prescribe birth control devices to married women only, the upper house refused to go along.

League members surveyed local prosecutors, however, and discovered none who really wanted to enforce the law. In 1935 the League recruited two woman doctors to operate a clinic in Hartford.

Although the League was a bit nervous about the possibility of being prosecuted in Hartford, these fears were never realized. The League's leaders knew that physicians prescribed birth control devices for private patients who could afford to pay their own doctors. They believed it was simply unfair that families who had to use clinics could not get the same services and they hoped that prosecutors—and, if prosecutions did occur, juries and judges—would respond to the unfairness by nullifying the 1879 law. By the late 1930s, public sentiment had moved to favor making birth control widely available; surveys repeatedly showed that around 70 percent of the public supported the birth control movement's goals.

By 1939, the League had opened clinics in all of Connecticut's major cities, hoping that the law would remain a dead letter. The prosecutor in Waterbury, though, decided that he had an obligation to enforce the law on the books. The clinic there was one of the state's smallest, open only one day a week, and most of its clients had already received birth control devices elsewhere. The doctors who staffed the clinic did occasionally prescribe and fit diaphragms, though, and that was enough to violate the law.

The prosecutor charged Roger Nelson and William Goodrich, the two doctors who worked at the clinic, and Clara McTernan, a former nurse and the wife of a local private-school headmaster who helped run the clinic, with violating the 1879 act. The defendants did not deny that they had prescribed birth control devices. They argued, though, that the statute should not be interpreted to apply to doctors who prescribed contraceptive devices as part of their medical practice. If it did apply to doctors, they continued, it was unconstitutional because it violated individual liberty. The defendants emphasized the statute's interference with the medical judgment of qualified physicians about what was in their patients' interests.

The trial judge agreed with the defendants' legal claims and dismissed the charges. The statute did not allow doctors to prescribe contraception, and, the judge wrote, "without these proper exceptions the statute is defective" on constitutional grounds. The state appealed this decision to the state supreme court.

In March 1940 the supreme court upheld the statute. The court divided three to two, although the dissenters did not explain the reasons for their disagreement. The majority pointed out that the legislature had repeatedly refused to repeal or even amend the 1879 act. The statute was constitutional, the majority said, because the legislature might have believed that using contraceptives "would be injurious to public morals," in part because some married people might be tempted to engage in extramarital affairs if they knew that they could use contraceptives to reduce the risk of pregnancy.

The prosecutor had won the legal battle. The Waterbury clinic closed, as did all the Birth Control League's other clinics. Interested only in closing the clinics, the prosecutor dismissed the criminal charges.

Birth control advocates tried to develop new strategies. They toyed with the idea of having a statewide ballot referendum on repealing the 1879 act. They tried to figure out how to get the state legislature to amend it to allow hospitals to prescribe contraceptives. They also developed a new test case.

The plaintiff was Wilder Tileston, a New Haven doctor and professor. The lawsuit asked the state courts to declare that Tileston could prescribe contraceptives to three of his patients, whose lives, he claimed, would be threatened if they became pregnant: One had very high blood pressure, another suffered from the aftereffects of tuberculosis, and the third had to care for three children already in impoverished circumstances. Because, the lawsuit claimed, the statute barred Tileston from prescribing contraceptives to avoid the women's deaths or severe injury to their health, it was unconstitutional.

This case went directly to the Connecticut Supreme Court, which decided once again that the statute applied to doctors and was constitutional. Tileston appealed to the United States Supreme Court, which had its first opportunity to consider the constitutionality of restrictions on contraceptive sale and use. In 1943 the Court refused to decide whether Tileston's constitutional rights had been violated.[2] As the Court interpreted the documents filed in the case, the only issue was whether the Connecticut statute violated the constitutional ban on taking life without due process of law. Tileston might have had a valid claim that the statute deprived him of liberty or property without due process, but his lawyers had not mentioned liberty or property in the complaint. His patients might have had a valid claim that the statute might deprive them of life without due process, but they were not parties to the lawsuit.

Through the 1940s, the Connecticut legislature considered proposals to amend the 1879 act. Reform prospects depended on partisan politics: Connecticut's Democrats tended to support the 1879 act in its original form, while Republicans tended to support repeal or amendment. But the politics of birth control played little part in Connecticut's elections. As larger forces affected the composition of the state legislature—national politics, or the condition of the economy—the fortunes of reform proposals grew brighter or dimmer.

No candidate for governor was willing to make an issue of birth control legislation either. As liberal Democrats and Republicans all saw it, reform was a "religious issue" that might divide their supporters. Opposition to reform had become a "Catholic" issue in Connecticut and reformers repeatedly criticized what they called "Catholic domination in government" for preserving the anti-contraceptive law as a "symbol of Catholic power."

The lower house passed a modest reform bill in 1943; it was defeated in the state senate. In 1945 an even broader reform measure was defeated in committee. By 1947, though, the lower house voted for a bill allowing doctors to prescribe contraceptives to a married woman if pregnancy would endanger her life or injure her health. The senate again rejected the proposal, though the margin was clearly more narrow than it had been. But when Democrats won a large victory in the 1948 elections, reform prospects were again bleak, and no bills even reached the floor of either house for debate in 1949. Two years later a bill passed the lower house 121 to 62 and later died without reaching the senate floor. In 1953 the margin in the lower house was again about 60 votes and again the senate killed the bill, this time on a voice vote. Essentially the same votes occurred in 1955 and 1957.

Having failed in the legislature, because of what they believed was the excessive power of the Catholic church, birth control advocates turned again to the courts. Estelle Griswold now headed Connecticut's Planned Parenthood League and she became the driving force behind the next decade's litigation.

Estelle Griswold lived in New Haven (sometimes scholars wrongly assert that she was related to A. Whitney Griswold, president of Yale University in the 1950s and 1960s), where the Planned Parenthood League had developed working relations with members of the Yale medical and law school faculties. The League provided some funding for an infertility clinic at Yale, for example.

The League's failures in the legislature renewed interest in getting a good test case to challenge the anti-contraceptive law. As a temporary measure, the League set up a referral service that directed Connecticut women to a clinic across the state border in Port Chester, New York, and helped arrange to get them there. Griswold assembled a group of legal advisers, including Yale law professor Fowler Harper, a specialist in family law who was outraged at the anti-contraceptive statute, which he believed an unconstitutional government intrusion in family matters. The cost of operating the referral service meant that the League could not continue to fund the Yale infertility clinic.

Its director, C. Lee Buxton, who also headed Yale's obstetrical department, volunteered to be the plaintiff in a new test case.

In 1957 Buxton had three patients who suffered severe medical problems during their pregnancies. One had a serious stroke because her pregnancy drove her already high blood pressure to a dangerous level. Another's babies died shortly after birth, while the third woman had her fourth late-term miscarriage; the last two patients suffered serious psychological trauma, and Buxton believed they should not run the risk of further trauma from another pregnancy.

After talking with Fowler Harper, Buxton persuaded his patients to join him in challenging the 1879 statute. Harper recruited Catharine Roraback, a graduate of Yale Law School whom he knew from left-wing politics in Connecticut, to try the case in the Connecticut courts, while Harper would prepare the inevitable Supreme Court appeal. Harper also found a Yale law student and his wife who agreed to join the lawsuit as plaintiffs. Because the patients did not want to identify themselves publicly, they proceeded under fictitious names, as Paul and Pauline Poe, and Ralph and Rena Roe. The defendant would be Abraham Ullman, because the lawyers wanted the courts to declare that Ullman could not prosecute the Poes for violating the 1879 statute, or Buxton for assisting them. The cases thus became known as *Poe v. Ullman* and *Buxton v. Ullman*.

The legal challenge then could cover all the bases. The lawyers would argue that the 1879 statute unconstitutionally interfered with Buxton's right to provide medical services to his patients, unconstitutionally threatened the lives and health of the patients, and unconstitutionally interfered with decisions about reproduction that married couples should be allowed to make. The first was a claim about interference with property and liberty, the second about life and liberty, and the third about liberty alone. This complaint could not be thrown out for failing to raise some potential constitutional claims, as Tileston's had been.

Harper's briefs to the Supreme Court laid out the basics of the arguments he and his colleagues would pursue until the Court decided in their favor in 1965. Relying on *Meyer v. Nebraska*, the 1923 case in which the Supreme Court referred to "the right of the individual . . . to marry, establish a home and bring up children" when it invalidated a statute barring teaching German, Harper argued that the 1879 statute interfered with "normal marital relations . . . [and the] personal freedom or privilege to procreate or not." "When the long arm of the law reaches into the bedroom and regulates the most sacred relation between a man and his wife," Harper wrote, "it is going too far."

The oral argument before the Supreme Court revealed that the case had a problem. The lawsuit asked the court to declare the statute banning the *use* of contraceptives unconstitutional. Justice Felix Frankfurter wondered whether the case was not "a theoretical thing" and Justice Potter Stewart called it "an abstract attack" on a law that "has no impact." The 1879 statute was a criminal law, but none of the lawyers knew of any prosecutions for violating it. Even the criminal ban on prescribing contraceptives—aiding and abetting the ban on contraceptive use—had not been enforced for twenty years. Still, Harper argued, the 1879 law did keep clinics from operating even though some types of contraceptives were available in pharmacies all over the state.

When the justices discussed the case after the argument, Chief Justice Earl Warren picked up the concern for deciding an important constitutional question in what he called "contrived litigation." He did not like being used as a "guinea pig[ ] for an abstract principle." He was supported by Frankfurter, who thought that the plaintiffs were trying to get the Court to issue an advisory opinion against a statute no one enforced.

Justice Hugo Black had made a career out of criticizing his predecessors and colleagues for relying on substantive due process and unenumerated rights like the right of privacy to interfere with legislators' decisions, and he did not think that the patients had a valid constitutional claim. He did think, though, that Dr. Buxton's First Amendment right to free speech was violated when the state kept him from giving appropriate medical advice to his patients; unfortunately for the plaintiffs, Harper had expressly stated to the Court that this lawsuit did not bring a free speech challenge to the 1879 statute.

Justice William O. Douglas, the Court's most liberal member, stated that the Court ought to hold the statute unconstitutional. An even more forceful statement came from Justice John Marshall Harlan, one of the Court's more conservative and reflective members. According to one law clerk, Harlan "was outraged at this interference with personal privacy . . . It was government going into places it simply shouldn't." Saying that the Court "had no business dismissing these cases," Harlan called the statute "the most egregiously unconstitutional act I have seen since being on the Court" for the past six years. It interfered with a precious liberty, even if that freedom was not listed anywhere in the Constitution. Because the statute prohibited contraceptive use, it was "more offensive to [the] 'right to be let alone' than any [other statute] could possibly be."

When the votes were counted, six justices voted to dismiss the challenge on the ground that there was no real controversy, and three—Harlan, Douglas, and Potter Stewart—voted to find it unconstitutional. Chief Justice Warren asked Frankfurter to write the Court's opinion. The opinion emphasized that there was no specific threat of enforcing the ban on contraceptive use and that some types of contraceptives were easily available in Connecticut. The opinion was an essay about the importance of keeping the Court from ruling on constitutional issues before it had to.[3]

The case was "abstract," Frankfurter wrote, because the state had not tried to enforce the 1879 statute. This "undeviating policy of nullification" showed that there could be no "realistic fear of prosecution" for violating the statute. Dr. Buxton's asserted concern about being prosecuted for aiding and abetting a violation of the 1879 statute was "chimerical," in light of the fact that the 1879 act had "during so many years gone uniformly and without exception unenforced." "This Court," Frankfurter wrote, "cannot be umpire to debates concerning harmless, empty shadows."

Justice William Brennan was uncomfortable with the wide-ranging discussion in Frankfurter's opinion. Justice Douglas circulated a draft dissent that Brennan found persuasive. After criticizing Frankfurter's opinion for requiring doctors and patients to "[f]lout the law and go to prison" or "[v]iolate the law surreptitiously and hope they will not get caught," Douglas called the liberty protected by the due process clause "a conception that sometimes gains content from the emanations of other specific [constitutional] guarantees or from experience with the requirements of a free society." The 1879 statute, he wrote, "reaches into the intimacies of the marriage relationship" and could justify searches by police officers of married couples' bedrooms.

When Brennan suggested that he might go along with Douglas, Douglas actually urged Brennan to stay with his original vote to dismiss the case: Because of Black's focus on free speech, Douglas said, if Brennan joined the dissenters there would be no majority for any outcome, which Douglas thought would delay the Court's adjournment. Brennan stuck with his vote, but refused to join Frankfurter's opinion. He wrote a separate opinion saying that "the true controversy in this case is over the opening of birth-control clinics on a large scale; it is that which the State has prevented in the past, not the use of contraceptives by isolated and individual married couples. It will be time enough to decide the constitutional questions . . . when, if ever, that real controversy flares up again."

Justice Harlan circulated a long opinion, drafted by his law clerk Charles Fried (who later served as solicitor general, the government's chief lawyer before the Supreme Court, under Ronald Reagan). As Harlan understood the situation in Connecticut, state prosecutors had successfully deterred doctors from abetting violations of the 1879 statute. That, rather than any " 'tacit agreement' not to prosecute," was the reason that there had been no prosecutions. Frankfurter, Harlan wrote, had "indulged in a bit of sleight of hand to be rid of this case."

For Harlan, "a statute making it a criminal offense for married couples to use contraceptives is an intolerable and unjustifiable invasion of privacy in the conduct of the most intimate concerns of an individual's private life." The statute, as he had told his colleagues earlier, was "obnoxiously intrusive." Harlan's opinion spelled out why the Court could enforce rights that were not enumerated in the Constitution. The Court had the duty to enforce "the balance which our Nation, built upon postulates of respect for the liberty of the individual, has struck between that liberty and the demands of organized society." In doing so, the Court had to treat the nation's tradition as "a living thing."

For Harlan, liberty under the due process clause was infringed when the state passed laws that were "substantial arbitrary impositions and purposeless restraints." Like Douglas, Harlan emphasized the law's intrusion on "the most intimate details of the marital relation." He could not imagine "what is more private or more intimate than a husband and wife's marital relations." True, Harlan wrote, a state government could "concern[ ] itself with the moral soundness of its people," and "laws forbidding adultery, fornication and homosexual practices" were, in his view, constitutional even though they interfered with sexual practices.

Laws against contraceptive use, though, were different. The state was "asserting the right to enforce its moral judgment by intruding upon the most intimate details of the marital relation with the full power of the criminal law." The sexual relations between husband and wife, Harlan argued, were "necessarily an essential and accepted feature of the institution of marriage," which the state "fostered and protected." Perhaps the state might limit the sale and distribution of contraceptive devices, Harlan suggested, but it could not seek to enforce its moral judgments about contraceptives by "the obnoxiously intrusive means it has chosen to effectuate [its] policy" against contraceptives. He thought the "novelty" of Connecticut's approach to the issue "conclusive": No other government in the nation had made contraceptive use a crime, and even governments in Europe that disapproved of contraceptive use did not make the use alone a crime.

The Court Finds a Right to Privacy

The Court's decision in *Poe v. Ullman* made the next step apparent: Planned Parenthood had to open a clinic where doctors would prescribe contraceptives. If Justice Frankfurter was right, the 1879 law was a dead letter and the clinics would be allowed to operate freely. If he was wrong, someone would be prosecuted for violating the statute, and the defense could then raise the constitutional claims again.

Estelle Griswold signed a lease for clinic space in a New Haven building and Dr. Buxton lined up several doctors who volunteered to spend a few hours each week staffing the clinic. When police officers showed up at the clinic a few days after it opened, Griswold showered them with information she hoped they would use in building a case against her and the clinic. She even arranged to have some clinic patients talk with the police about how the clinic provided them with birth control pills and other contraceptives, a clear example of assisting a violation of the ban on using contraceptives. Ten days after the New Haven clinic opened, Griswold and Buxton were arrested, charged with assisting women to use contraceptives, and released on bail. The clinic shut down until the long-delayed constitutional challenge would be resolved.

Everyone knew that the proceedings in the state courts were only a rehearsal for the real performance in Washington, D.C. The clinic's lawyers added to the now-standard privacy argument a more complete argument that the statute violated the free speech rights of doctors by barring them from giving their patients their best medical judgment, and a new argument, drawn from Frankfurter, that the 1879 statute had been effectively nullified by a long history of nonenforcement. At the conclusion of a one-day trial on January 2, 1962, Griswold and Buxton were found guilty and fined $100. A year later they lost the first round of their appeals, and sent the case on to the state supreme court, which in turn upheld the convictions in May 1964. The case was finally ready for the Supreme Court.

Fowler Harper prepared the first set of Supreme Court briefs. A law review article written after *Poe* persuaded Harper to rely on the Ninth Amendment as well as substantive due process ideas and the First Amendment's protection of free speech. The dissents by Justices Douglas and Harlan in *Poe* also helped shape the new arguments. Harper now knew that the case against the Connecticut statute could be strengthened by arguing that the Constitution's specific guarantees helped define unenumerated rights, that their "emanations," as Douglas had put it, indicated other fundamental rights deserving the same degree of protection.

When the Court agreed to hear the appeal, though, Harper was in the hospital with terminal cancer. He arranged for his Yale Law School colleague Thomas Emerson to draft the final briefs and argue the appeal. Harper and Emerson were longtime collaborators in Connecticut's progressive politics; Emerson, sometimes called "Tommy the Commie" by both friends and enemies, had run for governor of Connecticut on Henry Wallace's Progressive Party ticket in 1948.

Harper died in January 1965 and Emerson completed the work on the Supreme Court brief. Even more clearly than the prior briefs, Emerson's connected the right of privacy to specific constitutional guarantees as well as to the Ninth Amendment and substantive due process. Modern conditions, Emerson argued, "require that the composite of these specific constitutional protections be accorded the status of a recognized constitutional right." That right encompassed "the sanctity of the home and the wholly personal nature of marital relations."

Emerson was a staid and unemotional lawyer, with an almost dull manner. But the justices drew him into a vigorous exchange at the oral argument. Just as the argument in *Poe* indicated some interest among the justices in resting a decision on the First Amendment, an argument that no one had made before, so the argument in *Griswold* indicated interest in resolving the case on the ground that the Connecticut statute violated the constitutional guarantee of equal protection of the laws. The First Amendment argument was a bit strained, but the equal protection argument was not. At least it directed attention to the important fact that the Connecticut statute's practical effect was to deny contraceptive services to women who could not afford their own doctors and so had to use clinics, while allowing relatively affluent women to get those same services from doctors in private practice.

Near the end of his oral presentation, Emerson responded to one question that his argument "would not cover the abortion laws" because "[t]he conduct that is being prohibited in the abortion cases takes place outside of the home." Justice Byron White interjected that abortion was different as well because it "involves killing a life in being." When Emerson agreed, Justice Black asked, "Are you saying that all abortions involve killing or murder?" Emerson qualified his earlier claim, now saying that abortion "involves taking what has begun to be a life." These questions would arise again, when the abortion issue came directly before the Court.

Chief Justice Warren led off the justices' discussion of the case.[4] He was, he said, "bothered with the case." He was unsympathetic to the claim that the statute violated the doctors' free speech rights. He did not want to say that the state had no permissible interest in banning contraceptive use because, he said, that "could apply to abortion laws." Nor did he like the substantive due process approach or the equal protection argument or even the privacy argument. But, having rejected nearly all the arguments Harper and Emerson had made, Warren nonetheless was inclined to hold the Connecticut statute unconstitutional, perhaps on the theory that it was a denial of equal protection to enforce it only against clinics but not against private physicians. He also thought that any statute regulating contraceptive use had to be written more narrowly than Connecticut's, because "we are dealing with a confidential association, the most intimate in our life."

Proceeding in the order of seniority, Justice Black went next. The First Amendment was not involved. That amendment guaranteed a right of assembly, but "the right of husband and wife to assemble in bed is a new right of assembly to me." Justice Douglas replied that constitutional rights had emanations and peripheries, and the right of marital association ought to be protected: "There's nothing more personal than this relationship and it's within First Amendment protection, if on the periphery." Justice Tom Clark relied on the 1923 decision in *Meyer v. Nebraska* to show that there was a right to marry and have children, with which the Connecticut statute interfered. "This is an area where we have the right to be let alone," he said. Justice Harlan restated his views from *Poe*.

Now that the case of a clinic was before the Court, Justice Brennan went along with Harlan and Douglas, but Justice Potter Stewart, who in *Poe* suggested that he agreed with them, voted to uphold the statute. The problem was one the Connecticut legislature should resolve, he said. Justice White voted to reverse. When Frankfurter retired in 1962, Arthur Goldberg had been named to fill Frankfurter's seat. Unlike Frankfurter, Goldberg did not worry much about "judicial activism." In *Griswold*, Goldberg voted to reverse the convictions. He pointed out that the Court had recently struck down statutes penalizing members of the Communist Party on freedom of association grounds, and if people could join the Communist Party, surely, Goldberg thought, a man "can join his wife and live with her as he likes."

The vote was seven to two to reverse the convictions. Chief Justice Warren had to decide who should write the Court's opinion. There were two obvious candidates, Douglas and Harlan, both of whom had written in *Poe* that the statute was unconstitutional. Warren decided to ask Douglas to write for the Court for personal and doctrinal reasons. Douglas was a very fast writer, and the Court had only a couple of months to go before it had to adjourn for the summer. Harlan, in contrast, was meticulous and, perhaps more important, almost blind. There was some risk that he could not produce a substantial opinion in the time available.

Or, at least, not an opinion that the other justices would join. Harlan was far more comfortable with the idea of substantive due process than anyone else in the majority. His opinion in *Poe* defended the idea, and said relatively little about the Constitution's enumerated rights. In contrast, Douglas's opinion, and even more his oral comments to his colleagues, showed that he wanted to connect the right to privacy in *Griswold* to a number of specific constitutional guarantees. That approach, Warren believed, was more likely to go down easily with other justices than Harlan's would have.

Douglas quickly drafted a very short opinion. It relied solely on the First Amendment, saying that the Court would not respond to the "overtones" of arguments suggesting that it rely on substantive due process. Douglas acknowledged that "[t]he association of husband and wife is not mentioned in the Constitution," but, he wrote, neither were the rights protected in *Meyer* and *Pierce*. Those cases showed that "the First Amendment has been construed to include certain . . . peripheral rights . . . Without those peripheral rights the specific rights would be less secure."

Douglas then called the family "an instruction unit," and parents "both teachers and pupils," to draw the right of association as family members closer to *Meyer* and *Pierce*. Those cases, and others involving rights of political association, were not precisely the same as *Griswold*, of course, but Douglas said "they place it in the proper frame of reference." Marriage was "a form of association as vital in the life of a man or woman as any other, and perhaps more so." It was "the essence of one form of the expression of love, admiration, and loyalty. To protect other forms of such expression and not this, the central one, would seem to us to be a travesty."

Douglas then lyrically described the institution of marriage: It was "a coming together for better or for worse, hopefully enduring, and intimate to the degree of being sacred. This association promotes a way of life, not causes; a harmony in living, nor political faiths; a bilateral loyalty, not commercial or social projects." Then, returning to matters closer to the core of the First Amendment, Douglas said that the family "flourishes on the interchange of ideas," in which each spouse educated the other about the family's health and well-being. The opinion ended rather abruptly. "The prospects of police with warrants searching the sacred precincts of marital bedrooms for telltale signs of the use of contraceptives is repulsive to the idea of privacy and of association that make up a goodly part of the penumbra of the Constitution and Bill of Rights."

Douglas sent this draft to Justice Brennan, who did not like it. His law clerk Richard Posner (later a prominent conservative federal judge and a leading force behind bringing economic theory to bear on legal questions, including questions of sexuality) drafted a letter to Douglas. Brennan was concerned that Douglas's language might make the family unit "unreachable by the State." And, he suggested, it was straining quite a bit to connect the association of husband and wife to "advocacy and expression," as Douglas had.

"Instead of expanding the First Amendment right of association to include marriage," Brennan suggested, "why not say that what has been done for the First Amendment can also be done for some of the other fundamental guarantees of the Bill of Rights?" Douglas should treat specific constitutional guarantees as "expressions or examples" of more fundamental rights: "The guarantees of the Bill of Rights do not necessarily resist expansion to fill in the edges where the same fundamental interests are at stake." Douglas could "create[ ]" a right to privacy "out of the Fourth Amendment and the Fifth, together with the Third, in much the same way as the right to association has been created out of the First." Looking at all the amendments together, one could see "a fundamental concern with the sanctity of the home and the right of the individual to be let alone." This approach, Brennan wrote, had "a better chance that it will command a court."

Three days later Douglas sent a revised version of the opinion to Brennan and Warren. The new draft showed the influence of Brennan's letter. It included several new paragraphs adding the Third, Fourth, and Fifth Amendments to the list of specific provisions that had "penumbras, formed by emanations from those guarantees that help give them life and substance." It restated the concern that Connecticut's law authorized searches of bedrooms, calling the idea repulsive. Instead of relying on a right of association, though, the new draft relied explicitly on "a right of privacy older than the Bill of Rights." The lyrical description of marriage ended the opinion, with the new line, "[I]t is an association for as noble a purpose as any involved in our prior decisions."

Chief Justice Warren's law clerk did not like the revised opinion. He thought that the courts would be unable to define any sensible limits on the right to privacy. The law clerk suggested that Warren "wait and see what is written." If necessary, he would draft a short opinion saying that the Connecticut law was unconstitutional because "it is only against the clinics that the law is enforced."

Without waiting for Warren's response, Douglas then sent the draft to the rest of the Court. Justice Clark was enthusiastic, writing that the opinion "emancipates femininity and protects masculinity." Justice Goldberg also joined the opinion. Harlan said that he would concur in the judgment—that is, agree with the result but not with Douglas's opinion—and might write a separate opinion.

Douglas had four votes, but there seemed little chance of his getting a fifth. The law clerks were nearly unanimous in thinking the Douglas draft badly reasoned. Douglas's law clerk later recalled that Douglas's references to "emanations" and "penumbras" "attracted the giggles" of the clerks. Warren discussed the case with Goldberg, who wanted to beef up the opinion's references to the Ninth Amendment. Prodded by the conversation, Goldberg had his law clerk Stephen Breyer (named to the Supreme Court in 1994) draft an extensive opinion dealing with that amendment. The amendment, Goldberg's opinion said, was written "to quiet expressed fears that a bill of specifically enumerated rights could not be sufficiently broad to cover all essential rights." It supported the proposition that the Court could protect unenumerated rights. But which rights were fundamental? Judges, Goldberg wrote, were not "left at large to decide cases in light of their personal and private notions." They had to rely on tradition and the "collective conscience of our people." Those sources—"the entire fabric of the Constitution"—led Goldberg to conclude that "the rights to marital privacy and to marry and raise a family are of similar order and magnitude as the fundamental rights specifically protected." Without such protection, states might "decree that all husbands and wives be sterilized after two children have been born to them."

For Goldberg, government intrusions on marital privacy had to have a strong justification. Connecticut argued that it wanted to discourage extramarital relations. Goldberg called this justification "dubious," because some contraceptives were widely available in the state. But, he wrote, the state could achieve its goal by "a more discriminately tailored statute," including the existing laws against adultery and fornication.

Brennan joined Goldberg's opinion as well as Douglas's. Although Warren's law clerk thought Goldberg's draft "good," he still was concerned that it had the same problem as Douglas's: It left the contours of the right to marital privacy "disturbingly unclear." When White sent around a separate opinion finding the statute unconstitutional because banning the use of contraceptives did nothing to "reinforce[ ] the State's ban on illicit sexual relationships," Warren's law clerk called it "the best opinion which has yet been circulated," because it did not try to rely on an unenumerated right of privacy. Instead, White argued, the state's theory was the implausible one that by making it hard to a married person to get a contraceptive, the state made it riskier for such a person to engage in extramarital affairs—even though the state also made adultery a crime. Warren agreed, and joined White's opinion.

Meanwhile, Justices Black and Stewart sent around their dissents. Black criticized his colleagues for even attempting to enforce unenumerated rights. "I like my privacy as well as the next one, but I am nevertheless compelled to admit that government has a right to invade it unless prohibited by some specific constitutional provision," Black wrote. He rejected what he called the "philosophy" that the Court had a duty "to keep the Constitution in tune with the times." The right to privacy rested on "subjective considerations," which were "no less dangerous when used to enforce this Court's views about personal rights than those about economic rights."

Justice Stewart pungently called Connecticut's statute "an uncommonly silly law." But, like Black, he could not find it unconstitutional unless it violated some specific constitutional provision. There was, he said, "no . . . general right of privacy" anywhere in the Constitution.

Without five votes, an opinion is only an opinion. It announces the judgment reached by the majority, but it stands only for the views of the justices who join it. A plurality opinion, with only four votes, does not have much force as a precedent. As things stood, Douglas's opinion had only four votes. Unexpectedly, perhaps simply to get the Court's term over with, Chief Justice Warren switched his vote. Abandoning White's concurrence in the judgment, he joined Goldberg's opinion. But, because Goldberg already had signed on to Douglas's draft, the effect was to give Douglas a five-justice majority.

The opinions were released on June 7, 1965.[5] A new clinic sponsored by Connecticut's Planned Parenthood League opened in New Haven on September 20. Estelle Griswold resigned as director of the League at the end of the year.

Reform or Repeal?

Griswold provided the foundation in constitutional doctrine for challenges to a wide range of laws dealing with sexual privacy. The justices understood that the rule they announced might later be used to challenge laws against adultery, abortion, and homosexual activity. The laws against adultery were rarely enforced, but the laws against abortion had effects as real as the effects of the 1879 statute in Connecticut. Even more, although Connecticut's anti-contraceptive statute was unique by 1965, laws restricting the availability of abortions were on the books, and enforced, throughout the country.

Supporters of birth control like the Planned Parenthood Federation of America were able to coordinate the challenge in *Griswold*. They had to deal with only a single state, and birth control activists had engaged in a sustained political and legal attack on the 1879 statute for decades. In contrast, coordinating efforts to reform or abolish restrictive abortion laws, either by legislation or through litigation, was extremely difficult. There were too many forums: states throughout the country, and within each state courts and legislatures. And there were too many activists: lawyers interested in bringing the law up to date, physicians who wanted more latitude in deciding when an abortion was medically justified, doctors who believed they and their patients should have unfettered control over the decision about abortion, and, of course, many women who believed they alone should control the decision.

Activists who wanted to change restrictive abortion laws proposed alternative solutions. Some wished to *reform* the laws, others to *abolish* them. The abortion laws on the books in most states in the 1960s were no different from the ones adopted in the second half of the nineteenth century. Before then, abortions were generally not a felony if they occurred before "quickening," that is, the time when the woman felt the fetus moving. After mid-century, doctors believed that advances in medical knowledge made it irrational to draw the line at quickening. The professional consensus was that fetuses were human beings from the start, and should be protected by the law.

The doctors supported new laws against abortion. These laws typically made it a crime for anyone to perform an abortion and also usually made it a crime for a woman to obtain one. They generally had an exception allowing abortions when they were necessary to save the woman's life. Most courts made it difficult to invoke that exception. Few doctors were willing to run the risk of prosecution for openly performing an abortion even though they might have some chance of persuading a jury that the abortion was necessary to save the woman's life.

That did not mean, however, that no one performed abortions. According to some estimates, the number of abortions—nearly all of them illegal—was well over 500,000 a year. Although doctors rarely performed them openly, there was a well-established "underground" of abortion providers. Some were highly trained doctors who treated patients able to pay enough for abortions in the doctor's office. By the 1960s, other doctors were connected to a network of activist women who referred patients to sympathetic physicians. But other abortion providers were so-called "back alley abortionists" with little medical training; they charged lower fees, and often performed the abortions under unsanitary conditions using techniques that posed a serious threat to the woman's life. Thousands of women died each year after trying to have an abortion.

Much of *Griswold*'s impetus came from a sense of unfairness, that well-to-do people could obtain contraceptives while poorer people could not. Similar sentiments fueled the movement to change abortion laws. *Reformers* proposed to expand the exception for lifesaving abortions to allow what were called therapeutic abortions, that is, abortions that would preserve the woman's physical or mental health. These reformers usually had an expansive view of when a pregnancy would harm a woman's health. For example, they usually believed that an abortion should be allowed when continuing the pregnancy would cause severe mental anguish to the woman or when the physical aspects of a normal pregnancy would pose some risk to her health through elevated blood pressure and the like.

Reformers understood that their position left a lot to doctors, who would be asked to decide whether the exceptions for physical or mental health applied to each woman seeking an abortion. Partly because they were concerned that their opponents would complain that some doctors would invoke the exceptions too often, and partly out of a principled concern that abortion should not become too readily available, many reformers proposed ways to limit doctors' decisions. The most common was that a doctors' committee would have to approve an abortion. That way, reformers believed, abortions would be performed only when there really was a medical consensus that the woman's life or health was seriously at risk. No single doctor, perhaps overly concerned about a patient with whom he or she had dealt for many years, perhaps overly affected by the prospect of charging a fee for the procedure, would be able to decide to perform an abortion.

The American Law Institute (ALI) proposed major reforms of abortion law in 1959. The ALI was a group of self-selected elite lawyers whose goal was the improvement of law in areas from property law to sales law to criminal law. During the 1950s its major effort was the development of what it called the Model Penal Code. The Model Penal Code was a comprehensive review of criminal law. It contained standards for distinguishing between, among other crimes, murder and manslaughter and between burglary and robbery. One item on the ALI's agenda was to ensure that the criminal law be used only when it should be. In the course of thinking about the proper scope of the criminal law, the head of the Model Penal Code project proposed a major reform of abortion law. The Model Code endorsed an exception for therapeutic abortions, where there was a "substantial risk that continuance of the pregnancy would gravely impair the physical or mental health of the mother," and required two doctors to agree on that conclusion. Proponents of abortion law reform used these provisions as the models for their legislative proposals.

For some, however, reform did not go far enough. They sought *repeal* of all restrictive abortion laws. This group continued to see abortion as a medical procedure, of course, and they did not urge that it be completely deregulated. Rather, repeal meant that the decision to have an abortion would be in the hands of the woman and the doctor she chose. Reform proposals were inadequate, in the view of proponents of repeal, for several reasons. The "life or health" standard was, they believed, far too vague. In practice, they argued, it would mean that the availability of abortions would depend too much on the subjective views of doctors in particular communities. Where doctors were hostile to abortion, the abortion committees were unlikely to find the standard satisfied very often; where they were not, abortions would be more easily available. Making the availability of abortions turn on where women happened to live was unacceptable.

Probably more important, though, advocates of repeal believed that reform proposals continued to intrude too much on highly personal matters. It was one thing for a woman to find a doctor she trusted; it was quite another for her to try to explain to a committee of three doctors she had never met before why continuing her pregnancy posed a threat to her mental health. In the contest between reformers and advocates of repeal, *Griswold*'s rhetoric of privacy came down on the side of repeal.

The Legislative Movement to Reform Abortion Law

As the movement to change abortion law developed, there were three groups of players. Many doctors and lawyers supported legislative proposals to reform the abortion laws. Abortion providers, doctors themselves, challenged reform laws as unconstitutionally vague. Women scattered across the country began lawsuits based on a right to privacy or a right to choose.

Many liberal lawyers in the 1960s had a model for litigation challenges to laws they believed unconstitutional. This model was the litigation campaign developed by the National Association for the Advancement of Colored People (NAACP), led by Thurgood Marshall, to eliminate racial segregation. It suggested that a successful litigation effort required some central direction and a guiding hand. But the attack on abortion laws was not coordinated at all. Even so, the women and their lawyers, working on individual lawsuits, were ultimately more successful than the legislative reform efforts.

In the early 1960s a steady, small stream of articles in medical journals and popular magazines presented the case against existing abortion laws. The issue burst into public attention, though, in July 1962. Sherri Finkbine was the hostess of a children's television show in Phoenix, Arizona. Pregnant with her fifth child, Finkbine read a news story about the risk that children of women who had taken the anti-morning-sickness drug thalidomide might have physical deformities. She discovered she had taken such a drug, which her husband had brought from England, where it was available, to the United States, where it had not yet been approved. In 1962, prenatal testing could not yet detect fetal deformities; Finkbine's doctor advised her to get a therapeutic abortion on the ground that the pregnancy would impair her mental health, and they started the process of getting committee approval.

Finkbine called a friend at the newspaper to thank the paper for providing the information she used. The newspaper's medical editor decided to play up Finkbine's story, as a follow-up to the initial story about thalidomide. When the story was published, the hospital canceled the planned abortion. It joined the Finkbines in a lawsuit to ensure that no one would be prosecuted if Finkbine had an abortion. The judge refused to help, saying that there was no real legal controversy. Instead of running the risk of a prosecution, the Finkbines flew to Sweden, where Mrs. Finkbine did have an abortion; the procedure showed that the fetus was quite deformed.

Scholars agree that Finkbine's case had a major effect on public views about abortion. Polls showed a majority of the public agreeing that Mrs. Finkbine had done "the right thing," even as prosecutors and newspapers pointed out that she could not have legally obtained an abortion in most states because the pregnancy did not endanger her life. An epidemic of German measles in 1965 kept the question of performing abortions as a way to avoid having children with birth defects alive, because pregnant women who contracted German measles ran a serious risk that their babies would be born deformed.

Doctors responded to these medical issues by redefining what would count as a threat to the woman's life. Before these developments, doctors usually understood the standard to mean that a continued pregnancy would, for example, raise the woman's blood pressure to life-threatening levels. Now they began to argue that women faced with the prospect of delivering and then raising a severely deformed child would commit suicide rather than continue the pregnancy. In that sense, continuing the pregnancy did threaten the woman's life. Most doctors knew, though, that they were stretching the statutory exception and many came to believe that abortion law reforms should be adopted.

By 1967, state legislatures all over the country were considering reform proposals that, for the first time, had some chance of being enacted. New York's Republican governor Nelson Rockefeller, leader of his party's liberal wing, called for the adoption of an ALI-type reform law. Leaders of the Roman Catholic church in New York spoke out vigorously against reform. Legislators and the public quickly came to believe that the battle for abortion law reform was between liberalizers and the Roman Catholic church, though some well-established Protestant journals expressed concern about abandoning the existing restrictive abortion law.

Colorado enacted the first ALI-type reform in April 1967. Sponsored by state representative Richard Lamm (who later became governor), the legislation proceeded smoothly through the legislature and drew little public attention. North Carolina was the second state to adopt a reform a few days later. Studies later showed that the new statutes had little impact on the availability of legal abortions, probably because, as the North Carolina legislator who sponsored the bill said, the laws "merely . . . [made] legal what doctors actually had been doing previously."

Abortion law reformers were, of course, interested in changing the laws in the nation's larger states. By 1967 the prospects in California were quite favorable. Governor Ronald Reagan objected to a provision in the proposed reform bill that would have allowed abortions in cases of fetal defects. Because the bill still allowed abortions to preserve the woman's life or physical or mental health, its chief sponsor believed that removing the provision that Reagan objected to would not make much difference. With that provision removed, Reagan signed the reform bill in June 1967. The new statute relied on the ALI model, with its potentially restrictive approach to the physical and mental health exceptions. Still, it was a victory for the reformers, unlike their defeats earlier that year in New York and elsewhere.

A pattern developed in the politics of abortion reform. Proponents of reform proposed an ALI-style reform bill and the legislation began to move ahead. Opponents, principally associated with the Roman Catholic church, then mobilized against reform. Reformers won preliminary victories but by the end of a legislative session the issue of reform became so contentious that nothing happened. For example, Georgia's lower house adopted a reform proposal by a vote of 129 to 3, but two weeks later the proposal died in a state senate committee. In New York the reform proposal lost in a house committee in March 1967. Reform proposals were defeated in Texas as well.

Still, public support for reform grew. In Georgia reformers modified their ALI-style bill to include provisions limiting abortions to women who had lived in Georgia for four months and requiring that abortions be performed in hospitals rather than clinics. As amended the statute was enacted in 1968. New Mexico, Arkansas, Kansas, Oregon, and Delaware adopted similar reforms in 1969.

Again, though, the enduring issue was how broadly prosecutors and doctors would construe the exception for therapeutic abortions. Most activists had come to believe that the exception would inevitably be too narrow. And, they argued, at the very least doctors would have wildly differing views about when a woman's life was threatened. If a woman found a sympathetic psychiatrist, she might get the doctor to agree that she might commit suicide if she had to continue her pregnancy. If she stayed with her regular gynecologist, she might not get the required medical approval. Proponents of repeal thought this disparity was another source of unfairness that repeal would eliminate.

New York's Governor Rockefeller appointed a committee in 1968 to study reform. Its report supported reform, defining threats to the woman's life and health rather broadly, and endorsing the idea of abortion for social or economic indications. Although the reform proposal had to be withdrawn in 1968, it was reintroduced in 1969. Activists continued to recruit respected legislators to sponsor their bills. By now, however, their primary focus was on bills that would repeal rather than reform the abortion laws, by allowing an early abortion whenever a woman found a doctor willing to perform it. Once again, though, the bill narrowly failed. Repeal proposals also failed, by narrow margins, in Nevada and Illinois, and a reform proposal lost in Michigan by four votes.

The Litigation Movement to Repeal Abortion Laws: Augmenting Griswold

While the legislative reform efforts were progressing, advocates of repeal were attempting to work out a strategy. They understood that most of the reform efforts would not actually make abortions more widely available, although the reforms might shift some abortions from back alleys to hospitals and clinics. The reformers had gained the upper hand in state legislatures, at least in part because public sentiment favored reform but not "abortion on demand." Advocates of more substantial changes wanted to allow abortions for what they called "social and economic indications," that is, when the pregnant woman believed that she was too poor to raise another child. These advocates began to focus on the courts.

The litigation challenges to restrictive abortion laws began when doctors in California and Washington, D.C., defended themselves against criminal prosecutions. A birth control activist contributed an essential element to the case against abortion laws when the Supreme Court agreed he could not be convicted for distributing contraceptives to unmarried women. Also, young lawyers in Texas and Georgia stumbled into the cases that the Supreme Court would use as the vehicles for invalidating the nation's abortion laws.

The vagueness challenge Leon Belous was a gynecologist practicing in Beverly Hills when a pregnant college student saw a television broadcast in which Belous advocated changing California's abortion laws. She called Belous, seeking help. After an emotional meeting at his office, during which he cautioned the student against getting an abortion in Tijuana, Mexico, Dr. Belous referred the student to a doctor from Mexico who performed abortions in California even though he did not have a U.S. medical license. Alerted to this fact, police brought charges of performing illegal abortions against the other doctor, to which he pleaded guilty; Dr. Belous was prosecuted for conspiracy to perform the student's abortion.

His lawyers appealed. They made two arguments. Restrictive abortion laws were unconstitutional interferences with the right to privacy recognized in *Griswold*, which logically had to extend to cover "early abortion by licensed physicians." As they put it, *Griswold* "reserves to the individual control of the procreative function free from unreasonable controls by the state." In *Griswold* the state sought to interfere with that right by denying access to contraceptives. Restrictive abortion laws interfered with the same right and were equally unreasonable.

In addition, the lawyers argued, the laws were unconstitutionally vague. Supreme Court cases make it clear that the Constitution is violated when the state has punished someone for violating a law so vague that no one could figure out when his or her actions violated the law. And, Belous's lawyers argued, no doctor could know what the California legislature meant when it banned abortions but created an exception for cases of threats to the woman's life or health.

The California Supreme Court agreed that the statute was unconstitutionally vague.[6] The statute said that abortions were permitted if they were necessary to preserve the woman's life, but, the court's majority said, the words *necessary* and *preserve* were too unclear. Prior decisions had established that the woman's death did not have to be imminent or inevitable. Then, however, the justices asked, *how* close to death did the woman have to be? And, if death was not close, how likely did it have to be? No one could know. The exception made the statute unconstitutionally vague. Three dissenters criticized the majority for "transform[ing] that which is simple and lucid into something complex and arcane."

The California Supreme Court's opinion discussed *Griswold* and the right to privacy in rather sympathetic terms, but it did not rely directly on that controversial right. It did say that prohibiting abortions, unless the woman's death was certain, would violate her constitutional rights. The court also described medical developments that made it "safer for a woman to have a hospital therapeutic abortion during the first trimester than to bear a child." And it recited evidence indicating that the risks from nonhospital abortions were enormous and unlikely to be eliminated by a criminal ban on such abortions. Its legal analysis was narrower, though. By invoking the more well-established ban on vague laws, the court suggested a line of attack against every restrictive abortion law that had some exceptions.

Milan Vuitch was an abortion provider in Washington, D.C., who received referrals from activists all over the East Coast. An immigrant to the United States from central Europe, Vuitch had been specializing in providing abortions since 1964. Although he had been arrested several times in Washington, D.C.; Maryland; and Virginia, he had been convicted only once of a minor offense. He was arrested again in 1968. A few months after the California decision, federal district judge Gerhard Gesell, the son of a well-known Yale psychiatrist, dismissed Vuitch's indictment on the ground that the federal statute against abortion, applicable in Washington, was unconstitutionally vague.[7] The statute's exception allowed abortions "necessary for the preservation of the mother's life or health." In a short opinion citing *Belous*, Gesell found that the word *health*, which some doctors used as a way to make abortions more readily available, was too vague: Did it cover threats to the woman's mental health, or only her physical health? And did health include general well-being, or did a threat to health require more severe impairments?

The government asked the Supreme Court to review Gesell's decision. The case turned out to be a procedural mess. The justices split on two issues. The first was technical: Could the government appeal Gesell's decision? Five justices agreed that it could. Unfortunately, they disagreed about the second issue: Was Gesell right?

Three justices, led by Hugo Black, believed that Gesell had misinterpreted the statute. As Black interpreted the statute, doctors could perform abortions "for mental health reasons." That was enough to eliminate the vagueness that bothered Gesell.

Justice Douglas thought Gesell was right. He argued that Black's approach allowed doctors to rely on the "highly subjective" judgments about whether a woman's mental health was really threatened. Could a doctor perform an abortion, Douglas asked, for women who wanted "to avoid the 'stigma' of having an illegitimate child? Is bearing a 'stigma' a 'health' factor? Is any unwanted pregnancy a 'health' factor because it is a source of anxiety?" Juries, Douglas argued, could not fairly decide whether the doctor's subjective answers to these questions were correct.

Finally, Justice Stewart thought the solution should be to make a licensed doctor's decision that there was a threat a complete defense. For him, the statute gave the doctor the exclusive right to determine whether there was a threat, "without the overhanging risk of incurring criminal liability at the hands of a second-guessing lay jury."

With four justices saying that the government should not be allowed to appeal, what could be done? Justice Harry Blackmun, appointed to the Court only a year earlier, broke the logjam by saying that, although he did not think the Court should hear the case, he would go along with Justice Black's interpretation of the statute. After that, Justice Harlan went along as well, giving Black a majority to send the case back to Gesell.[8] Most observers agreed that the new expansive definition, allowing abortions when a woman's health was threatened, would allow doctors to perform abortions in Washington, D.C., pretty much whenever they deemed it necessary.

The Court's decision did not eliminate the possibility of continuing to attack state abortion laws as unconstitutionally vague. It did suggest, though, that the "right to privacy" arguments would play a large role in the Court's ultimate decision. Throughout the oral arguments in *United States v. Vuitch*, justices asked about the right to privacy, even though the only real issue in the case was Gesell's decision that the statute was too vague. Their discussions among themselves repeatedly referred to pending lawsuits challenging abortion laws on privacy grounds. Justice Black, for example, told his colleagues that he "can't go with [a] woman's claim of [a] const[itutional] right to use her body as she pleases."

Privacy and unmarried people Bill Baird worked for a contraceptive manufacturer until he was let go because of his public advocacy of eliminating restrictions on contraceptive distribution. He began a crusade against such laws and in April 1967 gave a speech at Boston University. Saying that students were being "enchained by men who have no right to dictate to you the privacy of your bodies," Baird passed out packages of vaginal foam to a number of women. He was arrested for violating Massachusetts' ban on distributing and exhibiting contraceptives. As amended after *Griswold*, the statute allowed doctors and pharmacists to distribute contraceptives to married people, but barred anyone else from doing so, and continued to ban the distribution of contraceptives to unmarried people.

The Massachusetts Supreme Court upheld Baird's conviction for distributing the packages, but struck down his conviction for exhibiting them. The ban on exhibiting contraceptives, the court said, violated the free speech provisions of the First Amendment. But the distribution ban, the court said, was a permissible regulation aimed at promoting public health.

Baird then moved his case to federal court, using the procedure known as *habeas corpus*, which allows a person convicted of a crime in state court to get a federal court to consider constitutional challenges to the conviction. (The defendant in a habeas corpus case is the jailer or prison warden, so the case was known in the lower courts as *Eisenstadt v. Baird*, after the sheriff in charge of Boston's jail.) The federal appeals court rejected Baird's argument that the distribution ban also violated his free speech rights.[9] It agreed, though, that it was an unreasonable way of promoting public health. The statute allowed doctors to distribute contraceptive material to *married* people, if the doctor decided that the patient's health would be promoted by using contraceptives. The appeals court could not understand how public health would be promoted by denying the doctor the opportunity to distribute the same material under the same conditions to an *unmarried* person.

The prosecutors also argued, though, that the ban was designed to protect morals. They argued that unmarried people who could not get access to contraceptives would be deterred from engaging in sexual relations. The appeals court found that argument implausible. Before *Griswold*, the statute banned distribution to married people, so, the court said, it could not have been designed to deter fornication by unmarried people. The state could not try to deter fornication "by making the penalty a personally, and socially, undesired pregnancy."

The court believed the statute really expressed the judgment that using contraceptives was itself immoral. But, the court continued, once deterrence was out of the picture, it had to assume that the state was trying to say that people who "nevertheless persist in having intercourse" behave immorally when they use contraceptives. Such people had to risk "an unwanted pregnancy," which made the statute "the very mirror image of sensible legislation." Without a showing of "demonstrated harm," such morals regulations were unconstitutional.

Massachusetts appealed to the Supreme Court. By the time the Court heard the case in November 1971, Justices Black and Harlan had retired because of ill health. To fill their seats, President Richard Nixon nominated Lewis F. Powell, a prominent Richmond lawyer who had been head of the American Bar Association, and William H. Rehnquist, an Arizona conservative who was head of the office in the Justice Department that served as the "lawyers' lawyers." They had not been confirmed, though, when the Court considered *Eisenstadt v. Baird*.

When the remaining seven justices met to discuss the case, Chief Justice Burger said that he would uphold the statute because Baird was not a doctor. Douglas relied on the First Amendment, while Brennan thought that Baird's actions were protected by *Griswold*. Justice Stewart also relied on *Griswold*, saying that Massachusetts's statute was "complete[ly] irrational[ ]," because there was no health-based distinction between married and unmarried people. Justice Blackmun, still tentative in his first years on the Court, did not think the statute really was designed to promote public health and was "bothered" that the state allowed only doctors to distribute contraceptives.

Burger concluded the discussion by saying that he would not vote on the case because he could not "discover what the issue is."

Burger's action might have affected the power to assign someone to write the Court's opinion. If the Chief Justice is in the majority, he chooses the author; otherwise the most senior associate justice in the majority does. If Burger adhered to his initial vote to uphold the Massachusetts statute, Douglas could have chosen the author.

Assigning the opinion is important for two reasons. When some justices who initially vote with the majority are not firm in their judgments, a well-written opinion can solidify the majority and a badly written one can sometimes drive tentative votes away and create a new majority to go the other way. Even if the majority's votes are firm, one justice might write a broad opinion and another a narrow one. Burger's colleagues sometimes suspected he fudged his own votes so he could influence the outcomes in these ways by choosing the opinion's author.

But, as Douglas saw things, Burger had voted to uphold the statute, and within a week Douglas decided to assign the opinion to Justice Brennan, hoping for a short unsigned opinion describing the different reasons the justices had for finding the statute unconstitutional. Instead, Brennan sent his colleagues a more expansive opinion in December, but it got only two more votes when at least three were needed to make it a majority opinion of the seven sitting justices. And then the opinion simply sat around.

Eventually Justice Douglas, who stressed the importance of getting the Court's work done, signed on to Brennan's opinion. Much of Brennan's opinion tracked the arguments of the federal appeals court.[10] It relied on the Fourteenth Amendment's equal protection clause, finding that the statute's different treatment of married and unmarried people was unreasonable.

At its most basic level, the equal protection clause means that governments must have some reason to treat different people differently. The reasons have to be related to the purposes the government is trying to accomplish. For example, if a government wants to deter housebreaking, it can make it a crime for someone to possess housebreaking tools.[10] That statute does treat people differently—people who do not possess such tools get better treatment than people who do—but the government has a reason for the different treatment—it advances the purpose of deterring housebreaking.

This legal analysis makes it crucial for the courts to decide what a statute's purpose is. It might make sense to treat people differently if the purpose is deterring housebreaking, but it would not be reasonable to make the same distinction if the government's purpose is, for example, to deter extramarital sexual relations: There simply is no connection between having housebreaking tools and engaging in extramarital affairs, and so the different treatment of those who have and those who do not have such tools would be unreasonable in light of the purpose of deterring extramarital affairs.

What, then, was the purpose of Massachusetts's ban on distribution of contraceptives to unmarried people while allowing distribution to married people? The state might have been trying to deter premarital sex. But, Justice Brennan said, "[i]t would be plainly unreasonable to assume that Massachusetts has prescribed pregnancy and the birth of an unwanted child as punishment for fornication." The statute allowed married people to get contraceptives even if they were about to engage in sexual relations with unmarried people and it allowed distribution of contraceptives to unmarried people when the aim was to avoid disease rather than pregnancy. The statute, Brennan wrote, was "so riddled with exceptions that deterrence of premarital sex cannot reasonably be regarded as its aim."

Nor did banning distribution of contraceptives to unmarried people protect against the distribution of harmful materials. If the materials were harmful, they would hurt married people as well as unmarried ones. And, in any event, "not all contraceptives [for example, condoms] are potentially dangerous."

What about a ban on contraceptives as immoral? Here Justice Brennan wrote sentences that proved critical in the attack on abortion laws:

> [W]hatever the rights of the individual to access to contraceptives may be, the rights must be the same for the unmarried and the married alike.
> If under *Griswold* the distribution of contraceptives to married persons cannot be prohibited, a ban on distribution to unmarried persons would be equally impermissible. It is true that in *Griswold* the right of privacy in question inhered in the marital relationship. Yet the marital couple is not an independent entity with a mind and heart of its own, but an association of two individuals each with a separate intellectual and emotional makeup. If the right of privacy means anything, it is the right of the individual, married or single, to be free from unwarranted governmental intrusion into matters so fundamentally affecting a person as the decision whether to bear or beget a child.

These sentences transformed *Griswold* from a case about state intrusions on the sacred precincts of the marital bedroom into a case about the individual's right to make fundamental decisions connected to sexuality. In writing these sentences, Justice Brennan knew the Court would soon have to confront challenges to abortion laws. Law clerks at the time believed Brennan inserted them to lay the foundation for a decision striking down existing abortion laws.

Justice Douglas wrote a concurring opinion relying, as he had said before, on the free speech clause. Justice White was joined by Blackmun in agreeing that the statute was unconstitutional when applied to Baird's distribution of vaginal foam, which on no view could be considered a risky product. Chief Justice Burger dissented, saying that the only issue in the case was whether Massachusetts could penalize Baird, who was not a doctor, from distributing material the state believed only licensed physicians or pharmacists should handle.

3

Abortion in the Supreme Court, 1973–1993

Roe *in the Supreme Court*

Norma McCorvey had drifted from job to job when in 1969 she discovered she was pregnant after a brief affair. She already had given birth to two children; her mother had custody of one and the other had been adopted. McCorvey was from Dallas, and she returned there to find someone who would provide her a safe and inexpensive abortion. At the office of an osteopath to whom she had been referred, another patient told her it would be easier for her to get an abortion if McCorvey said she had been raped. McCorvey did so, and held to that story for many years before acknowledging that her pregnancy arose from less dramatic circumstances. The doctor she consulted, though, told her it would cost her $500 to get an abortion and she would have to go to California or New York.

McCorvey could not afford to pay that much for an abortion and began to look once again for someone who could assist her in placing her child for adoption in exchange for payment of her medical fees. The lawyer she contacted did help with that. He also referred McCorvey to two young lawyers, Sarah Weddington and Linda Coffee, who had been trying to find a plaintiff for a lawsuit to challenge Texas's abortion law.

Weddington and Coffee were working with a women's group in Austin whose project to provide information about birth control had now started to refer women wanting abortions to Dr. James Hallford near Dallas, whose office became something of an abortion clinic for college students seeking abortions. The group wanted to know whether they could operate an abortion referral service openly. Weddington, recently graduated from the University of Texas Law School, could not come up with a clear answer.

The group then thought about challenging Texas's abortion law itself. After some hesitation, Weddington agreed to look into the possibility. Weddington got in touch with Coffee, a law school classmate, and they began to work out a strategy.

Their first problem was to find a plaintiff. The federal courts require that plaintiffs challenging state laws have *standing*. That is a technical doctrine whose central requirement is that the plaintiff be someone who is actually being hurt by the state law. Consider a law banning the sale of alcohol to young men. A liquor-store owner prosecuted for violating the law has standing to challenge the law as a denial of equal protection of the law because it unfairly discriminates between young men and young women. Even someone who is about to be charged with violating the law has standing. A young man who would like to purchase liquor most likely would have standing as well.

Who might be plaintiffs in the suit against the abortion law? Perhaps Dr. Hallford, who might say that he wanted to perform abortions but was deterred by the restrictive law. Perhaps a pregnant woman, who would claim that the Constitution gave her a right to an abortion. But no one in the women's group in Austin was pregnant. It was also not clear that a woman could get standing by claiming she had to take additional precautions when she had intercourse because she was afraid that if she got pregnant she would be unable to get an abortion; that might not count as a real injury under the doctrine of standing.

McCorvey, a pregnant woman, was probably the best kind of plaintiff. There was another problem, though. The federal courts do not decide *moot cases*. Suppose McCorvey had standing because she could not get an abortion. By the time Weddington and Coffee got in touch with her, McCorvey's pregnancy was well advanced, and she was certain to carry her pregnancy to term. By the time a court could decide her case, the baby would have been born. Her challenge to the Texas abortion law might be moot because she could get no benefit from a ruling striking the law down.

Fortunately for McCorvey and her lawyers, the Supreme Court has developed another rule about moot cases. If a problem is, as the Court puts it, "capable of repetition but evad[es] review," the fact that the harm has ended will not make the case moot. Pregnancies last only nine months, far shorter than the period necessary for judicial review. And they are capable of repetition. McCorvey, who had been pregnant three times, could easily become pregnant again.

McCorvey's case might get over the problems of standing and mootness, but there was yet a third procedural problem. The lawyers wanted the federal court to issue an order, known as an *injunction,* against enforcing the criminal ban on abortion. Courts usually treat injunctions as special remedies, to be used only when there is no other way to grant relief. With a criminal law, however, there is an obvious alternative to an injunction. As *Griswold* showed, someone prosecuted for violating the law can raise constitutional challenges as a defense. Traditionally, courts were reluctant to issue injunctions against ("enjoin") criminal prosecutions, relying on the *Griswold* route to get to the constitutional challenges. Even more, *federal* courts were particularly reluctant to enjoin prosecutions for violating *state* laws. When McCorvey's case reached the Supreme Court, the Court postponed ruling on the merits of her constitutional claim until it worked out new rules for enjoining state criminal prosecutions in a series of non-abortion cases.

Linda Coffee drafted the document that started McCorvey's lawsuit. To ensure privacy, it referred to McCorvey as Jane Doe. It also included as plaintiffs a married couple; the wife recently had obtained an abortion in Mexico because she was devastated by the physical and psychological effects of her pregnancy, and the couple alleged that their inability to obtain an abortion in Texas interfered with their "marital happiness." The case was filed in March 1970. Because Dr. Hallford had been indicted in 1969 for performing illegal abortions, he soon joined the lawsuit.

Weddington and Coffee were not part of the larger national network of pro-choice activists. Neither were the lawyers who challenged Georgia's ALI-type reform statute; they objected to the "red tape" a woman had to go through to get a therapeutic abortion under the reform law, and they supported abortion law repeal. But repeal failed in the state legislature in 1970, and the lawyers started looking for a plaintiff. The lawyers and their supporters asked the women operating the abortion service at Atlanta's main hospital to send them any woman who could not get through the red tape.

In early 1970 a woman, known in the litigation as Mary Roe, came to the hospital to get approved for a therapeutic abortion on psychological grounds: She was in the process of getting divorced from her abusive husband, her three children had already been taken away from her for adoption or foster care, she had been briefly treated at a state psychiatric facility, and she could not care for another baby. Over the course of six weeks Doe spoke with psychiatrists at the hospital. Eventually the hospital committee refused to approve the abortion. The Georgia lawyers filed their lawsuit in April 1970.

Throughout the national network, plans were proceeding for lawsuits against abortion laws. Lawyers filed challenges in New York, Connecticut, and Wisconsin. The case in New York became moot when the state repealed its abortion law. The lower courts in Connecticut and Wisconsin issued influential opinions holding traditional abortion laws unconstitutional. In Minnesota, Jane Hodgson, a respected obstetrician and gynecologist, was charged with performing an illegal abortion on a woman who had contracted German measles. Hodgson raised the constitutional claims in her defense.

Cases challenging traditional and ALI-type abortion laws were thus bubbling up all over the country, and the courts were divided over the statutes' constitutionality. In general, though, the opinions striking down the laws were written by judges who tended to be more well thought of among knowledgeable lawyers than the judges who wrote opinions upholding the statutes.

The Texas and Georgia lower courts found that each state's abortion law did violate the Constitution. Instead of enjoining prosecutions, though, the courts simply issued declarations that the statutes were unconstitutional. In Georgia, though, the court indicated that the state could require a hospital committee to approve an abortion or require the woman to consult with a minister or other counselor, even though it struck down the limited list of reasons the state allowed for abortions.

These holdings created a procedural problem for both sides. The states had lost the main battle so they planned to appeal. Under the existing procedural rules, they had to appeal to the federal circuit court, one level below the Supreme Court. The plaintiffs, however, had lost a relatively minor issue, because the courts had rejected their requests for injunctions. And under the procedural rules, *they* could appeal directly to the Supreme Court. Because the plaintiffs knew the cases would not be resolved until the Supreme Court ruled, they decided to appeal even though the lower courts had struck down the statutes they challenged.

The appeals in *Roe* and *Doe* were surrounded with complicated procedural issues: Who had standing? Were the cases moot? Should the federal courts stay out of cases challenging state criminal laws and wait for someone who was being prosecuted, like Dr. Hallford in Dallas or Dr. Hodgson in Minnesota, to raise constitutional challenges as part of the defense? And, of course, underlying all this was the question of whether either traditional or ALI-type reform abortion laws were unconstitutional.

The procedural issues delayed the cases' resolution. When the abortion cases got to the Supreme Court, the justices were already considering a group of six cases about the federal courts' power to enjoin state prosecutions. The justices found these cases quite difficult and they had to be argued several times. When the dust settled, the Court held that the federal courts could not stop a prosecution once it had begun, which meant that Dr. Hallford's part of the Texas case had to be dismissed. The Court also began to develop restrictions on standing to challenge state statutes, which suggested that Roe and Doe themselves might not be allowed to challenge the statutes.

The justices postponed the abortion cases until they decided *Vuitch* in the spring of 1971. When a case comes to the Court, the justices first have to decide whether to dismiss it without further proceedings. Most cases come to the Supreme Court by *writ of certiorari*. The abortion cases, though, came under a procedure—now mostly abandoned—with the technical label *appeal*. The Court's decision not to hear a case that comes to it by certiorari has no legal significance. In contrast, in cases coming to the Court by appeal, the Court was technically supposed to rule on the merits. If the justices decided not to hear the case, they issued an order saying that the appeal was "dismissed for failure to present a substantial federal question." Four justices did vote to dismiss the appeals in *Roe* and *Doe*, arguing that the only issue really being appealed was whether the lower courts made a mistake in refusing to enjoin prosecutions and that this issue presented no substantial federal question. Five justices, though, voted to hear full argument.

When the Court got around to considering the appeals in *Roe* and *Doe*, it still had only seven members. Texas's lawyer asked the Court to delay its hearing until Powell and Rehnquist could participate, but the Court refused.

The oral arguments in December 1971 were rather routine. Sarah Weddington, arguing her first important case, stumbled a bit when asked to specify which constitutional provisions her case rested on. Georgia's lawyer, Dorothy Beasley, probably was the most effective advocate, at least in part because she began her argument by focusing on the issue of "the value which is to be placed on fetal life." Her opponents spent little time on that issue in their briefs, and none at oral argument. But, because Beasley went last in the arguments, Weddington did not have to respond to the questions Beasley raised.

Chief Justice Warren Burger opened the justices' discussion of *Roe* and *Doe* with a rambling summary of the issues, including the procedural ones. After saying that the underlying question was the "balance . . . between state's interest in protecting fetal life and woman's interest in not having children," he concluded that the Texas statute, though "certainly archaic and obsolete," was not unconstitutionally vague. His colleagues thought Burger also said that it was not unconstitutional on any other ground either, but their interpretation of his position became controversial within a few weeks.

Justice Douglas went next, saying that abortion was a "medical [and] psychiatric problem." He and Justice Brennan thought the Texas statute was unconstitutionally vague. Justice Stewart continued to hold the position he had developed in *Vuitch*, that licensed doctors could not be punished for performing abortions that, in their own judgment, they found medically appropriate.

As Justice Byron White saw the case, the issue was whether the government had the power "to protect [a] fetus that has life in it as opposed to [the] desire of the mother." Although he said that he was "not at rest" on the case, he clearly inclined in favor of upholding the Texas statute. Justice Thurgood Marshall noted that the "time problem concern[ed] him." He did not see any state interest in barring abortions one week after conception, but he wondered about late-term abortions.

Justice Harry Blackmun had served as general counsel to the Mayo Clinic in Rochester, Minnesota, before he was appointed to the federal bench. He was particularly sensitive to the impact of restrictive abortion laws on doctors who sometimes felt a conflict between the law's demands and their own medical judgment. He thought that a "strong argument" could be made that the government could outlaw all abortions if it could protect fetal life. He also thought that there was "no absolute right to do with one's body what you like." But, he said, the Texas law did "not go far enough to protect doctors." And there were other "opposing interests"—the woman's right "to life and to mental and physical health," for example. In the end, Blackmun voted to hold that the Texas statute violated constitutionally protected privacy rights.

Blackmun observed that Georgia's statute was "fine" and Burger agreed. There the state had responsibly performed its "duty to protect fetal life at some stage." White also thought that Georgia had "struck the right balance here." Justice Douglas worried that the Court did not "know how this statute operates, . . . What about the poor?" Marshall agreed: What would happen to African-American women needing abortions in rural areas where there were "no [African-American] doctors," he asked. Brennan said that he would strike down the Georgia statute's hospital committee requirement and Stewart agreed.

Blackmun also took up a suggestion Douglas made. He thought the Court's opinion should "recognize[ ] opposing interests in fetal life and [the] mother's interest in health and happiness." The Georgia statute appeared to "strike[ ] a balance that is fair," but Blackmun would like more information about how the statute actually operated, particularly with regard to poor women. Perhaps, Blackmun suggested, the Court's opinion should "paint some standards" and then send the case back to the lower court for additional factual findings.

Adding up the votes was difficult. In *Roe*, the Texas case, five justices clearly indicated their conclusion that the statute was unconstitutional, but some thought the opinion should rest on a vagueness argument and others on a "right to privacy" argument. Justice White clearly voted to uphold the statute. Burger's position was unclear: For him the statute was not unconstitutionally vague, but he had not said precisely what he thought about the right to privacy argument. The outcome in the Georgia case was even more murky. Brennan, Stewart, and Marshall voted to strike down the statute, and Burger and White voted to uphold it. Douglas and Blackmun appeared to want more information.

Douglas, a prickly personality, thought he had the right to assign the opinions in both cases, because—as he understood the votes—the Chief Justice had been outvoted. He also thought that Blackmun had voted against a majority that would *strike down* the Georgia statute. He was outraged when Burger assigned both opinions to Blackmun. Douglas would have given the Texas opinion to Blackmun, but he told Burger that Blackmun was in the minority in the Georgia case: "I would think, therefore, that to save further time and trouble, one of the four [in the majority], rather than one of the three [in the minority], should write the opinion."

Burger replied that he found the justices' discussion so confusing that he could not "mark up an accurate reflection of the voting" in both cases. The cases, he said, "would have to stand or fall on the writing." Indeed, they were so "sensitive" that they were "quite probable candidates for reargument." Burger's liberal colleagues, and particularly Douglas, were periodically suspicious of Burger's vote shifts. Sometimes they thought they resulted from Burger's inability to administer the Court's procedures; sometimes they thought they were conscious attempts by Burger to manipulate outcomes. Burger's comments raised those suspicions: If the cases were to turn on the writing, assigning the opinion to Blackmun was likely—so Douglas thought—to result in an opinion that failed adequately to protect the right to choose.

Douglas quickly drafted a short opinion relying heavily on *Griswold*. Women had fundamental rights that could be restricted only by "narrowly drawn" regulations. The hospital committee requirement was not narrow enough. By making the "final decision" turn on approval by doctors "in whose selection the patient has no part," the "freedom of association between physician and patient and the privacy that entails" would be destroyed. Douglas's draft also argued that the Georgia statute was unconstitutionally vague because it "does not give full sweep" to the criteria of psychological and

65

physical health that "saved the concept 'health' from being void for vagueness" in *Vuitch*.

After speaking with Brennan, Douglas decided against sending this draft to his colleagues, at least until after Blackmun circulated his own draft in the Texas case. In a long letter to Douglas, Brennan raised questions about relying on the right of association rather than the right of privacy. Treating the cases as involving privacy would mean that the right was clearly an individual one not shared with the doctor. Brennan identified three "fundamental freedoms" implicated in the abortion cases:

> [F]irst, freedom from bodily restraint or inspection, freedom to do with one's body as one likes, and freedom to care for one's health and person; *second*, freedom of choice in the basic decisions of life, such as marriage, divorce, procreation, contraception, and the education and upbringing of children; and, *third*, autonomous control over the development and expression of one's intellect and personality.

Brennan then said that finding a fundamental right was "only the beginning of the problem," because, as Douglas's draft recognized, the next question was whether the state had "a compelling interest in regulating abortion." This would be "the most difficult part of the opinion," because it should deal not only with the woman's health but also with "the material interest in the life of the fetus and the moral interest in sanctifying life in general." For Brennan, these interests were not strong enough to overcome the woman's interest. He would find no government interest at all "in the early stages of pregnancy," and he "would leave open the question when life 'is actually present'—whether there is some point in the term before birth at which the interest in the life of the fetus does become subordinating." In the end, Douglas incorporated much of Brennan's analysis in the opinion he published.

Before that, however, Blackmun had to come up with something. When Burger asked his colleagues in January for a list of cases that should be reargued with Powell and Rehnquist participating, Blackmun leaped at the chance to delay decision and suggested including the abortion cases on the list. His more liberal colleagues tended to think it unnecessary to reargue cases where the Court had divided five to two. Even if Powell and Rehnquist joined the two dissenters, the outcome would not change. And, as they saw it, *Roe* was at least five to two. Hearing another argument in the case could make a difference only if Burger thought that somehow a shaky vote could shift from the majority. And they believed that Burger thought the shakiest vote was Blackmun's. Once again, then, the liberals' suspicion that Burger was manipulating the Court's internal processes came to the fore.

Still, with Blackmun suggesting reargument and drafting an opinion, there was little the liberals could do but wait. Blackmun, a notoriously slow opinion writer in his first years on the Court, finally produced a draft of *Roe* in May. It argued that the Texas statute was unconstitutionally vague and stayed away from what Blackmun called "the more complex Ninth Amendment issue." The draft called the Texas statute "insufficiently informative to the physician." Other justices and their law clerks thought this draft "awful." Its central problem was *Vuitch*. There the Court interpreted the statute to allow abortions to protect the woman's mental and physical health and found that those standards were not unconstitutionally vague. How could a statute that was *more* restrictive, limiting abortions to situations in which the woman's *life* was at risk, be vague?

Justices Brennan and Douglas quickly responded to Blackmun's draft. In separate letters they asserted that Blackmun's draft ignored the majority's view that states could not restrict abortions performed by doctors early in the pregnancy. This was the "core issue," there was a majority to address it, and there was no reason to reargue even the Georgia case.

Three days later, Blackmun sent his colleagues a draft opinion in *Doe*. It struck down the hospital committee requirement and the residency requirement. "What essentially remains," Blackmun told his colleagues, "is that an abortion may be performed only if the attending physician deems it necessary 'based upon his best medical judgment' . . . and if the abortion is performed in a hospital licensed by the State." He was troubled in barring the use of hospital committees because his experience at the Mayo Clinic convinced him that such committees "serve a high purpose in maintaining standards and in keeping the overzealous surgeon's knife sheathed."

The draft followed the lines that had by then become clear. It found that "a woman's interest in making the fundamental personal decision whether or not to bear an unwanted child" was protected by the Ninth and Fourteenth Amendments. The woman's right was not absolute, because "somewhere" during pregnancy "another being becomes involved." The government's interest therefore "grows stronger as the woman approaches term." Some restrictions on late-term abortions might be justified, but Georgia's system of regulation was "unduly restrictive of the patient's rights and needs."

To avoid the risk that the cases *would* be reargued, Justices Douglas, Brennan, Stewart, and Marshall quickly signed on to Blackmun's draft in *Doe*. With five votes there was, they thought, no reason for reargument.

The picture changed, though, when Justice White circulated a short dissent in *Roe* that powerfully attacked Blackmun's vagueness theory, saying that it "necessarily overrules" *Vuitch*. As White put it, "if a standard which refers to the 'health' of the mother . . . is not impermissibly vague, a statutory standard which focuses only on 'saving the life' of the mother would appear to be *a fortiori* acceptable."

Blackmun believed that White's analysis severely undercut the draft he had circulated. He strongly urged that both cases be reargued. "I believe, on an issue so sensitive and so emotional as this one, the country deserves the conclusion of a nine-man, not a seven-man court . . ." He also thought that some important issues were unresolved: Should *Doe* be the main case, with *Roe* redrafted to fit? "Should we spell out . . . just what aspects are controllable by the State and to what extent?"

Brennan told Blackmun, "I see no reason to put these cases over for reargument." So did Douglas, who said that the cases had been "as thoroughly worked over and considered as any cases ever before the Court in my time." Blackmun had done "yeoman service," Douglas wrote, and had "a firm 5" votes that would "be behind you in these two opinions until they come down."

Burger pressed for reargument, saying that he "had a great many problems with these cases from the outset," because he could not find a "specific provision of the Constitution" limiting state power. Douglas, still believing that Burger was manipulating procedures in the hope that the initial outcomes in the cases would be reversed after reargument, threatened that, if the Court ordered reargument, he would publish a statement "telling what is happening to us and the tragedy it entails." However, when Powell and Rehnquist decided that they had been on the Court long enough to vote on the question of reargument, the cases were set for reargument: Burger, Blackmun, Powell, Rehnquist, and White voted for it.

Douglas did draft a statement saying that Burger, who had "represented the minority view," had assigned the opinions, "an action no Chief Justice in my time would ever have taken." Burger's actions showed that "there is a destructive force at work in the Court. When a Chief Justice tries to bend the Court to his will by manipulating assignments, the integrity of the institution is imperiled." Because there were five firm votes in both cases, they should be announced. Reargument was "merely strategy by a minority . . . with the hope that exigencies of time will change the result. That might be achieved of course by death or conceivably retirement. But that kind of strategy dilutes the integrity of the Court and makes the decision here depend on the manipulative skill of a Chief Justice." Douglas was prepared to make his views public. Brennan tried to tone down Douglas's draft statement, and advised Douglas not to publish it in any form. In the end Douglas took that advice.

Justice Stewart, though, leaked the story to the *Washington Post* after Douglas left the city for his summer vacation home. Stewart was as angry as Douglas. After the vote to reargue occurred, Stewart called Burger "high handed" and said that he "want[ed] to make an issue of these things." Douglas wrote Burger that he was "appalled" at the leak. "I have never breathed a word concerning these cases, or my memo, to anyone outside the Court. I have no idea where the writer got the story," Douglas said.

Justice Blackmun spent the summer of 1972 working on the abortion cases at the Mayo Clinic's library. Despite what Burger might have hoped, Blackmun never wavered in his view that both the Texas and Georgia statutes were unconstitutional. The formal reargument was almost pointless. The only significant point in the reargument was Weddington's concession that "if it were established that an unborn fetus is a person," she "would have a very difficult case." But, Justice Stewart prodded her opponent, can a legislature decide that a fetus is a person? Were fetuses treated as persons in any other area of law? And, perhaps more important, if a fetus was a person, wouldn't laws *allowing* abortions be unconstitutional, because they would deny the fetus its right to life without due process of law?

The justices who had gone through the case in the spring stood by their positions. The oral arguments had clarified three points, though. First, the opinions had to say something about the state's interest in protecting fetuses. Not even Justice White thought that the fetus was a person itself entitled to constitutional protection, but that did not resolve the constitutional question. The public, acting through its representatives, can protect lots of things that are not *entitled* to constitutional protection, like bald eagles and historic houses. The real questions were whether the state could *choose* to protect fetuses, and if so, how much that choice counted when compared to the impact of restrictive abortion laws on women's right to choose.

Second, the justices decided that the opinions ought to say something about why late-term abortions *could* be banned even though early-term ones could not. And third, with everyone uncomfortable with Blackmun's effort to rely on vagueness doctrine, something had to be done about identifying the constitutional source of the limits on state power the majority was going to endorse.

The two new justices weighed in with their views. Justice Rehnquist simply endorsed White's position and, to the surprise of at least some law clerks, Justice Powell agreed that both statutes were unconstitutional. Later, Powell said that his views had been shaped by an experience he had while in private practice. An office boy at his law firm asked him for help after the older woman he had been seeing died from a botched abortion. Powell talked with the prosecutor and persuaded him not to bring charges against the office boy. Powell said this incident convinced him that making abortions illegal only drove them underground and made them dangerous. Powell's daughter backed those views and added that abortion had to be understood in the wider framework of birth control and child welfare.[1]

Blackmun told his colleagues that his summer's work had already led him to revise his earlier drafts, though not his conclusions. He said that his new opinion would say that "there is a point where other interests are at stake where [the] state can regulate." Because he still thought that the Texas statute was unconstitutionally vague, he planned to make the Georgia case the lead opinion. After Powell said that he too did not like the vagueness theory, Blackmun said that he would be willing to rely on the basic privacy theory in both cases.

Blackmun circulated his proposed opinion in late November. After a rather rambling discussion of the history of abortion and its regulation, the opinion made a key distinction. Responding to his colleagues' desire to distinguish between early and late-term abortions, Blackmun proposed to draw the line after the first three months. Before then, the draft said, the decision had to be left "to the best medical judgment of the pregnant woman's attending physician." After that, the states were free to limit abortions to "stated therapeutic categories that are articulated with sufficient clarity so that a physician is able to predict what conditions fall within the stated classifications."

Although the other justices in the majority were generally satisfied with Blackmun's new approach, Justices Brennan, Stewart, and Marshall were concerned that it might allow too much regulation after the first trimester. In response, Blackmun suggested that it might make as much sense to draw a line at viability, "when independent life is presumably possible." There were "logical and biological justifications" for drawing the line there, and there was, he said, "a practical aspect" because "many pregnant women, especially younger girls, . . . may refuse to face the fact of pregnancy" and therefore delay seeing a doctor until after the first trimester.

Justice Marshall replied the next day in a letter that had been discussed with Justice Brennan's law clerks. Expressing his concern that Blackmun's approach "would lead states to prohibit abortions completely" after the first trimester, Marshall's letter endorsed drawing the line at viability, largely for the practical reasons Blackmun mentioned. Marshall, though, added a new suggestion. Blackmun was worried about ensuring that abortions be performed under safe conditions after the first trimester, when the procedure became somewhat more complicated. Marshall suggested that the opinion could draw *two* lines. As in Blackmun's draft, essentially no regulations would be permitted in the first trimester. But, between the end of that period and viability, "state regulations directed at health and safety alone [would be] permissible."

The next day Brennan supported Marshall's suggestion, although he thought it would be helpful to abandon the word *viability*. Using that word suggested that the focus was on the state's interest in protecting the fetus, whereas the entire analysis otherwise focused on the woman's interests and the state's interest in protecting *her* health and safety. So, Brennan suggested, during the first phase the government could not regulate at all, during a second phase of uncertain extent—when "abortions become medically more complex"—the government could regulate to protect the woman's health and safety, and during a third phase—after viability—"the state may well have an interest in protecting the potential life of the child" and could regulate much more broadly.

Blackmun readily agreed with these suggestions. In a new draft, he said, he would "associat[e] the end of the first trimester with an emphasis on health, and associat[e] viability with an emphasis on the State's interest in potential life. The period between the two points would be treated with flexibility." The new draft quickly got five more votes. In early January 1973, Justices White and Rehnquist circulated short dissents. Burger finally signed on, with a short separate opinion saying that the Court had not endorsed "abortion on demand."

Two minor flaps occurred before the opinions were released. Blackmun proposed to issue a statement about the decisions in which he offered a short summary of what he thought they meant, and particularly stressing that "the Court does not today hold that the Constitution compels abortion on demand," or "that a pregnant woman has an absolute right to an abortion." Although the justices do sometimes summarize opinions when they announce them, Blackmun's proposal went farther than the Court's usual practice, and

Brennan persuaded Blackmun to do no more than announce the decisions.

Time magazine's issue for January 22, 1973, published a story summarizing what the Court was about to do. The story was based on an interview with one of Justice Powell's clerks, who had talked with a reporter on the assumption that the decision would be announced on January 17, before the magazine appeared. Burger's slowness in circulating his concurring opinion delayed the decision day. Burger, always a stickler for protocol and suspicious of the press, law clerks, and leaks, was furious.

The leak did not matter, though. Although advance copies of the magazine were available over the weekend of January 20, the issue was not widely available until January 22, 1973. And, on that morning, the Supreme Court met and released the decisions themselves.

Justice Blackmun's opinion began by acknowledging the Court's "awareness of the sensitive and emotional nature of the abortion controversy, of the vigorous opposing views, even among physicians, and of the deep and seemingly absolute convictions that the subject inspires."[2] It said that the Court "earnestly" sought to "resolve the issue by constitutional measurement, free of emotion and of predilection." After disposing of the issues of standing and mootness, the opinion examined the history of legal regulation of abortion. Modern restrictive laws, the opinion said, originated in the nineteenth century, primarily as a way of responding to the medical risks of abortions. "Modern medical techniques," the opinion continued, "have altered this situation by making abortion less risky to the woman than childbirth."

After recognizing the government's interest in protection of life from the moment of conception and the "less rigid claim" of an interest in protecting potential life, Justice Blackmun turned to the Constitution. Saying that the Court had recognized a right to privacy, either "in the Fourteenth Amendment's concept of personal liberty" or "in the Ninth Amendment's reservation of rights to the people," Justice Blackmun stated that the right was "broad enough to encompass a woman's decision whether or not to terminate her pregnancy." Restrictive regulations imposed a "detriment" on pregnant women: medical harm in early pregnancy, psychological harm, "the distress, for all concerned, associated with the unwanted child."

Because the right to choose was "fundamental," the government could restrict it only for compelling reasons. One reason might be that the fetus was a person itself, within the Constitution. Justice Blackmun spent some time explaining why that was not so: The census had never counted fetuses as persons, for example, and abortions were more freely available when the Fourteenth Amendment was adopted.

The state also argued that, because life "begins at conception," it had "a compelling interest in protecting that life from and after conception." Justice Blackmun said that the Court "need not resolve the difficult question of when life begins." The courts could not "speculate as to the answer" when specialists in medicine, philosophy, and theology had not been able to agree. He suggested that the states could "adopt[ ] one theory of life," but their decision to do so could not "override the rights of the pregnant woman."

But, Blackmun continued, the states did have two "important and legitimate" interests—protecting the health of the pregnant woman and "protecting the potentiality of human life." These interests "grow[ ] in substantiality as the woman approaches term and, at a point during pregnancy, each becomes 'compelling.'" This analysis laid the basis for the Court's guidelines. The interest in protecting the woman's health became compelling at the end of the first trimester, after which the states could adopt regulations that "reasonably relate" to protecting the woman's health. Such regulations might specify the provider's qualifications, and "the facility in which the procedure is to be performed," but the woman and her doctor had to be "free to determine" that the procedure should be performed. The interest in protecting potential life became compelling at viability, after which the states could outlaw abortions.

Justice Douglas wrote a concurring opinion that tracked the letter Justice Brennan had sent him. Justice Stewart, who had dissented in *Griswold* even though he called the anti-contraception law "uncommonly silly," now concurred. He "accepted" that *Griswold* rested on ideas of substantive due process, and said that Justice Blackmun's opinion "thoroughly demonstrated" that the states' interests "cannot constitutionally support the broad abridgement of personal liberty" in restrictive abortion laws.

Justices White and Rehnquist dissented. Rehnquist's opinion pointed out that abortions were not " 'private' in the ordinary usage of that word." He agreed that the Constitution gave some protection to women wishing "to be free from unwanted state regulation of consensual transactions," but believed that the protection was quite limited. All the states had to do was adopt "rational" regulations. The Court's "conscious weighing of competing factors" showed, Rehnquist said, that it was exercising a legislative rather than a judicial role. He pointed out as well that thirty-six states had restrictive abortion laws in 1868, when the Fourteenth Amendment was adopted. This showed that its drafters "did not intend" that the Amendment would "withdraw from the States the power to legislate with respect to this matter.

Justice White's opinion reiterated the argument that he had made during the Court's deliberations: Under the majority's analysis, the Constitution "values the convenience, whim or caprice of the putative mother more than the life or potential life of the fetus." White said that there was nothing in the Constitution's "language or history" to support that conclusion. "The Court simply fashions and announces a new constitutional right . . . and, with scarcely any reason or authority for its action, invests that right with sufficient substance to override most existing state abortion statutes." He continued, "As an exercise of raw judicial power, the Court perhaps has authority to do what it does today; but in my view its judgment is an improvident and extravagant exercise of the power of judicial review . . ."

Despite the controversy *Roe* produced in succeeding years, the justices did not believe they were striking out on a new constitutional path. The rulings from lower courts throughout the country against restrictive abortion laws meant that the Court's decisions in *Roe* and *Doe* fit comfortably into the existing pattern. Over the next years, the cases became increasingly contentious.

From Roe to Webster and Casey

Inside the Court *Roe* did not generate much tension until 1989. Outside the Court the story was different. Even before *Roe*, antiabortion activists had begun to mobilize against abortion law reform and had been able to block reform in several important states.

A long lobbying effort in New York ended in 1970 with a very contentious debate in the state's assembly, which was divided evenly over repeal. As the votes added up until only one more vote was needed to repeal the state's abortion law, Assemblyman George Michaels, an upstate Democrat, addressed the assembly: "I realize, Mr. Speaker, that I am terminating my political career, but I cannot in good conscience sit here and allow my vote to be the one that defeats this bill." New York, the nation's second largest state, had eliminated restrictions on abortions: There was no residency requirement and no requirement that abortions be performed in hospitals. Michaels did lose his seat when party leaders refused to renominate him at the next election.

In 1972 antiabortion activists tried to overturn the new statute. The state assembly voted to return to the old law by 79 to 68; the senate agreed, by a vote of 30 to 27. Governor Rockefeller, a long-standing supporter of abortion law reform, vetoed the bill.

Michigan had a referendum on abortion law repeal in 1972. A few weeks before the referendum, polls showed nearly 60 percent in favor of repeal. After an extensive advertising campaign asking voters to heed the "voice of the unborn," though, the referendum was defeated; instead of 60 percent in favor, when the votes were counted, 60 percent opposed repeal.

The experiences in New York and Michigan signal several related developments.

Reform successes: By 1970 the trend toward abortion law *reform* was clear. Fifty-six percent of Washington state's voters approved a referendum liberalizing the state's abortion laws. The new statute had a residency requirement and allowed abortions in the first sixteen weeks of pregnancy.

Repeal activism: But as reform began to succeed in legislatures throughout the country, advocates of changes in abortion laws shifted their focus. Now they sought to repeal the abortion laws and leave the decision to the woman and her doctor. *Roe* came down firmly on the side of repeal, when reform was likely to prevail in legislatures.

Antiabortion activism: The rising interest in abortion law reform generated a countermovement among defenders of restrictive abortion laws. Their opposition to repeal was one factor contributing to the legislative trend to reform: Legislators saw reform as a compromise between the status quo and complete repeal. The events in Michigan and New York in 1972 suggest that the balance of forces might even have shifted decisively in favor of antiabortion sentiment. *Roe* eliminated the possibility of compromises, and effectively stripped antiabortion activists of their political agenda.

Roe further impelled antiabortion activists into a new kind of political action. They mobilized to get legislatures to enact whatever restrictions might be compatible with *Roe* and pushed unsuccessfully for a constitutional amendment to overturn *Roe*.

They did succeed in getting state legislatures and Congress to bar public funding for abortion services provided to women receiving public assistance. The Supreme Court upheld these restrictions, saying that *Roe* did not create an affirmative right to have an abortion, but only barred government interference with a woman's "freedom to decide."[3] Denying public support for abortions "imposed no restrictions on access to abortions that was not already there." The fact that women were too poor to afford to pay for abortions was not "created nor in any way affected" by the government's decisions. "Although the government may not place obstacles in the path of a woman's exercise of her freedom of choice, it need not remove those not of its own creation."

(Pro-choice activists have argued that denying public assistance for abortions creates a "class" system of medical care: Well-to-do women can easily get abortions, while poor women must struggle to do so. Studies indicate, however, that the impact of denying public funding has been relatively small.[4] Some states continued to provide public assistance for abortion services, either by choice or because their state supreme courts interpreted the *state* constitution to require such funding. Some abortion providers charge reduced fees to women on public assistance, or work out monthly payment schedules. Many poor women have found it possible to borrow whatever they need to pay for an abortion.)

Roe expressly said that it did not hold that there was a constitutional right to abortion on demand. In many states, legislatures responded to *Roe* by enacting new restrictions that attempted to reduce the number of abortions without challenging what came to be called *Roe*'s "central premise"—that the Constitution barred states from making it a criminal offense to have or perform *any* abortion. Almost all of the Court's decisions *invalidating* restrictions on abortions have been displaced by its 1992 decision in *Casey v. Planned Parenthood of Pennsylvania*, but it will be helpful in understanding how the Court dealt with the abortion issue to have a catalogue of the Court's decisions between 1973 and 1992.

Restricting public financing of abortions Our tax system means that people sometimes have to pay taxes to support activities they personally find offensive. Antiabortion advocates argued that abortions were *so* offensive to their fundamental beliefs that *no one*'s tax money should be used to pay for abortions. Congress enacted the so-called Hyde Amendment in 1976, which bars federal financing aid through the Medicaid system for abortion services, even where a doctor would certify that the abortion was medically necessary. After upholding a state's restriction on public funding for purely elective abortions (*Maher v. Roe*, 1977),[5] the Supreme Court upheld the Hyde Amendment (*Harris v. McRae*, 1980).[6]

Hospitalization requirements Once criminal laws against abortion were removed from the books, doctors and pro-choice advocates saw an opportunity to provide abortions in clinics rather than hospitals. Because clinics need not maintain the full range of equipment that hospitals do, they are able to provide abortions at a substantially lower price. Antiabortion advocates urged states and cities to adopt rules requiring that abortions be performed in hospitals, on the ground that clinics could not effectively handle the complications that sometimes arose in connection with abortions. The Supreme Court found such rules unconstitutional (*City of Akron v. Akron Center for Reproductive Health*, 1983).[7]

Parental and spousal consent laws In *Planned Parenthood of Missouri v. Danforth* (1976), the Court invalidated a statute requiring the consent of the woman's spouse, saying that "giving the husband a veto power" would rarely serve the asserted state interests in "fostering mutuality and trust in a marriage."[8] When spouses disagreed, one would necessarily prevail and that, the Court said, should be the woman.

When women who are minors seek abortions, should the law require that their parents be involved in the decision? The laws could involve parents by requiring their consent or by requiring that they be notified.

Parental consent In a series of cases the Court adopted the position that states could require *either* parental consent or approval by a state judge before an abortion was performed on a minor (*Bellotti v. Baird*, 1979; *Planned Parenthood of Kansas City v. Ashcroft*, 1983).[9] The judge had to decide whether the woman was mature enough to make the abortion decision on her own or, if not, whether the abortion was in the minor woman's best interests. Experience has shown that, although each judge's decision is strongly affected by his or her view about the morality of abortion itself, in general these "judicial bypass" proceedings, as they are called, end with the judge permitting the abortion.[10] That seems to be because many pregnant young women are mature enough, and in the remaining cases involving immature young women it is ordinarily quite hard to show that requiring an immature woman to bear a child would be in the woman's best interests.

Parental notification The Court upheld a Utah statute requiring that the parents of unmarried minor women living at home be notified before an abortion was performed, although it indicated that in some individual cases—for example, where parental notification might produce an assault by a parent on the woman—it might be unconstitutional to require notification.[11]

Informed consent laws In *Planned Parenthood of Missouri v. Danforth* (1976), the Court upheld a state law requiring that the woman certify in writing that she consented to the abortion.[12] Antiabortion advocates used the idea of informed consent to urge the adoption of regulations specifying particular information abortion providers had to give to women before they consented to the procedure. The Court held these regulations unconstitutional, finding it unreasonable to insist that only a doctor provide the information and finding it impermissible to provide skewed information designed to persuade the woman not to have the abortion (*City of Akron v. Akron Center for Reproductive Health*, 1983).[13]

Waiting periods In the same case the Court invalidated a requirement that no abortion be performed until twenty-four hours had passed after the woman signed the consent form. The Court said that the waiting period increased the cost of abortions, and it could see no state interest served by what it called "an arbitrary and inflexible waiting period."

Record-keeping laws and similar laws Although the Court allowed legislatures to define "viability," a concept that was important under *Roe*, it was uncomfortable with using legislative definitions to determine criminal liability. It therefore held unconstitutionally vague a Pennsylvania statute requiring doctors to make every effort to "preserve the life and health of the fetus" where the fetus "may be viable" (*Colautti v. Franklin*, 1979).[14] The Court also upheld a number of record-keeping requirements in the *Danforth* and *Ashcroft* cases, but it held unconstitutional a state law barring doctors from using a particular medical procedure (saline amniocentesis) in performing abortions.

These cases formed the background against which the Court ultimately confronted the question of whether to overrule *Roe*. Taking them as a group, the cases allowed states to impose relatively small restrictions on the availability of abortions, but not to restrict the availability too severely.

In the long run, antiabortion activists had their greatest successes in their efforts to influence the Supreme Court. Until the Court's membership changed, of course, there was little they could expect. But antiabortion activists believed that, over time, they *could* change the Court's membership, if not the minds of any sitting justices.

Ronald Reagan's election in 1980 provided the first opportunity. (Justice Douglas retired in 1975; president Gerald Ford appointed John Paul Stevens, a Chicago lawyer and judge who turned out to be a strong supporter of *Roe*.) Potter Stewart had been a lukewarm supporter of *Roe* and, like Burger, his views began to change as the Court confronted the funding cases and cases involving requirements that parents consent to abortions for their children. Justice Blackmun privately noted his "disappointment" with this drift, saying, "I fear that the forces of emotion and professed morality are winning some battles. That 'real world' continues to exist 'out there' . . ."

When Stewart retired in 1981, President Reagan nominated Sandra Day O'Connor to be the first woman Supreme Court justice. O'Connor had served in the Arizona state legislature before becoming a state judge and one of her votes there could be construed as support for abortion law reform. Some antiabortion activists therefore opposed her nomination.

Shortly after she joined the Court, though, Justice O'Connor severely criticized *Roe* as a decision "on a collision course with itself."[15] She argued that medical advances might make it possible to preserve the fetus's life rather early in pregnancy—before the time when, under *Roe*, the state could regulate abortions to preserve fetal life. As a result, O'Connor argued, *Roe*'s holding that the states could restrict abortions after viability would conflict with its holding that states could not restrict early abortions. She urged that the Court replace its approach in *Roe* with one that would invalidate restrictions on abortion only when the restrictions placed an "undue burden" on the right to choose.

Chief Justice Burger had drifted away from his endorsement of *Roe*'s holding and eventually suggested that the Court's decisions after *Roe* had gone so far in the direction of making abortion available on demand that the Court should reconsider and probably overrule *Roe* itself. When Burger retired in 1986, President Reagan named William Rehnquist as chief justice, and Antonin Scalia as the new associate justice. Scalia was an adamant opponent of *Roe*, but his appointment did not shift the balance on the Court: With O'Connor, there were four justices who disagreed with *Roe*, but still five who supported it.

That changed in 1987, when Justice Powell retired. President Reagan nominated Robert Bork to fill the seat. Bork was probably the nation's most prominent conservative academic and judge, who had spoken out against *Roe* and many other liberal decisions of prior years. Concerned that Bork's appointment would decisively shift the Court in a conservative direction, liberal interest groups mounted a substantial campaign against his confirmation. When the nomination was defeated, President Reagan eventually settled on Anthony Kennedy as Powell's replacement. Kennedy was a California lawyer and lobbyist who had served for several years as a federal appeals court judge. He was reliably conservative, but did not reveal his views on abortion before he took his seat on the Supreme Court.

In January 1989 the Supreme Court agreed to hear an appeal by the state of Missouri from a lower court decision striking down several provisions of Missouri's law regulating abortions (*Webster v. Reproductive Health Services*, 1989).[16] One provision, which the justices eventually decided had no legal significance, declared that "the life of each human being begins at conception." Another, following on the funding cases, barred the use of state facilities for abortions, even if the woman paid for it herself. The most significant provision required doctors to perform tests on women seeking abortions after the twentieth week to determine whether the fetus was viable. This was a regulation of second-trimester abortions and so seemed inconsistent with *Roe*'s ruling that such regulations were justified only if they were designed to protect the woman's health or life.

The federal Justice Department urged the Court to overrule *Roe*. At first a majority—Chief Justice Rehnquist and Justices White, O'Connor, Scalia, and Kennedy—were inclined at least to substantially modify *Roe*. Rehnquist took on the job of writing the Court's opinion. His draft criticized the "rigid *Roe* framework." It argued that *Roe* itself recognized that at some point the state had an interest in protecting potential human life, and said, "we do not see why the State's interest . . . should come into existence only at the point of viability." It would have replaced *Roe*'s "compelling interest" standard with a much weaker requirement that a regulation "permissibly further[ ] the State's interest in protecting potential human life." But, the draft said, the Court would "leave [*Roe*] undisturbed" because the case did not provide the "occasion to revisit the holding of *Roe*."

Justice Stevens told Rehnquist that the new standard was too weak. "A tax on abortions, a requirement that the pregnant woman must be able to stand on her head for fifteen minutes, . . . or a criminal prohibition would each satisfy your test." Justice O'Connor too had some misgivings. Most of the time a justice will indicate rather quickly that she or he agrees with a draft opinion; Justices White and Kennedy, for example, had immediately signed on to Rehnquist's draft. Justice O'Connor, in contrast, waited to see what Blackmun's draft dissent would say.

Blackmun's draft was severely critical of Rehnquist. In light of the standard Rehnquist stated, "*Roe* no longer survives." By denying that fact, "the majority invites charges of cowardice and illegitimacy . . . I cannot say that these are undeserved."

Justice O'Connor concluded that Rehnquist's draft reached out to undermine *Roe*. In an opinion circulated just after Blackmun's, O'Connor pointed out that there always was some uncertainty about what week a pregnancy was in. Missouri required tests, she argued, within the range of uncertainty, and so really imposed no regulations on second trimester abortions at all. She therefore concurred in the result but not in Rehnquist's revision of the *Roe* approach. Justice Blackmun toned down his dissent, but he continued to note that "a chill wind blows" to threaten "the liberty and equality of the millions of women who have lived and come of age" since *Roe*.

Justice Scalia was furious with O'Connor. Her analysis, he said, "cannot be taken seriously." As he saw it, Rehnquist had drafted an opinion that did not explicitly overrule *Roe* only because Rehnquist believed that O'Connor would join it. By the time the dust had settled, though, it was too late for Rehnquist to start over and write an opinion—perhaps only for four justices rather than five—that took on *Roe* directly. Scalia quickly drafted a sharp opinion saying that *Roe* should be overruled. The compromise reflected in Rehnquist's standard was not "a triumph of judicial statesmanship" because it left the Court "in a field where it has little proper business."

The scenario in *Webster* was replayed in 1992, with a few new participants. This time the case came from Pennsylvania (*Planned Parenthood of Southeastern Pennsylvania v. Casey*).[17] By then Justices Brennan and Marshall had retired and had been replaced by David Souter and Clarence Thomas. Souter had been a state supreme court justice, only recently appointed to the federal court of appeals in Boston. His views on abortion were largely unknown. However, because he was sponsored by presidential adviser John Sununu, a leading conservative voice in the Bush administration, many observers believed he would eventually vote to reject *Roe*. Thomas's nomination was accompanied by enormous controversy. His critics believed he was unqualified for the Supreme Court. Some were particularly troubled by his assertion that he had never discussed *Roe v. Wade*, even though he had been active in conservative legal circles—where *Roe* was a symbol of improper judicial activism—for a decade. These misgivings were compounded by late-emerging charges that Thomas had harassed his assistant, Anita Hill. After a bitter debate, the Senate voted to confirm Thomas's appointment by the narrowest vote on a Supreme Court nomination in a century.

O'Connor had cast her first vote against a restrictive abortion law in 1990, agreeing that it was unconstitutional to require that both parents be notified of an impending abortion on a minor.[18] By the time *Casey* reached the Court, she had become concerned that overruling *Roe* would indeed threaten gains in women's lives she regarded as important.

The statute challenged in *Casey* went back over the Court's rulings after *Roe*. The Court previously held unconstitutional two of its requirements: a twenty-four-hour waiting period between a woman's decision to have an abortion and the procedure itself, and a requirement that doctors provide information about fetal development designed to persuade women not to have an abortion. It also required that a married woman seeking an abortion notify her spouse of her plans. Except for making abortion a criminal offense, the statute was as direct an attack on *Roe* as possible.

The prediction that the Court would overrule *Roe* seemed well founded. With Thomas on the Court, Rehnquist would not have to shade his opinion to get a fifth vote: White, Kennedy, and Scalia would be enough. He had not counted on what Justice Scalia sarcastically called the pull of "statesmanship," though. Precisely because *Casey* made it clear that the Court was on the verge of overruling *Roe*, Justice Kennedy backed away.

The arguments in *Casey* were hard-edged. No one suggested that the statute in *Casey* was somehow distinguishable from the ones the Court had dealt with before. The pro-choice advocates wanted *Roe* reaffirmed or abandoned; so did antiabortion advocates. Each side preferred a clear victory, of course. But each also preferred a clear defeat to a muddled compromise, because each believed that its supporters would be mobilized for further political action: If *Roe* was overruled, pro-choice activists hoped to enact a national statute protecting the right to choose; if *Roe* was reaffirmed, antiabortion activists hoped to elect a president and Congress that would even more forcefully advance their goals.

"Statesmanship" prevailed, however. Justices O'Connor, Kennedy, and Souter collaborated on an opinion reaffirming what it called the "central holding" of *Roe*, that "a State may not prohibit any woman from making the ultimate decision to terminate her pregnancy before viability." Yet the opinion simultaneously abandoned *Roe*'s analytic framework. Instead of allowing regulations only when there were compelling reasons, the joint opinion would permit any regulation that did not impose an "undue burden" on the right to choose. States could not "place a substantial obstacle in the path of a woman seeking an abortion" before viability. According to the joint opinion, that standard made sense because it allowed states to advance their "profound respect for the life of the unborn" without interfering with the ultimate right to choose.

Neither the waiting period or the required information were undue burdens, the joint opinion concluded. In contrast, the spousal notification requirement was, because studies of spousal abuse showed that a notification requirement would lead to more assaults on women.

Legal scholars could easily criticize the joint opinion's analysis. The opinion did not do a very good job of specifying the content of the undue burden standard. It also criticized the rigidity of *Roe*'s trimester framework, but did not explain why it should be replaced by an undue burden standard rather than, as Rehnquist wanted, a standard that would allow states to impose "reasonable" regulations on abortions.

But the joint opinion was concerned more with crafting a statesmanlike compromise than with developing a clear standard. After a defense of substantive due process, the joint opinion moved to an extended essay on the importance of *stare decisis*, the requirement that courts follow precedents even if they disagree with them. The Supreme Court does not have a rigid rule against overruling precedents, of course. That would make constitutional law too inflexible. But, the joint opinion said, the Court should be cautious about abandoning precedents.

The opinion's analysis stressed several points. Returning to Justice O'Connor's earlier point about advances in medicine, the opinion argued that these changes might have impaired *Roe*'s trimester framework and might affect the determination of when a fetus was viable, but they had "no bearing" on *Roe*'s rule that women had a right to choose before viability.

The opinion also discussed whether overruling *Roe* would be unfair "to those who have relied on it" or do "significant damage to the stability of the society governed by the rule." Here, the opinion said, it had to recognize "the fact that for two decades, . . . people have organized intimate relationships and made choices that define their views of themselves and their places in society, in reliance on the availability of abortion in the event that contraception should fail. The ability of women to participate equally in the economic and social life of the Nation has been facilitated by their ability to control their reproductive lives." People who had "ordered their thinking and living around" *Roe* would bear the cost of overruling it.

Even more expansively, the joint opinion asserted the important role the Court had, in its authors' view, in settling deep social conflicts. The Court sometimes "calls the contending sides of a national controversy to end their national division by accepting a common mandate rooted in the Constitution." When it does, overruling the decision is particularly unwise. Overruling "under fire" would almost inevitably seem to be "a surrender to political pressure, and an unjustified repudiation of the principle on which the Court staked its authority in the first instance." The Court had faced the divisive issue of abortion in 1973. "Whether or not a new social consensus is developing on that issue, its divisiveness is no less today than in 1973, and pressure to overrule the decision, like pressure to retain it, has grown only more intense." Overruling *Roe* "under the existing circumstances" would do "profound and unnecessary damage to the Court's legitimacy, and to the Nation's commitment to the rule of law."

Finding the joint opinion's defense of stare decisis unconvincing, four justices stated they would explicitly overrule *Roe v. Wade*. The "newly-minted variation on stare decisis retains the outer shell of *Roe v. Wade*, but beats a wholesale retreat from the substance of that case." After all, they pointed out, the joint opinion praised stare decisis even as it explicitly overruled cases striking down waiting periods and mandated information. Further, the new undue burden standard was just as much a departure from *Roe* as the alternative "reasonableness" standard would have been, and it was "created largely out of whole cloth by the authors of the joint opinion," rather than having roots in earlier decisions.

Justice Scalia, saying that it was "beyond human nature to leave [the joint opinion] unanswered," criticized the opinion's "epic tone." He referred to the Supreme Court's notorious *Dred Scott* decision before the Civil War, when the Court came down decisively on the side of Southern slavery. Its author, too, might have believed that the Court was "calling the contending sides . . . to end their national division," but that belief was "unrealistic." Issues "involving life and death, freedom and subjugation," cannot be settled by the Supreme Court. Treating the issue as a constitutional one, Scalia said, "banish[ed it] from the political forum that gives all participants, even the losers, the satisfaction of a fair hearing and an honest fight." To Scalia, the abortion question should be left to the political process.

Justice Harry Blackmun, in his last opinion on abortion, took comfort that "the flame has grown bright" with the joint opinion's acknowledgement that women had a fundamental right to reproductive choice. But, he wrote, he continued to "fear for the darkness as four Justices anxiously await the single vote necessary to extinguish the light." He could not "remain on this Court forever, and when I do step down, the confirmation process for my successor well may focus on the issue before us today."

Blackmun's prediction was wrong. When *Casey* was announced, spokesmen and women on both sides of the issue claimed they had lost, because both sides knew that the joint opinion's compromise probably made it impossible for them to make abortion a major political issue. With the election of President Bill Clinton, the replacement of Justice Blackmun by Ruth Bader Ginsburg and of Justice White by Stephen Breyer, the issue of abortion left the Court's docket and, at least for a few years, became less important in national politics as well. "Liberty finds no refuge in a jurisprudence of doubt," the joint opinion in *Casey* began. The *Casey* decision appears to have resolved the doubts about treating abortion as a constitutional issue, at least for a while.

4

Perspectives on Abortion as a Constitutional Issue

The United States experience dealing with abortion as a constitutional issue has opened additional perspectives on constitutionalism and abortion. Examining the treatment of abortion in the constitutional law of other nations, law professor Mary Ann Glendon suggests that the United States experience shows the distinctively individualistic character of U.S. constitutional law. She and others also argue that pro-choice groups, in relying on the courts to protect their interests, may have contributed to a heightening of tension over the abortion issue and may have obstructed the emergence of a resolution of the issue that would have been acceptable to all sides. Other scholars challenge Glendon's arguments. They suggest that, although in the United States the law is nominally more pro-choice than elsewhere, in fact abortions are available on roughly the same terms, and to roughly the same extent, in the United States and the nations on whose experience Glendon relies. They also suggest that the use of the courts by pro-choice activists may not have had much impact on the contours of political controversy.

These arguments place the U.S. constitutional law of abortion in two broader contexts. They direct attention to experiences elsewhere and to the interaction between constitutional adjudication and politics.

International Perspectives: Ireland

Every nation has some law regarding abortions and most nations have written constitutions. Not every nation, though, has a constitution that its courts can interpret to determine whether legislation is consistent with the constitution. But, when nations have constitutional courts exercising the power of judicial review, they are likely to have to face the question of abortion at some point. The constitutional abortion experiences in Ireland, Canada, and Germany are particularly illuminating.

Ireland's laws, influenced by the nation's Roman Catholic heritage, made abortions generally illegal.[1] In one widely reported 1938 case, a celebrated trial judge instructed a jury considering a criminal charge against a person who performed an abortion that a physician was *required* to perform an abortion if carrying the pregnancy to term would leave the woman a "physical and mental wreck." The jury then acquitted the defendant, who had performed the abortion on a fourteen-year-old rape victim. The "physical and mental wreck" standard might have made it relatively easy to obtain a legal abortion in Ireland. But Irish lawyers disagreed over whether the jury instruction accurately described Irish law and Irish doctors almost uniformly refused to perform abortions. They adhered to Catholic interpretations of the principle of double effect and would not perform abortions where the destruction of the fetus was the directly intended effect.

In 1974 the Irish supreme court decided the counterpart to *Griswold v. Connecticut*, holding that married persons had a constitutional right to privacy encompassing a right to obtain contraceptive devices.[2] The Irish supreme court's decision referred to *Griswold* and other U.S. cases. Those references alerted Irish antiabortion groups to what they thought might be a real threat, even though the Irish supreme court rather clearly implied that the contraceptive case implicated different interests from abortion. Antiabortion groups feared that, just as the U.S. Supreme Court had extended the right to privacy announced in *Griswold* to cover the right to choose in *Roe v. Wade*, so too the Irish supreme court might extend *its* decision.

After several years of organizing political support, antiabortion groups in Ireland put a "right to life" constitutional amendment on the ballot. Only 54 percent of the eligible voters cast their votes on the referendum, which was approved in 1983 by a margin of approximately two to one. The Eighth Amendment to the Irish Constitution states, "The State acknowledges the right to life of the unborn and, with due regard to the equal right to life of the mother, guarantees in its laws to respect, and, as far as practicable, by its laws to defend and vindicate that right."

Because few Irish doctors had been performing abortions, the right-to-life amendment had no immediate direct effects. But abortion was not unknown in Ireland. Abortions were easy to obtain in Great Britain, a short and familiar plane flight away. Some estimates indicate that each year in the 1980s, between five and ten thousand Irish women travelled to Great Britain to have abortions. A number of groups, many serving university communities, offered information about the availability of abortions in Great Britain. Antiabortion groups, led by the Society for the Protection of the Unborn Child (SPUC), saw the amendment as an opportunity to restrict the operation of these counseling centers: Closing them down would "defend" the right to life of unborn Irish children, as the Eighth Amendment required.

The SPUC went to court and received orders requiring the counseling services to stop "assisting" in providing abortions by making travel arrangements for women or by giving information about the availability of abortions at specific clinics outside Ireland. The counseling services then moved the controversy outside of Ireland as well. They called on European international courts to overturn the Irish decisions.

The European Convention on Human Rights, which Ireland has signed, protects a right of free expression "regardless of frontiers." The counseling services went to the European Court of Human Rights claiming that the injunction against distributing information about abortions in Great Britain violated this guarantee. A majority of that court agreed that the injunction violated freedom of expression. Most of the judges relied on the technical ground that freedom of expression is violated when courts issue injunctions without a specific statute authorizing them to do so; they believed that the Eighth Amendment itself was not specific enough. Some of the judges, though, said that limiting freedom of expression regarding abortion information was excessive, even if the government had a right to prevent abortions. They noted that telling people not to distribute information was likely to be ineffective unless those who received the information could be barred from leaving Ireland. A few years later the court adopted that position, noting that information about abortions could be obtained not simply from counseling services but from magazines and telephone directories. Barring counseling services from providing information was, the court said, ineffective in protecting unborn life.

Another European court also disapproved Ireland's policy. As a member of the European Community (the Common Market, now known as the European Union), Ireland may not interfere with the provision of commercial services across national borders, or with international travel. The counseling services argued that banning distribution of information interfered with the commercial operations of abortion providers in Great Britain. This claim went to the European commercial court, the European Court of Justice. Here, the counseling services lost on technical grounds. The Court of Justice agreed that injunctions against providing information interfered with commerce, but it pointed out that the counseling services in the case before the court were university student groups. Because they had no ties to commercial abortion providers, *their* rights to free commerce were not violated by the injunction against them.

The commercial decision was a victory in name only for the Irish government. It meant that foreign abortion services could advertise in Ireland. The Irish government therefore tried to renegotiate its international obligations. As these cases were proceeding, the members of the European Community were negotiating a new treaty to strengthen their commercial ties. The Irish government insisted that the new treaty, called the Maastricht Treaty, include a provision, Protocol Seventeen, stating that nothing in the treaty would affect the application of the "right to life" amendment in Ireland. The government's goal was to ensure that the Irish courts could continue to bar the distribution of information about the availability of abortions in Great Britain. As a technical matter, it might not have. Some lawyers argued, for example, that the court's decision did not deal with the application of the amendment "in Ireland," but rather dealt with the effects of the amendment in Great Britain.

A more serious defeat for Irish antiabortion groups lay ahead. A fourteen-year-old young woman, known throughout the litigation only as X, was sexually assaulted and made pregnant by the father of a friend whom she had been visiting. She and her parents decided they should go to Great Britain for an abortion. They were concerned, though, that the friend's father not escape punishment, so they went to the police and asked whether DNA test evidence taken from the aborted fetus would be admitted into evidence in an Irish prosecution of the father. The police said they would ask the public prosecutor. When the prosecutor learned of the plans being made by X and her parents, he went to court—not to prosecute the rapist, but to get an order barring X from leaving the country for nine months. (Later the friend's father was convicted of criminal assault and was initially sentenced to fourteen years in prison; a judge reduced the sentence to four and a half years.)

In February 1992, ten days after the Maastricht Treaty was signed, the judge issued such an order. The judge said that the travel plans posed a "real and imminent danger to the life of the unborn," and that the risk that X would commit suicide was "much less" and was "of a different order of magnitude than the certainty that the life of the unborn will be terminated."

The judge's order created a huge public outcry. The Irish electorate had to ratify the Maastricht Treaty and the X case became bound up in the ratification controversy. One-third of the public had opposed the "right to life" amendment, but many were able to live with it because women could at least go abroad for abortions. The

European Union treaties ordinarily protected the right to travel. Right-to-life proponents argued, though, that the provision saying that the Union agreements did not affect the application of the "right to life" amendment in Ireland authorized a travel ban as well.

Claiming that the order violated her constitutional right to travel, X and her parents immediately appealed. After lifting the injunction against travel, the court issued its opinion in March.[3] Two justices said that the order did *not* violate X's right to travel. As they saw it, the case presented a conflict of constitutional rights. On the one side there was X's right to travel and on the other the fetus's right to life. These judges thought it easy to strike the balance: in favor of life. As the court's chief justice put it, "If there were a stark conflict between the right of a mother of an unborn child to travel and the right to life of the unborn child, the right to life would necessarily have to take precedence over the right to travel."

Two other justices, though, thought that the courts did not have to "balance" competing rights. If the woman had a right to travel abroad, she had the right to do whatever was lawful in Great Britain. They thought that she could not be said to be "conspiring" to violate any law and therefore could not be barred from leaving Ireland.

Then, in an analysis that few observers had expected, these four justices said that X was nonetheless entitled to have an abortion *in Ireland*. She had threatened to commit suicide and, the court held, that created a risk to her own life. The risk did not have to be "inevitable or immediate," but only "real and substantial." The chief justice noted that sometimes the woman's life was *physically* threatened by her pregnancy. In such cases the woman's physical condition could be monitored and, if "diagnostic warning signs" appeared, an abortion could then be performed. In contrast, the chief justice said, it was impossible to monitor the woman to see if she was about to commit suicide. Another judge made the same point by saying that suicide threats meant that it was not "practicable" to protect the life of the unborn. Because the "right to life" amendment required the government to defend the fetus's right to life "as far as practicable," the amendment did not require the state to prohibit abortions in circumstances like X's.

Only one justice dissented. He argued that in making a "choice . . . between the certain death of the unborn life and a feared substantial danger of death but no degree of certainty of the mother by way of self-destruction," the courts should respond to the certainty of death rather than its probability. "If there is a suicidal tendency then this is something which has to be guarded against" by putting X under appropriate supervision with "loving and sympathetic care and professional counseling and all the protection which the State agencies can provide or furnish." He thought that "suicide threats can be contained." The dissenter also agreed that the woman's right to travel had to be subordinated to the fetus's right to life.

X's plight had caught the attention of the Irish public. The Supreme Court decision ended a major public controversy, but few were completely satisfied with the outcome. Right-to-life proponents believed that the X decision made abortions more freely available in Ireland than they thought proper. Pro-choice activists were worried about what a majority of the court had said about the right to travel. Three of the court's five judges said the right to travel *could* be overridden to protect the life of the unborn. That seemed to mean that the majority of women who went to Great Britain for abortions—who ordinarily did not face a "real and substantial" threat of death—might be barred from travel. Perhaps the same European commercial treaties that protected the distribution of information also protected the right to travel. The pending Maastricht Treaty, though, had Protocol Seventeen immunizing Irish abortion law from attack under the commercial treaties.

The Irish government tried to get around the pro-choice objections by getting Protocol Seventeen amended to make it clear that rights to information and travel were not affected. Unfortunately for the government, its treaty partners refused to amend the protocol. The Maastricht Treaty was controversial in many nations and the governments feared that opening the treaty to one change would open it to others. Instead, all the governments that signed the agreement issued a "Solemn Declaration" saying that "it was and is their intention" that Protocol seventeen would not limit freedom to travel or make information available in Ireland "relating to services lawfully available" elsewhere in Europe. They did this even though the Irish government had initially insisted on Protocol Seventeen *after* the European international courts had already protected the right to information; the Solemn Declaration apparently meant that Protocol Seventeen never really was intended to overcome the European courts' decisions.

Ireland's antiabortion groups had serious objections to the X decision. In its political campaign for ratification of the Maastricht Treaty, the Irish government promised to hold a referendum on abortion and the rights to travel and information. Three constitutional amendments were placed on the ballot in November 1992. Two would insert new language in the "right to life" amendment to protect the rights to travel and information. The third would have strengthened the ban on abortions: "It shall be unlawful to terminate the life of an unborn unless such termination is necessary to save the life, as distinct from the health, of the mother where there is an illness or disorder of the mother giving rise to a real and substantial risk to her life, not being a risk of self-destruction." This amendment would repudiate the X decision and place in the Irish constitution a stringent standard for determining when abortions would be lawful.

After another heated political campaign, the Irish voting public approved the amendments protecting the rights to travel and information and rejected the stronger "right to life" proposal. Approximately 68 percent of the electorate voted and over 65 percent of the voters opposed the amendment. Pro-choice groups, and those satisfied with the X decision, opposed the amendment. According to Irish political observers, some antiabortion voters did so as well because they disagreed with its limited recognition that sometimes "direct" abortions—intended to kill the fetus to preserve the woman's life—would be legal.

Several features of the Irish experience with abortion as a constitutional issue stand out.

- *International effects:* International influences affected the development of local constitutional law. The Eighth Amendment went into the Irish Constitution because of fears that the Irish supreme court would follow the path from *Griswold* to *Roe*. Its interpretation was influenced by the decisions of the two European international courts.
- *The power of dramatic facts:* There seems little doubt that the dramatic circumstances of X's case made the argument for a right to choice in such circumstances quite powerful. And the Irish public seems to have believed that attempting to keep X in Ireland until her baby was born was an egregious example of overreaching.
- *The complexity of the constitutional politics of abortion:* Even in a country with a population as committed to Roman Catholicism as Ireland, some facets of the abortion issue can be deeply divisive. Looked at from some distance, both in time and space, it seems almost as if inserting a "right to life" amendment in the Irish Constitution made it easier to obtain abortions in Ireland.

International Perspectives: Canada

Canada's constitutional treatment of the abortion issue resembles the Irish one in some ways. Dramatic facts had their effects, as did some examples of overreaching by antiabortion forces. In Ireland the result was to make abortions somewhat more easily available. In Canada the result was to eliminate any regulation of abortion entirely.

Canada saw the same revisions of traditional abortion law in the 1960s that occurred in the United States.[4] Prodded by doctors and law reformers, and supported by the Liberal Party's prime minister Pierre Trudeau, Canada's parliament enacted abortion law reform as part of a comprehensive revision of the nation's criminal laws. The new statute reduced the penalties for performing illegal abortions. More important, it allowed abortions if they were approved by a hospital's "therapeutic abortion committee," consisting of three doctors. The committee could approve an abortion if the doctors found that the pregnancy would endanger the woman's life or health. (Unlike the United States, where state governments make and administer most criminal laws, Canada's criminal law is made by the national government, but it is enforced in provincial courts.)

As in the United States, by 1969 the forces supporting abortion law reform saw this sort of liberalized abortion statute as inadequate. Even an official Commission on the Status of Women criticized the reforms. In the public eye, though, the most prominent opponent of the new law was Henry Morgentaler. Morgentaler, born in Poland, survived the Nazi concentration camps and, after receiving his medical degree in Belgium, emigrated to Canada in 1950. Later he said that his experience with the Nazis made him suspicious of all government actions. In Canada, Morgentaler practiced medicine and became active in the Montreal Humanist Fellowship. As its president in 1967, he testified in favor of abortion on demand during the first three months of pregnancy.

After Morgentaler testified, he was flooded with requests that he perform abortions. He decided that his principled support for the right to choose was more important than his fear of prosecution for violating the restrictive abortion laws. In January 1968 Morgentaler performed his first abortion and a year later announced that he was abandoning his general medical practice to concentrate on family planning, including performing vasectomies and abortions.

Because Morgentaler never got a hospital committee to approve the abortions he performed, all were illegal. In June 1970 he was arrested. Although Morgentaler initially wanted to get his case before a jury, where he thought he could challenge the law, his lawyers persuaded him to let them make all sorts of procedural motions that delayed his trial. In the meantime, he continued to perform abortions. By March 1973, Morgentaler announced, he had performed over five thousand illegal abortions. A few months later, Canadian television broadcast a program showing Morgentaler performing an abortion from start to finish.

Not surprisingly, Morgentaler's open defiance of the law brought further prosecutions. In August 1973 the police raided his clinic, forcing him to face the 1970 charges and ten new ones. In 1973 Canada did not have a constitution that the courts enforced to protect individual rights; as a result, Morgentaler could not challenge the constitutionality of the nation's abortion laws. Instead, he and his lawyers treated his trial as a political trial, where the lawyers would seek to persuade both the jurors and the public that even the reformed abortion laws were unjust.

Morgentaler and his lawyers created two kinds of political defenses. First, they focused the jurors' attention on the facts of the cases in which Morgentaler had performed the abortions: One, for example, involved a twenty-six-year-old student from Sierra Leone who had come to Morgentaler only after she discovered that a hospital abortion would cost much more than Morgentaler charged, would require a three-day stay and could not be scheduled for three weeks. Morgentaler was, the jurors were told, a compassionate doctor providing a necessary service to desperate women, not a back-alley abortionist.

Second, the lawyers argued that, as a matter of law, Morgentaler's actions were justified under the traditional defense of necessity. That defense protects someone who breaks one law when the law violation is necessary to avert a greater evil. (More recently, in the United States, some antiabortion activists have raised the defense of necessity against charges that they illegally have destroyed or damaged abortion clinics; in their view, their illegal actions are justified to avoid the greater evil of the destruction of human life through abortions.) Judges are usually skeptical about allowing the defense of necessity. In Morgentaler's case, however, the judge found enough evidence to allow the jury to decide whether Morgentaler's actions were justified by necessity.

To the surprise of many, the jury acquitted Morgentaler. In the United States, that would have been the end of the case. The double jeopardy clause of the Fifth Amendment says that no person shall "be subject for the same offence to be twice put in jeopardy of life or limb." The Supreme Court has interpreted this to mean that prosecutors are not allowed to appeal jury acquittals. In Canada, however, prosecutors can appeal acquittals on the ground that the judge gave instructions that erroneously favored the defense. The instructions about the necessity defense, the prosecutors argued, were precisely that sort of error.

In April 1974 the appellate court agreed with the prosecutors. Ordinarily the result would have been a second trial for Morgentaler. The judges on the appellate court did not send the case back for a new trial, though. Invoking a provision of Canadian law that had almost never been used before, they entered a verdict of guilty and sent the case back only for sentencing. This action turned Morgentaler's legal defeat into a political victory. He was sent to jail, but public outrage at the judges' refusal to let a jury decide the case strengthened the political position of those who thought the reformed abortion law was still too restrictive.

Meanwhile, Morgentaler closed his clinic and appealed his conviction to the Canadian supreme court. In 1975 that court upheld his conviction. As the supreme court's justices saw it, the only issue in the case was whether the appellate court had made a mistake in its treatment of the necessity defense. A majority thought it had not and that was the end of it. Neither the majority nor the three dissenters discussed broader questions of constitutional rights.

Once again Morgentaler's case became part of a broader pro-choice movement. When the Quebec government went ahead with the other charges against Morgentaler, his support grew, at least in part because people began to think that he was being persecuted. Two months after the Canadian supreme court affirmed his first conviction, Morgentaler went to trial on these additional charges. Once again, the jury acquitted him. The prosecutors again appealed, but this time the appellate court sided with Morgentaler. Two days after that, the Canadian minister of justice announced that he was setting aside Morgentaler's first conviction and ordering a new trial. Morgentaler left jail at the end of January 1976, having served about ten months of his sentence. Over the next few years, the number of legal abortions performed in Canada more than doubled.

Morgentaler's lawyers had to rely on the strained defense of necessity, and the appeal the facts had to the jury, because they could not rely on any constitutional rights. Until 1982 Canada adhered to the system of parliamentary supremacy. Although there was a statute *called* the Bill of Rights, it had no binding legal effect. Whatever parliament enacted was the law, which courts had to enforce.

That changed in 1982. After a vigorous political battle in which Pierre Trudeau championed the adoption of a constitutional system that would protect fundamental rights against legislative incursions, Canada adopted its Charter of Rights and Freedoms. The process of enacting the Charter mobilized woman's groups and supporters of human rights, who believed that the courts would enforce individual rights vigorously.

The Charter does not deal with the abortion issue directly. Section Seven of the Charter states that "everyone has the right to life, liberty and security of the person and the right not to be deprived thereof except in accordance with the principles of fundamental justice." During the debates over the Charter's adoption, antiabortion activists contended that this section protected the fetus's right to life, while pro-choice activists argued equally forcefully that it had no bearing on the abortion question.

Two weeks after the Charter became law, Morgentaler announced that he would open abortion clinics in Toronto and Winnipeg, his first ventures outside of Quebec. The Charter provided him the occasion for a renewed effort to eliminate all restrictions on abortion, but he was emboldened as well by the increased political contention over the abortion issue. A strong feminist community in Toronto could be expected to support Morgentaler's work and his legal challenges; the party governing Winnipeg's province supported abortion rights and the province's attorney general was a celebrated civil liberties lawyer who could be expected to sympathize with Morgentaler as well.

Morgentaler opened his Winnipeg clinic in early May 1983. It was a freestanding clinic, not associated with any hospital, and Morgentaler and his staff performed abortions without prior approval from a hospital committee. The abortions performed there were, in short, still illegal. A month later Morgentaler was charged with conspiracy to violate the abortion laws. In July, Morgentaler's Toronto clinic was raided by the police as well.

The prosecutors in Winnipeg agreed to hold off on their case until the Toronto case finished. Morgentaler's lawyers moved to dismiss the charges, arguing that the law restricting abortions to hospitals violated the Charter. They presented an extensive factual case: Their witnesses testified about the difficulties of obtaining permission for abortions from hospital committees, about the delays those committees caused, and about the medical and psychological aspects of abortion. In contrast, the prosecution presented no evidence at all. It argued instead that the facts Morgentaler's lawyers presented had no bearing on the law's constitutionality, only on its wisdom.

The legal arguments took place in the trial court during the last half of January 1984. Morgentaler's lawyers drew their arguments fairly directly from United States abortion law and *Roe v. Wade*. For example, they contended that Section Seven's guarantee of a right to life and personal security included "psychological as well as bodily security."

The trial judge had grown up in the tradition of parliamentary supremacy and was not ready to take a leading role in constructing the new constitutional jurisprudence under the Charter. In July 1984 he rejected Morgentaler's constitutional challenge and set the case for trial in October. With the constitutional issue removed from the case, Morgentaler's lawyers once again tried to appeal to the jury on political grounds. Again they presented Morgentaler as a compassionate physician persecuted by politicians concerned only with winning votes. When the time came to instruct the jury, the judge fairly clearly leaned against Morgentaler. He told the jury about the defense of necessity, but defined it in quite narrow terms. And he told the jury that they should not acquit Morgentaler merely because they might think that the abortion law was unwise. Even so, the jury refused to convict Morgentaler.

Once again, Morgentaler's trial and its outcome became the focus for political demonstrations on both sides. Faced with the conflict, the government decided to appeal the acquittal but, at first, also decided to let Morgentaler's clinic continue operating. The political controversy, and divisions within the government, eventually led the government to change its position, and once again the clinic's operators were arrested.

Relying on a 1984 Canadian supreme court decision, the appeals court reversed the acquittal in October 1985, holding that the jury should not have been instructed at all about the necessity defense, which the court said was completely irrelevant in Morgentaler's case. The court also rejected Morgentaler's constitutional claims against the abortion law itself.

By the time Morgentaler's case reached the Canadian supreme court, that court had become comfortable with its new role in enforcing the Charter of Rights and Freedoms. As one commentator put it, "the Court had begun to carve out a bold new path of judicial activism." Still, it took the court sixteen months to decide what to do.

At the end of January 1988, the court held Canada's abortion law unconstitutional.[5] Only Justice Bertha Wilson based her decision on the Charter's protection of a fundamental right to choose. Her opinion was much like the leading United States opinions in *Roe* and later cases and relied heavily on U.S. constitutional decisions generally.

Justice Wilson "had no doubt" that the right to personal liberty and security protected by Section Seven guaranteed "a degree of personal autonomy over important decisions intimately affecting their private lives," which included the decision to terminate a pregnancy. She linked this argument to a broader one about the changing relations between men and women. "It is probably impossible," she wrote, "for a man to respond, even imaginatively, to . . [the] dilemma [facing pregnant women] not just because it is outside the realm of his personal experience . . but because he can relate to it only by objectifying it, thereby eliminating the subjective elements of the female psyche which are at the heart of the dilemma." The right to choose, according to Justice Wilson, was "an integral part of modern woman's struggle to assert *her* dignity and worth as a human being." At some point in the fetus's development, restrictions on the right to choose would be reasonable; "It seems to me," she wrote, "that it might fall somewhere in the second trimester."

The court's majority took a different approach. They found the law unconstitutional on what seemed to be procedural grounds. The statute seemed to authorize abortions when permitted by a hospital committee, but, the majority said, the procedures for getting committee approval were so cumbersome that, as a practical matter, abortions—even those the law said would be legal—were extremely hard to obtain.

Chief Justice Brian Dickson, for example, found a violation of Section Seven because the abortion law told pregnant women "[at] the most basic, physical and emotional level" that they could not obtain abortions unless they satisfied "criteria entirely unrelated to [their] own priorities and aspirations." The uncertainty about getting approval, and the delays associated with the requirement of committee approval, made the psychological stress even worse. The delays also increased the risk that women getting abortions would themselves be physically injured by the procedure. Finally, Dickson said, the committees were told to apply a vague standard—whether continuing the pregnancy would endanger the woman's life or health—without any real guidance. Dickson concluded that the abortion law purported to create a defense against a criminal charge, but made the defense "illusory or so difficult to attain as to be practically illusory."

A concurring opinion by two other justices even more clearly relied on procedural problems with the existing statute. Their opinion, like Dickson's, suggested that Parliament might be able to enact a restrictive abortion law without violating the Charter, particularly if it ensured that hospital committees would make their decisions quickly. But, they all concluded, the existing statute was inadequate. (Two justices dissented.)

 Crown v. Morgentaler eliminated the criminal law as a way to restrict abortions. Antiabortion turned to the provincial level to see what they could preserve. Several provinces refused to pay for abortions or paid only for abortions performed in hospitals rather than in clinics. One refused to allow doctors to perform abortions in its hospitals.

 The most serious challenge to the pro-choice position, though, came in two cases where men sought injunctions against abortions sought by their former girlfriends. In Toronto, a judge issued such an injunction, which was overturned within a week—but not before the case attracted a great deal of media attention.

 During the same week in the summer of 1989 a judge in Quebec issued an injunction barring a woman named Chantal Daigle from getting an abortion. This time, though, the appeals court upheld the injunction. The Canadian supreme court convened an extraordinary session in August to hear Daigle's appeal. On the day of the hearing, Daigle's lawyer told the justices that his client had just obtained an abortion, defying the injunction. After a brief discussion, the argument about the validity of the injunction continued. At the end of the day, the justices announced that they had voted unanimously to overturn the injunction barring Daigle from getting an abortion. Three months later the court released its opinion. The fetus was not a "human being" protected by the relevant law, the court said. (The applicable law was a provision of the Quebec Bill of Rights, rather than of the Charter of Rights and Freedoms, but the court's opinion spoke in such broad terms that it clearly resolved the question of the fetus's status throughout Canada.)

 Canada's government, controlled by the Conservative Party of Brian Mulroney, now had to decide what to do. Mulroney appointed a committee to draft a new abortion law. Under the proposal, abortions would be criminal unless a medical practitioner, not necessarily a doctor, decided that the woman's life or physical, mental, or psychological health would be endangered by continuing the pregnancy. The government presented this proposal as a compromise: The abortion decision would not be left to the woman alone, but she need only find a medical practitioner who could make an unreviewable decision about the threat the pregnancy posed to her health. Neither side was happy with this compromise. Although Canada's lower house approved the proposal by a narrow margin, it died in the Senate on an evenly divided vote. The government announced that it would propose no further legislation.

 As things stand in Canada, then, there is no criminal regulation of abortion at all. The outcome was the same as that in the United

States, even after *Casey*. The identical outcomes occurred, however, in the face of quite different constitutional rulings. The United States Supreme Court said directly that criminal regulation of abortion was unconstitutional. The Canadian supreme court did not. It said only that the existing statute was unconstitutional. Abortion politics in Canada, influenced, but not entirely constrained by Canadian constitutional law, prevented Canada from having some criminal regulation of abortion procedures.

International Perspectives: Germany

The United States Supreme Court's abortion decisions hold that the government cannot prohibit abortions. The German constitutional court, in contrast, held that under the German constitution the government *must* prohibit abortions. As law professor David Currie puts it, "the German constitution required what our Constitution forbade."[6] The differences in the outcomes in court, however, may not be as dramatic as they appear.

The United States Supreme Court decides many cases that do not involve constitutional law; it is what constitutional scholars call a *general* court. In contrast, Germany, like many other countries, has a *specialized* constitutional court that considers only constitutional claims. Another difference between the U.S. Supreme Court and the German one is procedural. The U.S. Supreme Court decides only "cases or controversies." That is, the court will decide cases only if there is a real conflict between two sides and some real person—like Norma McCorvey—whose interests are affected by the controversy. Some German cases like that get to the German constitutional court, but it can also exercise what scholars call "abstract norm control." If a state government or one-third of the members of Germany's parliament submits a request, the German constitutional court will resolve "differences of opinion or doubts on the procedural and substantive compatibility of federal or state law" with Germany's Basic Law (essentially, its constitution).

By the 1930s, women could obtain abortions in Germany for "medical indications"; that is, threats to their life or health, certified by their doctors. The Nazi regime made abortions legal for "eugenic" reasons: to purify the Aryan race by eliminating children with hereditary defects. After Germany's defeat in World War II, West German law returned to allowing abortions for medical reasons. Gradually, doctors began to interpret the requirement of medical indications broadly, by taking the woman's social situation—the impact of the pregnancy and a new child on the existing family, for example—into account in deciding whether the pregnancy was a threat to her health. Doctors who performed illegal abortions were fined or given probationary sentences.

In many ways, the situation in West Germany in the early 1970s resembled that in the United States before *Roe*. According to the law on the books, abortions were allowed only in limited circumstances, but in practice abortions were more freely available. Doctors in German states controlled by the Social Democratic Party tended to find lawful "indications" for abortions than doctors in states controlled by the Christian Democratic Party.

Until 1972 West Germany's government was in the hands of Christian Democrats, who were willing to live with the gradual expansion in practice of the grounds on which abortions were available. In 1972 the Social Democratic Party took office for the first time since World War II. In 1974, Parliament enacted a more expansive abortion law, by a margin of 247 in favor and 233 against, with 7 abstentions.

The old law, referred to as the "indications" approach, was replaced by what Germans called the "time-phase" solution, which resembled the rules *Roe v. Wade* put in place. The new law declared that abortions would no longer be punishable if they were performed during the first twelve weeks of pregnancy. (Interestingly, the law did not say that such abortions would be legal, but only that women obtaining them would not be punished.) Before the operation was performed, though, the woman had to be counseled by a doctor or a counseling service, which would inform her of the public and private assistance available to help pregnant women, mothers, and children. Abortions after the twelfth week of pregnancy remained illegal, except where medical, eugenic, or ethical indications (such as pregnancy resulting from rape) justified them.

The Christian Democratic minority in Parliament and five state governments controlled by Christian Democrats raised objections to the new abortion law and asked the constitutional court to resolve those objections. Three days after the parliament adopted the law, the court enjoined its operation.

German constitutional decisions frequently ask whether the challenged statute is consistent with the "hierarchy of values" or the "objective order of values" embodied in the Basic Law. Germany's Basic Law begins its declaration of rights with two provisions that suggest what that hierarchy is. The first states that "everyone has the right to life and to the inviolability of his person"; the second secures the right to "development of personality."

In a decision issued in 1975, the constitutional court found the new abortion law unconstitutional because it failed to protect the right to life.[7] Its analysis began by explaining that the Basic Law gave such high priority to protecting the right to life "as a reaction to the 'destruction of life unworthy to live' " during the Nazi regime. Just as Germany had abolished capital punishment because of respect for life, the first provision in the Basic Law "emphatically opposes the views of a political regime for which the individual life had little significance."

For the constitutional court, the "life" protected by the Basic Law was "the developmental existence of a human individual," which it said began fourteen days after conception, "according to established biological-physiological findings." After that, development was continuous with no sharp boundary lines. As a result, the court said, "no distinctions can be made between individual stages of developing life before birth." The court rejected the idea that the decision to bear or not bear a child was a private one. The fetus was an independent human being, which implied that abortion had "a social dimension which makes it accessible to and in need of state regulation."

The court acknowledged that the woman had a right to protection, as recognized by the provision guaranteeing a right to development of personality. That right "embrace[d] the woman's responsible decision against parenthood and its attendant duties." But "the rights of others, the constitutional order, and moral law" limited the right to development of personality. As the court saw it, "no compromise is possible that would both guarantee the protection of the unborn life and concede to the pregnant woman the freedom of terminating the pregnancy." The competing interests had to be balanced.

Where there were appropriate indications for abortion, the balance was in favor of the woman's right to development of personality. The court stated that "social" reasons—such as severe hardship during and after pregnancy—might also make abortion permissible. However, to obtain an abortion for social reasons, a woman must receive appropriate counseling. In all other circumstances, "the decision must come down in favor of the preeminence of protecting the fetus's life over the right of self-determination of the pregnant woman." Pregnancy might indeed limit the woman's self-development, but not as much as abortion limited the fetus's life.

This analysis led the court to conclude that the government had to treat abortions as wrong by "clearly express[ing] its disapproval" of abortion. It must "avoid the false impression that terminating a pregnancy involves the same social course of events as, for instance, a trip to the doctor to have an illness healed." The new abortion law, in saying that abortions before the twelfth week would not be punished, was not a strong enough expression of disapproval. And, even if many women were so firmly committed to having an abortion that the threat of criminal punishment would not deter them, or if many women knew how to get an abortion without risking punishment, still the criminal law had to *express* disapproval, to "influence the value concepts and the manner of conduct of the population."

The new law's counseling provisions were also inadequate, in part because the counseling could come from the doctor who would perform the abortion and in part because the abortion could be performed immediately after the counseling session. "For any woman resolved to terminate her pregnancy, it therefore is only a matter of finding a compliant physician; since he is permitted to carry out both the social as well as the medical counseling and finally also the operation, no serious attempt on his part may be expected to deflect the pregnant woman from her decision." Appropriate counseling had to be directive, emphasizing that abortion was wrong.

The court's decision had another side, however. The court's analysis was driven by the constitutional guarantee of a right to life. The government could use the criminal law to express its disapproval of abortion, but "punishment should never be an end in itself." Parliament could express its disapproval of abortion "by means other than the threat of penal sanctions." So, the court suggested, it had to consider how extensively the government encouraged women to carry their pregnancies to term.

Indeed, the court said, "the singular situation of the pregnant woman" posed special problems for the criminal system. The question was what a pregnant woman "may reasonably be expected to endure." So, even a criminal law against abortion had to allow abortions when the pregnancy would "force[the woman] to sacrifice her own values beyond reasonable expectations." Exceptions had to be made for pregnancies that threatened the woman's life or health.

The court lifted the threat of criminal punishment even more. It said that the government could "refrain from imposing penal sanctions" when pregnancy would subject the woman to "extraordinary burdens," whether those burdens were "ethical" or "social." If the legislature decided not to punish abortions obtained for social reasons, though, it had to describe the circumstances in some detail, and it had to "offer counseling and assistance so as to remind the pregnant woman of her fundamental duty to respect the unborn's right to life, to encourage her to go through with the pregnancy, and to support her—particularly in cases of social need—with practical assistance." That would make "the gravity of the social conflict . . clearly recognizable" and so would not violate the government's duty to protect life.

Two judges dissented. They agreed that the government had a duty to protect the fetus's life, but disagreed with the majority in thinking that the new abortion law satisfied that duty. For them, Parliament could choose between criminal penalties for abortions and the counseling system the new law established. The constitutional court, they said, should take a stance of "judicial self-restraint" when assessing Parliament's choices about how to protect developing life. As they saw it, the new law gave "sociopolitical measures priority over largely ineffective penal sanctions" and it was not for the constitutional court to say that this was an improper way of achieving the constitutionally required goals. They were at least as troubled, they said, by the majority's insistence that the government use criminal law, "the strongest imaginable interference with the citizen's sphere of freedom," to protect developing life.

Under the law after 1975, abortions were available for medical and social reasons and some students of abortion practices suggest that it was not difficult to obtain an abortion for those reasons. The reunification of Germany in 1990 again made the abortion issue a constitutional one. East Germany had allowed abortions freely and women there had become accustomed to the right to choose. Abortion rates in the two parts of Germany were not dramatically different, but the legal regulations of abortion were. Somehow West Germany's restrictions on abortions and East Germany's freedom to choose had to be accommodated. The reunification treaty provided that the unrestrictive laws of East Germany would continue in force in that region for two years, but it required the unified German parliament to come up with some solution quickly.

In 1992, the parliament adopted a new abortion law. Again it was quite divided between proponents of the existing indications approach and supporters of the time-phase approach, including representatives from the eastern states. A compromise proposal ended up with substantial majority support. The new statute adopted the time-phase approach, with some important modifications. It again declared that abortions in the first twelve weeks of pregnancy were not unlawful. It required women seeking abortions to be counseled by someone other than the doctor who would perform the abortion. The counseling had to be directive, stressing the value of unborn life. Finally, the law imposed a three-day waiting period after the counseling.

The law also took up the suggestion from the 1974 decision that what really mattered was that the government discourage abortions by a combination of criminal penalties and civil supports for pregnancy, childbirth, and child rearing. The statute therefore modified a wide range of social policies involving social security, medical insurance, vocational training, and job placement, all to the end of making it easier for women to carry their pregnancies to term.

Once again Christian Democrats asked the constitutional court to review the statute. The day before the statute was to take effect the court suspended its operation, leaving abortion on demand available in eastern Germany and the indications approach in effect in western Germany. Nearly a year later the court issued its decision striking the new law down because it attempted to make abortion legal.

The Basic Law, according to the court, required that the government somehow express its disapproval of abortion and it could not do so by expressly saying that some abortions were "not illegal."[8] Those words suggested that abortion was a lawful choice. But, the court said, any abortion statute had to make it clear that abortions were wrong and, in principle, illegal.

The constitutional court did modify its earlier approach, however. Although abortions had to be made criminal, that did not mean, according to the court, that women and doctors had to be *punished* for having or performing abortions. The court agreed with the "conceptual change in the state's protection of life" represented by the new statute. That change sought to protect unborn life by positive incentives to bear the child rather than by negative penalties for abortion.

In particular, the government could require that women be counseled in an effort to get them to change their minds about having an abortion. But, if they decided to go ahead after this directive counseling, which the court called "preventive protection through counseling," they could not be prosecuted for abortions obtained during the first twelve weeks of pregnancy.

Even more, once a woman had rejected the advice she received from the counselor, she had to be given a list of doctors and facilities where she could get an abortion. As one commentator summarizes the court's opinion, "the state may validly conclude that in view of the reality of abortion in modern society, the more effective solution to the problem of unwanted pregnancy is to stay the hand of would-be prosecutors, to make an ally and friend of the woman in distress, and to induce her to cooperate voluntarily with the state without any fear of retribution of loss of personal integrity."[9]

Agreeing with the 1975 dissenters, the constitutional court now held that the legislature had some leeway to decide that the fetus's right to life would be protected more effectively by directive counseling than by criminal punishment. Indeed, contrary to the 1975 decision, the court in 1992 held that women seeking abortions for "social" reasons did not have to show that her circumstances were "severe." The court went so far as to invalidate some of the social-support provisions of the new law because they did not go far enough to support pregnant women in stressful circumstances, or their children after delivery. It also suggested that some aspects of private law had to be changed as well. For example, the court said, landlords should not be allowed to demand that families with newborn children move out.

Another aspect of the court's treatment of social support is even more striking. Neither the government's medical insurance funds nor private insurers could pay for illegal abortions. Paying for such abortions would, again, send the wrong message about their wrongfulness. Nonetheless, the government *was* required to make "social assistance" payments—general welfare payments—to poor women who had abortions; otherwise they might try to get illegal abortions, endangering their own health and avoiding even the directive counseling a state-paid doctor would provide. As the court saw it, paying for abortions through the medical insurance fund would convey the message that abortion was an ordinary medical procedure like any other, while paying for them through the general welfare fund simply acknowledged the predicament a woman may have found herself in, after receiving directive counseling and concluding that she should have an abortion even so.

Three judges dissented. Two would have upheld the 1992 statute entirely, as a reasonable attempt to balance the interests of women and the unborn. A third would have allowed the state to pay for abortions from its medical insurance funds.

International Perspectives: The Glendon Argument

These international examples illustrate some of the ways in which nations regulate abortion. Drawing on an even wider range of illustrations, Harvard law professor Mary Ann Glendon developed a criticism of U.S. abortion law as "extreme."[10] According to Glendon, the United States regulates abortion less than any other Western country and provides less social support for pregnant women, mothers, and children. Glendon connects this to the fact that abortion was

treated as a constitutional rather than a political issue in the United
States.

Glendon's argument directs attention to two dimensions of
social regulation of abortion and childbirth.

Social support: Nations vary in the amount of social support
they provide to pregnant women, mothers, and their children. As the
German constitutional court suggested, such social support comes in
many forms: medical and health insurance, maternity and parental
leave, social welfare payments for women and their children in need,
and "child benefit" payments made available to every child without
regard to need. Glendon notes that the United States provides very
few of these supports. Its social welfare system is much less generous
than that of Western European countries. A national parental leave
statute, enacted in 1993, requires employers to offer unpaid leaves to
new parents, in contrast to many Western European parental leave
statues, which provide for paid leaves.

Degree of regulation: Abortion regulations take many forms
as well.

- *Abortion on demand at any point.*
- *Abortion on demand during early pregnancy and abortion
  for reasons related to maternal health thereafter.* This was
  the system set in place by *Roe v. Wade.*
- *Abortion on demand during early pregnancy and restrictions on abortion thereafter in the interest of the fetus.* This
  is part of the system set in place by *Casey.* One scholar
  calls the categories up to this one "time limit" models
  based on self-determination.
- *Abortion for "social distress" or for reasons related to
  maternal health during early pregnancy.* Glendon praises
  French abortion law, which allows abortion for "social
  distress" in early pregnancy. A woman can obtain an
  abortion after counseling simply by asserting that continuing the pregnancy would cause her such distress; no
  one checks to see whether that assertion is true.
- *Abortion for such reasons, coupled with directive counseling.* A study of the effects of directive counseling in
  Germany concluded that such counseling had almost no
  effect on the choices made by women "who were determined to abort from the outset," but that about half of the
  women who were uncertain about whether to carry the
  pregnancy to term decided to do so after counseling.[11]
- *Abortion for social or medical indications, with certifica-
  tion of those indications required.* "Medical indications"

show that continuing the pregnancy would cause harm to the woman, or that the fetus, if delivered, would be severely deformed. The post-unification German abortion law falls in this category.

- *Abortion for medical indications only.* Irish abortion law is an example of this category. Here much depends on how generously doctors interpret the requirement that the woman's health be endangered by continuing the pregnancy. If doctors find dangers rather easily—for example, if they believe that "health dangers" include threats to the woman's mental health, or if in Ireland they are quick to conclude that a woman's threat to commit suicide is credible—these regulations in practice resemble systems allowing abortion for social distress.

    There is one important difference, though: Where doctors must decide whether the medical indications exist, sometimes women with access to sympathetic doctors will be able to obtain abortions when women—in otherwise similar circumstances—might not. This possibility is greater in a system like the United States, where the medical profession is largely private and substantially unregulated. Even in Germany, however, with extensive social welfare support for medical care, under the law before 1992 there were wide variations in the availability of abortions depending on which German state a woman lived in; doctors in states with Christian Democratic governments were more reluctant to certify medical indications than were doctors in states with Social Democratic governments.[12]

- *Abortions banned in all circumstances.*

    (There is one final variant to note: Some governments may *require* women to have abortions in some circumstances. The People's Republic of China reportedly does so in pursuit of its policy to limit explosive population growth.)

Does it matter what sort of abortion regulation a nation has? Not surprisingly, abortion rates in nations with relatively restrictive laws tend to be lower than the rates in nations with relatively unrestrictive laws. The tendency is not perfect, though. According to one analysis, the abortion rate in Hungary, with a "moderately restrictive" law, was twice that in Poland in 1987 when it had a "rather permissive" law.[13]

107

Although Glendon is somewhat concerned with the level of abortions in the United States, her argument is directed even more at the cultural and political consequences of the U.S. system of abortion regulation. Glendon believes that the U.S. system, by focusing entirely on the woman's choice, fails to take account of fetal interests at all. She points out that most women who have abortions regret having done so, indicating—in Glendon's view—that women regard abortion as a morally problematic event. She argues that the law can reflect that moral ambiguity even if it allows abortions and, in doing so, the law could communicate a message about the seriousness of abortions to the society at large. Abortion regulations like those in France and Germany can "combine compassion with affirmation of life." Here Glendon's arguments draw on a view of political morality that emphasizes people's ties with one another—the woman's ties to her family and her community in particular.

Glendon's political argument focuses on the fact that abortion regulation in the United States results from legislation within the severe constraints placed on regulation by *Roe*'s interpretation of the Constitution. According to Glendon, constitutionalizing abortion limited the possibility that compromises similar to those in Europe might emerge. For Glendon, the Hyde Amendment's ban on public financing of abortion symbolizes the tradeoff made in the United States: a strong pro-choice policy in exchange for no social support.

Glendon suggests that women would benefit from a weaker pro-choice policy, which could then take the concerns of antiabortion voters seriously. If states could adopt directive counseling and similar requirements stressing the seriousness of the abortion decision, Glendon suggests, antiabortion voters might be persuaded to support a more extensive scheme of public assistance to needy pregnant women and their children.

Glendon supports her argument by suggesting that *Roe* actually cut off promising developments. In the early 1970s, Glendon argues, gradual reforms in abortion law were being developed through political action. Some states, like Georgia, had abandoned their nineteenth-century restrictive abortion laws in favor of the more modern "medical indications" statute invalidated in *Doe v. Bolton*. California had extensive experience with such a statute and doctors were quite generous in finding medical indications for abortion there. New York had gone further by adopting a pure time-phase system. *Roe* mandated the time-phase solution for the entire country. As a result, according to Glendon, the possibility of working out compromises state by state, with some having restrictive medical indication laws and others having less restrictive ones, disappeared.

Glendon's argument has been criticized on several grounds.

Glendon's cultural analysis Like Germany's constitutional court, Glendon emphasizes the impact that legal messages send to the wider culture. Glendon's colleague at Harvard Law School, Laurence Tribe, argues that Glendon may have misinterpreted the messages sent by European abortion regulations.[14] He suggests that no strong antiabortion message could really be sent by abortion regulations like those in France, where a woman can obtain an abortion simply by stating that she is in a situation of social distress. The messages sent by more restrictive medical indications statutes are clouded by variability in interpretation: What can a culture learn about itself when a woman can obtain an abortion for medical reasons in one German state but not another? In Tribe's view, "the codification of a truly empty promise, one whose vision is belied by the people's daily experience, one that is utterly at variance with the substance of the law in which it is contained, . . . seems to teach mostly hypocrisy."[15]

Tribe and other critics have also focused on Glendon's rejection of the individualism that underlies United States constitutional law. They agree with Glendon that individualism explains the U.S. combination of a strong pro-choice abortion law with a weak social welfare system, but defend individualism itself. According to these critics, individualism in the United States is the foundation of our understanding of liberty and it ought not be rejected in favor of an ill-defined communitarian alternative. Perhaps our culture of individualism ought to be transformed. But, these critics suggest, it is not clear that it makes sense to begin that transformation by rejecting the pro-choice outcome of abortion litigation. A better place to start, in their view, would be with increases in the levels of social support for pregnant women, mothers, and children.

Glendon's political analysis Glendon's analysis of abortion politics before *Roe* has been questioned. David Garrow, the leading historian of abortion politics and law before *Roe*, argues that Glendon overestimates the amount of movement on abortion law reform. Attempts to repeal abortion laws in Michigan were defeated before *Roe*. The New York statute, enacted by a single vote, survived only because New York's Republican governor Nelson Rockefeller vetoed legislation to restore the prior restrictive abortion law. According to Garrow, antiabortion voters even before *Roe* were not interested in compromising or reforming abortion law in the direction of a "medical indications" model.

Nor were pro-choice or pro-reform voters. Chapter 2 showed the movement for abortion law reform went through two stages. Until the late 1960s, activists supported abortion law reform, mostly in favor of a medical indications model. After that, however, they switched to favor abortion law repeal. The change occurred largely because activists were troubled by the fact that the availability of abortions under medical indications statutes varied dramatically.

Abortion reform activists knew that what one scholar calls a "gray market" in abortions existed even under quite restrictive statutes.[16] Relatively well-to-do women, with family connections to sympathetic doctors, could obtain abortions without too much difficulty. Sometimes the police and prosecutors turned a blind eye to "respectable" doctors whom they knew were performing illegal abortions, enforcing the statutes only against doctors who served poor and minority women. Sometimes doctors concealed the abortions they performed by describing their medical interventions as if they occurred after the woman had begun a spontaneous abortion. Those efforts could succeed because spontaneous abortions were, at least in the 1950s and 1960s, not uncommon events.

Abortion law reformers were unsatisfied with the status quo of "gray market" abortions, in part because using the gray market was traumatic even for women who could afford to do so, but also because they thought it unfair that well-connected women could obtain abortions when poor and minority women could not. By the late 1960s, abortion reformers concluded that medical indications statutes like Georgia's were likely to increase the gray market they sought to eliminate. Getting a doctor to certify the medical indications might be nearly as traumatic as trying to locate a doctor willing to perform a gray-market abortion. Further, poor and minority women were likely to have as much difficulty getting an abortion under a medical indications statutes as they had under restrictive statutes.

Here, much turned on the vagueness of medical indications statutes allowing abortions to protect the woman's physical or mental health. *United States v. Vuitch* held that such statutes were not unconstitutionally vague. Nonetheless, some doctors would find a threat to a woman's mental health when others would not. Abortion law reformers were concerned that the availability of abortion depended on a woman's ability to locate a sympathetic doctor, who would adopt a definition of mental health that made it easy to satisfy the statutory requirement.

Garrow's review of the history of abortion law reform suggests, then, that by the time *Roe* was decided, neither antiabortion nor pro-choice activists were interested in the kinds of compromise Glendon favors.

Glendon wrote in 1987, when *Roe* was the law. *Casey* changed the law and it may provide the opportunity to see whether Glendon's political and cultural arguments are right. *Casey* does not require states to adopt directive counseling statutes, but it does allow them to do so. In this way it at least moves U.S. constitutional law in the direction Glendon favors. How far that movement goes, and whether it will lead to the kinds of compromises Glendon prefers, remains undetermined.

Abortion Law and the "Critique of Rights"

On one interpretation, Glendon's political analysis emphasizes the effect *Roe v. Wade* had in bringing antiabortion voters to the polls. Another political analysis emphasizes the effects the abortion decisions had on pro-choice voters. This analysis is sometimes described as part of the "critique of rights" developed by legal scholars interested in critical legal studies, a leftist approach to legal analysis. In its broadest terms, the critique of rights is skeptical about the political usefulness of traditional civil rights strategies focused on advancing left or liberal political positions through litigation like *Roe*.

The critique of rights in the abortion setting has two components.

Ideological effects: To prevail in the litigation, pro-choice lawyers had to make the strongest legal arguments they could, using the Supreme Court's precedents. The best precedent they had was *Griswold*, which described a fundamental right to privacy. But according to the critique of rights, the interests of women may not be best protected by finding a constitutional right to privacy expansive enough to cover women's choices about abortion and child-bearing.

Privacy, on this view, is an inherently *individual* right. By describing the right to choose as an aspect of a right to privacy, *Roe* isolates women from the broader social setting in which they make their choices. It reinforces the idea that there is a private domain in which such choices are made and a public domain in which other decisions are made. Two specific effects are said to be connected to this ideological division.

- The right to choose is located in the private domain and is exercised by women. This reinforces the idea that women are properly concerned primarily with the private sphere, especially the home, and should not be as concerned with what happens in the public sphere, including politics and employment outside the home.

111

- The fundamental institution of the public sphere is the market. By treating the right to choose as part of the private domain, *Roe* and a rights-based litigation strategy made it easier for the Court to uphold the Hyde Amendment in *Harris v. McRae*. The Court saw the problem posed by the Hyde Amendment as a question about whether Congress could leave abortion financing to the market. Because the market is the public sphere and the right to choose is part of the private domain, the Court found it easy to accept Congress's separation of the two domains.

This component of the critique of rights has supported efforts, described in Chapter 1, to redefine the fundamental issue in *Roe* as gender equality.

Political effects: Proponents of the critique of rights argue that *winning* a legal victory, as in *Roe*, may have adverse political effects. Once pro-choice lawyers persuaded the Supreme Court to protect a constitutional right to choose, pro-choice *voters* had no need to protect that right through political action. Instead of locating and voting for candidates who promised to protect the right to choose, they could make their voting decisions based on candidates' positions on other issues, such as the economy. If antiabortion voters continued to support antiabortion candidates, perhaps legislatures would adopt antiabortion statutes, but, pro-choice voters believed, the courts would strike those statutes down.

In the short run, this political calculation by pro-choice voters may have made sense. In the longer run, the critique of rights argues, it resulted in substantial defeats for pro-choice interests. These defeats came in two forms.

- Many pro-choice voters were interested in a broader agenda of issues of interest to women, and particularly poor and minority women. Others sought to protect only a right to choose and were less interested in that broader agenda. If the latter group retreated from politics, believing that the courts would protect the only thing they cared about, the coalition supporting the broader agenda was weakened. Even worse from the pro-choice point of view, some pro-choice voters were rather conservative on economic issues and found their natural political home in the Republican party. So long as the courts would invalidate restrictions on abortion pressed by antiabortion Republican legislators, these voters could support Republicans without having to worry that their pro-choice preferences would be overridden after the election.

- More important, pro-choice voters lost sight of the fact that the Court would not necessarily continue to protect their interests. Antiabotion voters became an important part of the Republican Party coalition. The president nominates federal judges, including Supreme Court justices. The Senate must confirm the president's nominees, but the party that controls the presidency controls the appointments. With Ronald Reagan's election as president, the composition of the federal courts began to change. Nearly all of President Reagan's appointees were uncomfortable with the judicial activism they believed *Roe* exemplified. Some of them, like Justice Antonin Scalia, firmly believed that *Roe* should be overruled. Others, like Justices Sandra Day O'Connor and Anthony Kennedy, were less sure about that, but were reluctant to defend *Roe* vigorously. Pro-choice lobbyists played an important part in the rejection of Judge Robert Bork's nomination to the Supreme Court in 1987, but a single dramatic victory was not enough to keep *Roe* standing.

The political analysis in the critique of rights, then, argues that the apparent victory pro-choice litigators won in *Roe* eventually turned into a defeat for the pro-choice side and, more broadly, for the liberal agenda of women's issues.

The critique of rights has been challenged.

- Its critics claim that the critique overstates the degree to which pro-choice voters retreated from politics, or turned their attention to other issues, after *Roe*. They can point to the Canadian experience to show that judicial declarations of rights do not necessarily impair the pro-choice political position.

- The critics point out that in the early 1970s, when the legal attack on restrictive abortion laws was developing, precedents invoking privacy rights, like *Griswold*, were the only ones available to pro-choice litigators. The Supreme Court first struck down a statute as discriminating on the basis of gender in 1971 and only began to develop a full-fledged explanation of why such statutes were unconstitutional later in the 1970s. Even today, it is not clear that the present Supreme Court—much less the one sitting in 1973—would accept the argument that restrictive abortion laws discriminate on the basis of gender.

- The critics note that public policy from 1973 to the present was a substantial advance, from the pro-choice point of view, over public policy before 1973. As political scientist Gerald Rosenberg points out, *Roe* turned abortion services into an unregulated market. Those who provided the services became important players in the political arena. In this connection, it is noteworthy that the plaintiffs in lawsuits challenging restrictive abortion laws shifted. *Roe* and *Doe* were brought by lawyers representing individual women like Norma McCorvey; *Webster* and *Casey* were brought by institutional providers of abortions like Planned Parenthood. For the critique of rights to be effective as a left or liberal criticism of *Roe v. Wade*, the critique would have to establish that the pro-choice side would have been better off if the Supreme Court had rejected the constitutional challenge in *Roe*. Presumably, the critique of rights would have to endorse an argument like Glendon's, that ordinary legislative politics would have yielded a better outcome, from the pro-choice point of view, some time after 1973. But, the critics contend, it is unclear that legislative politics would have done so.

• Even if *Roe* is ultimately rejected, those who reject the critique of rights argue, still there would have been a period of several decades in which choice was available. It is not clear, the critics say, that the pro-choice side would have been better off if that had never happened.

The Future of Abortion Law in the United States

Under the *Casey* decision, state regulations of abortions are constitutional if they do not place an "undue burden" on the woman's right to choose. What might happen to the constitutional law of abortion over the next decade?

Applying Casey *Casey* found that requirements of mildly directive counseling and a twenty-four-hour waiting period did not place an undue burden on the right to choose. At some points the plurality opinion indicated that its conclusion was based on the record compiled in the lower court. The first question, then, is whether precisely the same requirements might yet be found unconstitutional if challengers put more evidence before the court.

The lower court in *Casey* invalidated the twenty-four-hour waiting period based on findings that the distances some women had to travel, their limited financial resources, and the possibility of harassment outside an abortion clinic meant that the requirement's "practical effect will often be a delay of much more than a day." The plurality called these findings "troubling in some respects," but declined to invalidate the requirement without a finding by the lower court using the term *undue burden*. In contrast, it did invalidate a requirement that women seeking abortions must inform their spouses. Here the factual findings about the prevalence of spousal abuse led the plurality to conclude that the notification requirement *was* an undue burden. It was "likely to prevent a significant number of women from obtaining an abortion."

Future litigation may clarify the meaning of *undue burden* in light of these holdings. The basic question is how to measure burdens to find out whether they are undue. To see the problem, it is useful to consider two scenarios.

State-by-state variation Suppose there is only one abortion provider in a state with a twenty-four-hour waiting period. Challengers might be able to show that far more women than in Pennsylvania would have to wait more than one day to obtain an abortion. Is the waiting period an undue burden in that state even though it is not an undue burden in Pennsylvania?

Impact on an individual woman Suppose a woman in Pennsylvania shows that, because of her particular circumstances, requiring her to wait twenty-four hours before obtaining an abortion would almost certainly make it impossible for her to have the abortion. For example, she might show that she lives far from an abortion provider, that she faces substantial social pressures not to reveal her pregnancy to those in her hometown, that her financial condition requires her to take no more than one day off from her job, and perhaps more. The waiting period requirement, she argues, has a substantial impact *on her,* even though it might not have as severe an impact on the entire group of women seeking abortions. Is the requirement unconstitutional as applied to such a woman?

Perhaps under *Casey* there are general *types* of burdens. Some of the types are undue while others are not. The types would be distinguished by the goals the state sought to achieve. For example, according to the *Casey* plurality, states could adopt regulations "to further the health or safety of a woman seeking an abortion" and "to promote the State's profound interest in potential life" by "tak[ing] measures to ensure that the woman's choice is informed." An analysis based on types of regulations would uphold any regulations truly aimed at protecting health or promoting informed choice.

The *Casey* plurality's emphasis on the factual record, though, suggests that the Constitution requires that states are limited by more than a requirement that their purposes be acceptable. The plurality also said that regulations would be unconstitutional if they had the "effect" of placing "a substantial obstacle in the path of a woman seeking an abortion." As a result, it seems that identical regulations might be constitutionally permissible in one state and impermissible in another.

Casey's analysis also makes it difficult to know whether a regulation might be permissible in general but an undue burden on an individual woman. At some points the *Casey* plurality speaks of individuals, "a woman seeking an abortion." That is consistent with the idea that the Constitution protects individual rights. Yet, in striking down the spousal notification requirement, the plurality said that the requirement was an undue burden because it affected "a significant number of women": "[F]or many women, it will impose a substantial obstacle." This suggests that requirements that did not adversely affect "many women" would be permissible even if they *did* adversely affect a few.

The plurality's treatment of the spousal notification requirement raises another question. On one reading of the decision, the requirement was invalid because it would "prevent a significant number of women from obtaining an abortion." Does this imply that abortion regulations are constitutionally permissible under *Casey* only if they prevent only a small number of women from obtaining abortions? According to this interpretation of *Casey*, states can enforce only those abortion regulations that have little impact on the number of abortions. If this interpretation is correct, *Casey* was not a large victory for the antiabortion side.

It may take several years of litigation to clarify what *Casey* means. Perhaps the most important unresolved legal issue under *Casey* is whether a state could require that all abortions be performed in fully-equipped hospitals rather than in free-standing clinics. *Roe* changed the way in which abortions were performed not merely by eliminating criminal punishment, but more significantly by allowing abortions to be provided at a significantly lower cost, in clinics rather than in hospitals with their large overhead costs.

Under *Casey* the state may protect the woman's health or safety if the regulations do not place an undue burden on her right to choose. A state might defend a hospitalization requirement on the ground that some abortions lead to medical complications that cannot be effectively treated in clinics. Yet, because hospitals charge more for abortions than clinics, a hospitalization requirement might reduce the number of abortions significantly.

The question of a hospitalization requirement's constitutionality points to a deeper, less legal issue. The practical issues for the future of abortion policy may not be constitutional but social. Even before *Casey* the Court held that public hospitals need not perform abortions. Many hospitals affiliated with churches whose teachings oppose abortions also refuse to perform them. Many doctors have moral qualms about the procedure. Even if no further legal regulations are widely adopted, many women may find it difficult to locate a doctor close enough who is willing to perform an abortion.

Such concerns have made new forms of abortion of great interest to supporters of abortion choice. The most important of these is the so-called "abortion pill," RU-486. Taken in early pregnancy, this drug induces a miscarriage. At present the drug is not widely available in the United States and in its present form must be administered under a doctor's supervision to reduce risks to the woman's health. Further development of RU-486 and similar drugs, however, may make it possible for women to terminate pregnancies without medical supervision. If a black market for RU-486 develops, women who use the drug can present themselves at hospitals and doctors' offices with all the indications of a spontaneous miscarriage and doctors would have to treat those women just as they do any other women with miscarriages.

Pro-choice advocates hope that drugs like RU-486 will take the issue of legal regulation of abortion out of public controversy. Until then, the ambiguous *Casey* decision provides the constitutional framework of abortion law.

Abortion law and privacy law *Roe* and *Casey* are cases about the constitutional law of sexual autonomy or privacy. How might that law develop?

The concept of sexual autonomy that underlies *Griswold* and *Roe* led some gay-rights advocates to believe they could use those precedents to invalidate state laws making homosexual conduct unlawful. They failed, in *Bowers v. Hardwick* (1986), which may have eliminated the possibility that a more elaborate constitutional law about sexual autonomy would be developed.[17] After *Bowers*, constitutional law includes some restrictions on states' ability to regulate abortion and to regulate some aspects of personal privacy, but not a general ban on interferences with sexual autonomy.

Bowers began when a police officer in Atlanta, Georgia, went to Michael Hardwick's apartment to serve a warrant for failing to appear in court on a charge of carrying an open bottle of beer in public. (Actually, Hardwick had paid his fine already, but the police department's paperwork had not caught up with the officer.) After a friend of Hardwick let the officer into the apartment, the officer saw Hardwick having sexual relations with another man and arrested Hardwick for violating Georgia's statute prohibiting sodomy.

The state prosecutor eventually dropped the charge, but Hardwick, supported by the local American Civil Liberties Union, decided to challenge the sodomy statute. (Hardwick had standing to challenge the statute because he had been arrested once for violating it even though the charge against him had been dropped.)

After the appeals court ruled in Hardwick's favor, Georgia's attorney general, Michael Bowers, asked the Supreme Court to review the decision.[18] At first the justices voted seven to two against hearing the case. Justice White drafted a dissent, explaining why the Court should hear it and Justice Rehnquist joined him. Because it takes four votes to get the Supreme Court to hear a case, Justice Brennan thought that he too could now say that the Court should hear the case without running the risk that the Court would uphold the sodomy statute. When Justice Marshall saw Brennan's new vote, he too decided to vote to hear the case. Now there were four votes and the Court would hear it. Alarmed, Justice Brennan sent a memo to his colleagues changing his vote, leaving only three votes to hear *Bowers*. Finally, Chief Justice Burger, who, like Brennan and Marshall had initially voted against hearing the case, switched. With that, the four votes to hear it were settled.

Harvard law professor Laurence Tribe represented Hardwick in the Supreme Court. His argument tied together two lines of cases. One drew on the long tradition of respect for a person's home (or apartment). Although governments could prohibit the sale of obscene materials, for example, they could not make it a criminal offense for a person to possess such material in his own home.[19] The other cases were, of course, *Griswold* and *Roe*.

The key figure within the Court was Justice Lewis Powell. He had a traditional conservative's distaste for homosexual activity.[20] Indeed, he told one of his law clerks that he had never "met a homosexual." The clerk, himself gay, replied, "Certainly you have, but you just don't know that they are." Powell's views on homosexuality were bolstered by his views on constitutional interpretation. Although he was a firm supporter of *Roe* and had written important opinions defending it against criticism, Powell was uncomfortable with judicial innovation. Abortion rights were important to Powell because he understood what they meant to women; gay rights were less important because, according to one of his clerks, Powell "found homosexual sodomy abhorrent."

At first Powell felt that the constitutional theory justifying *Roe* was strong enough to justify some protection for gay rights. He did not want to develop a comprehensive theory of sexual privacy, though, and tried to figure out a more limited way of dealing with *Bowers*. An earlier Supreme Court case held that the Eighth Amendment's ban on cruel and unusual punishments was violated when

California made it a crime simply to be a drug addict (rather than to possess or sell drugs).[21] Powell thought he could use that precedent to strike down Georgia's ban on sodomy.

After the Court heard argument, the justices discussed the case. The other justices divided evenly. Powell said he did not support a general right of sexual autonomy covering homosexual sodomy, but he thought it would be cruel and unusual punishment "to punish [Hardwick] criminally . . for conduct based on a natural sexual urge, privately and with a consenting partner." That led him to vote to strike down Georgia's statute.

Justice Brennan immediately assigned the opinion to Justice Blackmun. Chief Justice Burger was incensed at Powell's vote, and sent Powell a personal letter criticizing Powell. According to Burger, "surely homosexuals are not 'sex crazed' automatons who are 'compelled' by their 'status' to gratify their sexual appetites only by committing sodomy." Burger said that "Western Civilization has for centuries viewed [sodomy] as a volitional, reprehensible act."

Powell thought that Burger's letter was "mostly" "nonsense," but he remained uneasy about the decision. The balance was tipped by one of his more conservative law clerks, who pointed out that Hardwick had *not* been sentenced to prison for his acts. After a weekend reflecting on the case, Powell returned to the Court and announced that he had changed his vote. He would uphold the Georgia statute in this case, but indicated that he still thought it might be unconstitutional to imprison a person for homosexual sodomy.

Justice Byron White quickly drafted an opinion that treated Hardwick's claim dismissively. *Griswold* and *Roe* involved "family, marriage, or procreation," and so did not "bear[ ] any resemblance" to Hardwick's activity. The argument that there was a fundamental right to engage in homosexual sodomy was "at best, facetious." Justice White, who had dissented in *Roe* and continued to oppose its theoretical underpinnings, refused "to take a more expansive view of [the Court's] authority to discover new fundamental rights," because the Court was "most vulnerable and comes nearest to illegitimacy when it deals with judge-made constitutional law having little or no cognizable roots in the language or design of the Constitution." Justice Blackmun's opinion, which for a few days was designed to speak for the majority, now became the dissent.

Initially Justice Powell was put off by the peremptory tone of White's opinion and planned to concur in the result without joining the opinion. He changed his mind, giving White's opinion the status of a full majority opinion. Powell also wrote a short concurring opinion saying that "a prison sentence for such conduct—certainly a sentence of long duration—would create a serious Eighth Amendment issue." Even here, Powell did not say that *any* prison sentence, even a long one, would in fact violate the Eighth Amendment.

Powell's biographer calls *Bowers* Powell's "greatest defeat." Four years after the decision, Powell said publicly that he "probably made a mistake in that one," and told a reporter that, when he reread the opinions, he thought that Justice Blackmun's dissent "had the better of the arguments."

Bowers expressed discomfort with judicial enforcement of unenumerated rights, although it did not completely disclaim the power to do so. A Court that remains committed to the view of unenumerated rights stated in *Bowers* is unlikely to develop a general constitutional law of privacy beyond its present contours.

New reproductive technologies and other variants on the right to life and death RU-486, the abortion pill, stands as a symbol for broader developments in reproductive technology. Controversies about surrogate mothers—who carry in their wombs fetuses created by the union of sperm and egg from two other people—already have attracted a great deal of public attention. A few judges have ordered women convicted of child battering or drug abuse to choose between a term in prison and having a long-acting contraceptive like Norplant embedded in their bodies. Some legislators have proposed increasing a woman's public assistance payment if she agrees to use a long-acting contraceptive; others have proposed reducing such payments unless recipients use such contraceptives.

Few of the recent controversies, however, have been framed in constitutional terms. The Supreme Court has not decided any questions raised by these controversies. The legal issues in the controversies decided so far have been whether state law permits or prohibits the new reproductive technology involved in the case. Although scholars and other observers know that constitutional issues lurk just below the surface of these cases, the constitutional issues have not as yet become the major feature of litigation.

Further, regulation of these techniques—when it occurs at all—usually results from applying existing law to new technologies. That often results in a mismatch between the law and the techniques. As technology develops, Congress and state legislatures may address the problems it raises through specific legislation. Because we cannot know today what tomorrow's legislatures will do, any attempt to assess the constitutionality of regulation of new reproductive technologies is premature.

The Court's only confrontation to date with these emerging issues was a "right to die" case and the Court chose to avoid the fundamental issues.[22] Nancy Beth Cruzan was driving home from her job on January 11, 1983, when her car skidded off the road and crashed. She was thrown facedown into a ditch; deprived of oxygen, Cruzan's brain was permanently damaged and Cruzan never regained consciousness, although she continued to breathe without mechanical support. She was placed in a state-run rehabilitation center, where she remained for seven years, receiving food and water through a stomach tube.

In 1988 Cruzan's parents, believing that their daughter would not have wanted to survive under the conditions she was in, asked a local probate judge for permission to remove the feeding tube. Without it, Nancy Cruzan would gradually—although probably painlessly—starve to death. The probate judge granted the request. The state attorney general intervened in the case and appealed. According to him, the state had an interest in assuring that life support not be terminated without a strong showing that withdrawing support was what Nancy Cruzan would have wanted.

The Missouri Supreme Court, dividing four to three, agreed that life support could be withdrawn only if there was "clear and convincing evidence" about Nancy Cruzan's wishes. The Cruzans took their case to the United States Supreme Court, which also found the case difficult. It divided five to four and issued a quite narrow opinion. The Court held only that, given the state's interest in ensuring that a patient's wishes would really be followed, the state could insist on proof of her wishes by clear and convincing evidence. Other states, the Court emphasized, could make different choices.

Justice O'Connor wrote a concurring opinion saying that the Constitution protected the "liberty interest in refusing unwanted medical treatment." The Court's opinion did not go quite as far as that. It "assume[d] that the . . Constitution would grant a competent person a constitutionally protected right to refuse lifesaving hydration and nutrition."

Justice Scalia wrote his own concurring opinion, which began with the proposition that states would not violate the Constitution in prohibiting suicide. He inferred from that proposition that states could regulate the manner of dying however they chose: "the federal courts have no business in this field."

Nancy Cruzan's case went back to the probate court, to see whether there was clear and convincing evidence of her wishes. Some of Cruzan's friends testified about conversations they had with her in which she said she would not want to stay alive on machines. No one appeared to oppose the order, because the state's attorney general withdrew from the case. The probate judge allowed the hospital to remove the feeding tube on December 14, 1990, and Nancy Cruzan died twelve days later.

The Court did get into the field, but it refrained from addressing Justice Scalia's assumption about the constitutionality of a ban on suicide. That issue is bound to return to the Supreme Court. The primary issues are likely to involved physician-assisted suicide. The Court will have to decide whether people have a constitutionally protected right to commit suicide. If they do, does that right imply that people have a right to assistance in committing suicide? The Court in *Cruzan* emphasized the wide range of choices states could make. Does that mean that states can *permit* physician assisted suicide?

These questions might seem far removed from the questions about abortion that have concerned the Court. They are not. Deciding them will require the Court to consider what the fundamental right to privacy, first announced in *Griswold* and later expanded, then contracted, in *Roe* and *Casey*, really means.

Chapter Notes

CHAPTER ONE

1. Roe v. Wade, 410 U.S. 113 (1973); Doe v. Bolton, 410 U.S. 179 (1973).

2. Articles dealing with the Ninth Amendment are collected in *The Rights Retained by the People* (vols. 1 & 2) (Randy E. Barnett, ed., Fairfax, Virginia: George Mason University Press, 1989, 1993).

3. 32 U.S. (7 Pet.) 243 (1833).

4. 6 F.Cas. 546 (1823).

5. 83 U.S. (16 Wall.) 36 (1873).

6. Herbert Hovenkamp, *Enterprise and American Law, 1836–1937* (Cambridge: Harvard University Press, 1991), pp. 118–24.

7. John Hart Ely, *Democracy and Distrust* (Cambridge: Harvard University Press, 1980), p. 18.

8. Wynehamer v. People, 13 N.Y. 378 (1856).

9. Dred Scott v. Sanford, 60 U.S. (19 How.) 393 (1857).

10. For example, compare Laurence Tribe's 1973 article, "Foreword: Toward a Model of Roles in the Due Process of Law and Life," *Harvard Law Review* 87 (1973), with his 1988 book *American Constitutional Law* (2nd ed., Mineola, New York: Foundation Press, 1988), p. 1350.

11. Ronald Dworkin, *Life's Dominion* (New York: Knopf, 1993).

12. Calder v. Bull, 3 U.S. (3 Dall.) 386 (1798).

13. Fletcher v. Peck, 10 U.S. (6 Cranch) 87 (1810).

14. Lochner v. New York, 198 U.S. 45 (1905).

15. Muller v. Oregon, 208 U.S. 412 (1908); Holden v. Hardy, 196 U.S. 366 (1898).

16. Coppage v. Kansas, 236 U.S. 1 (1915).

17. Adkins v. Children's Hospital, 261 U.S. 525 (1923).

18. Ives v. South Buffalo R. Co., 201 N.Y. 271 (1911).

19. Meyer v. Nebraska, 262 U.S. 390 (1923).

20. Pierce v. Society of Sisters, 268 U.S. 510 (1925).

21. Skinner v. Oklahoma, 316 U.S. 535 (1942).

22. Gerald Gunther, "Foreword: In Search of Evolving Doctrine on a Changing Court: A Model for a Newer Equal Protection," *Harvard Law Review,* 86 (1972), p. 8.

23. Griffin v. Illinois, 351 U.S. 12 (1956); Douglas v. California, 372 U.S. 353 (1963).

24. Moore v. City of East Cleveland, 431 U.S. 494 (1977).

25. Michael H. v. Gerald D., 491 U.S. 110 (1989).

26. Laurence Tribe & Michael Dorf, *On Reading the Constitution* (Cambridge: Harvard University Press, 1991), p. 98.

27. 381 U.S. 479 (1965).

28. Donald Regan, "Rewriting *Roe v. Wade*," *Michigan Law Review* 77 (1979): 1569.

29. Judith Thompson, "A Defense of Abortion," *Philosophy and Public Affairs* 1 (1971): 47.

30. John T. Noonan, Jr., "The Experience of Pain by the Unborn," in *Abortion, Medicine, and the Law* (J. Douglas Butler & David F. Walbert eds., 3rd ed., New York: Facts On File, 1986), p. 360.

31. Craig v. Boren, 429 U.S. 190 (1976).

32. Cass Sunstein, "Neutrality in Constitutional Law (with Special Reference to Pornography, Abortion, and Surrogacy)," *Columbia Law Review* 92 (1992): 1.

CHAPTER TWO

1. David J. Garrow, *Liberty and Sexuality: The Right of Privacy and the Making of* Roe v. Wade (New York: Macmillan, 1994). The narrative in this and the next chapter is drawn heavily from Garrow's account, which is now indispensable. It has supplanted all earlier works on the topic.

2. Tileston v. Ullman, 318 U.S. 44 (1943).

3. Poe v. Ullman, 367 U.S. 497 (1961).

4. In addition to Garrow's discussion, see Bernard Schwartz, with Stephan Lesher, *Inside the Warren Court* (Garden City, N.Y.: Doubleday, 1983), pp. 229–30.

5. 381 U.S. 479 (1965).

6. People v. Belous, 71 Cal. 2d 954 (1969).

7. United States v. Vuitch, 305 F. Supp. 1032 (D. D.C. 1969).

8. United States v. Vuitch, 402 U.S. 62 (1971).

9. Baird v. Eisenstadt, 429 F. 2d 1398 (1st Cir. 1970).

10. Eisenstadt v. Baird, 405 U.S. 438 (1972).

CHAPTER THREE

1. John F. Jeffries, *Justice Lewis F. Powell: A Biography* (New York: Charles Scribner's Sons, 1994), p. 347.

2. Roe v. Wade, 410 U.S. 113 (1973).

3. Maher v. Roe, 432 U.S. 464 (1977); Harris v. McRae, 448 U.S. 297 (1980).

4. Mark Graber, *Equal Choice* (Princeton: Princeton University Press, 1996).

5. Maher v. Roe, 432 U.S. 315 (1977).

6. Harris v. McRae, 448 U.S. 297 (1980).

7. City of Akron v. Akron Center for Reproductive Health, 462 U.S. 416 (1983).

8. Planned Parenthood of Central Missouri v. Danforth, 428 U.S. 52 (1976).

9. Bellotti v. Baird, 443 U.S. 622 (1979); Planned Parenthood of Kansas City v. Ashcroft, 462 U.S. 476 (1983).

10. See Patricia G. Barnes, "Minors Seeking Abortions Find No Court Resistance," *National Law Journal,* March 13, 1995, p. A8.

11. H.L. v. Matheson, 450 U.S. 398 (1981).

12. Planned Parenthood of Central Missouri v. Danforth, 428 U.S. 52 (1976).

13. City of Akron v. Akron Center for Reproductive Health, 462 U.S. 416 (1983).

14. Colautti v. Franklin, 439 U.S. 379 (1979).

15. City of Akron v. Akron Center for Reproductive Health, 462 U.S. 416, 458 (1983).

16. Webster v. Reproductive Health Services, 492 U.S. 490 (1989).

17. Planned Parenthood of Eastern Pennsylvania v. Casey, 505 U.S. 833 (1992).

18. Hodgson v. Minnesota, 497 U.S. 417 (1990).

CHAPTER FOUR

1. An overview of the Irish constitutional developments is provided in J. M. Kelly, *The Irish Constitution* (3rd ed., Gerard Hogan & Gerry White eds., Dublin: Butterworths, 1994), pp. 790–810.

2. McGee v. Attorney General, [1974] Irish Rep. 284.

3. Attorney General v. X, [1992] Irish Rep. 1.

4. F. L. Morton, *Pro-Choice v. Pro-Life: Abortion and the Courts in Canada* (Norman: University of Oklahoma Press, 1992), provides an overview, on which the account here relies heavily.

5. R. v. Morgentaler, 44 Dominion L. Rep. (4th) 385 (1988).

6. David Currie, *The Constitution of the Federal Republic of Germany* (Chicago: University of Chicago Press, 1994), p. 310.

7. Excerpts from the decision are translated in Donald Kommers, *The Constitutional Jurisprudence of the Federal Republic of Germany* (Durham: Duke University Press, 1989), p. 347.

8. The decision is discussed in Donald P. Kommers, "The Constitutional Law of Abortion in Germany: Should Americans Pay Attention?," *Journal of Contemporary Health Law & Policy* 10 (1994): 1.

9. *Id.*, p. 20.

10. Mary Ann Glendon, *Abortion and Divorce in Western Law* (Cambridge: Harvard University Press, 1987), p. 62.

11. Albin Eser, "Abortion law reform in Germany in international comparative perspective," *European Journal of Health Law* 1 (1994): 15, 24.

12. Kommers, "Constitutional Law of Abortion in Germany," p. 10

13. Eser, "Abortion law reform," p. 26.

14. Laurence H. Tribe, *Abortion: The Clash of Absolutes* (New York: W. W. Norton, 1990), pp. 73–76.

15. *Id.*, pp. 73–74.

16. Mark A. Graber, "The Ghost of Abortion Past: Pre-*Roe* Abortion Law in Action," *Virginia Journal of Social Policy & the Law* 1 (1994): 309.

17. Bowers v. Hardwick, 478 U.S. 186 (1986).

18. David J. Garrow, *Liberty and Sexuality: The Right to Privacy and the Making of* Roe v. Wade (New York: Macmillan, 1994), pp. 656–67.

19. Stanley v. Georgia, 394 U.S. 557 (1969).

20. John C. Jeffries, Jr., *Justice Lewis F. Powell, Jr.: A Biography* (New York: Charles Scribner's Sons, 1994), pp. 514–30.

21. Robinson v. California, 370 U.S. 660 (1962).

22. Cruzan v. Director, Missouri Department of Health, 497 U.S. 261 (1990).

Appendixes

TABLE OF CONTENTS

Appendix A

POE V. ULLMAN

367 U.S. 497 (1961)
(DISSENT OF JUSTICE HARLAN)
(EXCERPTS)

PART TWO

CONSTITUTIONALITY

I consider that this Connecticut legislation, as construed to apply to these appellants, violates the Fourteenth Amendment. I believe that a statute making it a criminal offense for *married couples* to use contraceptives is an intolerable and unjustifiable invasion of privacy in the conduct of the most intimate concerns of an individual's personal life. I reach this conclusion, even though I find it difficult and unnecessary at this juncture to accept appellants' other argument that the judgment of policy behind the statute, so applied, is so arbitrary and unreasonable as to render the enactment invalid for that reason alone. Since both the contentions draw their basis from no explicit language of the Constitution, and have yet to find expression in any decision of this Court, I feel it desirable at the outset to state the framework of Constitutional principles in which I think the issue must be judged.

I.

In reviewing state legislation, whether considered to be in the exercise of the State's police powers, or in provision for the health, safety, morals or welfare of its people, it is clear that what is concerned are "the powers of government inherent in every sovereignty." *The License Cases,* 5 How. 504, 583. Only to the extent that the Constitution so requires may this Court interfere with the exercise of this plenary power of government. *Barron v. Mayor of Baltimore,* 7 Pet. 243. But precisely because it is the Constitution alone which warrants judicial interference in sovereign operations of the State, the basis of judgment as to the Constitutionality of state action must be a rational one, approaching the text which is the only commission for our power not in a literalistic way, as if we had a tax statute before us, but as the basic charter of our society, setting out in spare but meaningful terms the principles of government. *McCulloch v. Maryland,* Wheat. 316. But as inescapable as is the rational process in Constitutional adjudication in general, nowhere is it more so than in giving meaning to the prohibitions of the Fourteenth Amendment and, where the Federal Government is involved, the Fifth Amendment, against the deprivation of life, liberty or property without due process of law.

It is but a truism to say that this provision of both Amendments is not self-explanatory. As to the Fourteenth, which is involved here, the history of the Amendment also sheds little light on the meaning of the provision. Fairman, Does the Fourteenth Amendment Incorporate the Bill of Rights, 2 Stan. L. Rev. 15. It is important to note, however, that two views of the Amendment have not been accepted by this Court as delineating its scope. One view, which was ably and insistently argued in response to what were felt to be abuses by this Court of its reviewing power, sought to limit the provision to a guarantee of procedural fairness. See *Davidson v. New Orleans,* 96 U.S. 97, 105; Brandeis, J., in *Whitney v.California,* 274 U.S. 357, at 373; Warren, The New "Liberty" under the 14th Amendment, 39 Harv. L. Rev. 431; Reeder, The Due Process Clauses and "The Substance of Individual Rights," 58 U. Pa. L. Rev. 191; Shattuck, The True Meaning of The Term "Liberty" in Those Clauses in the Federal and State Constitutions Which Protect "Life, Liberty, and Property," 4 Harv. L. Rev. 365. The other view which has been rejected would have it that the Fourteenth Amendment, whether by way of the Privileges and Immunities Clause of the Due Process Clause applied against the States only and precisely those restraints which had prior to the Amendment been applicable merely to federal action. However, "due process" in the consistent view of this Court has ever been a broader concept than the first view and more flexible than the second.

Were due process merely a procedural safeguard it would fail to reach those situations where the deprivation of life, liberty or property was accomplished by legislation which by operation in the future could, given even the fairest possible procedure in application to individuals, nevertheless destroy the enjoyment of all three. Compare, *e. g., Selective Draft Law Cases,* 245 U.S. 366; *Butler v. Perry,* 240 U.S. 328; *Korematsu v. United States,* 323 U.S. 214. Thus the guaranties of due process, though having their roots in Magna Carta's *"per legem terrae"* and considered as procedural safeguards "against executive usurpation and tyranny," have in this country "become bulwarks also against arbitrary legislation." *Hurtado v. California,* 110 U.S. 516, at 532.

However it is not the particular enumeration of rights in the first eight Amendments which spells out the reach of Fourteenth Amendment due process, but rather, as was suggested in another context long before the adoption of that Amendment, those concepts which are considered to embrace those rights "which are . . . *fundamental;* which belong . . . to the citizens of all free governments," *Corfield v. Coryell,* 4 Wash. C. C. 371, 380, for "the purposes [of securing] which men enter into society," *Calder v. Bull,* 3 Dall. 386, 388. Again and again this Court has resisted the notion that the Fourteenth Amendment is no more than a shorthand reference to what is explicitly set out elsewhere in the Bill of Rights. *Slaughter-House Cases,* 16 Wall. 36; *Walker v. Sauvinet,* 92 U.S. 90; *Hurtado v. California,* 110 U.S. 516; *Presser v. Illinois,* 116 U.S. 252; *In re Kemmler,* 136 U.S. 436; *Twining v. New Jersey,* 211 U.S. 78; *Palko v. Connecticut,* 302 U.S. 319. Indeed the fact that an identical provision limiting federal action is found among the first eight Amendments, applying to the Federal Government, suggests that due process is a discrete concept which subsists as an independent guaranty of liberty and procedural fairness, more general and inclusive than the specific prohibitions. See *Mormon Church v. United States,* 136 U.S. 1; *Downes v. Bidwell,* 182 U.S. 244; *Hawaii v. Mankichi,* 190 U.S. 197; *Balzac v. Porto Rico,* 258 U.S. 298; *Farrington v. Tokushige,* 273 U.S. 284; *Bolling v. Sharpe,* 347 U.S. 497.

Due process has not been reduced to any formula; its content cannot be determined by reference to any code. The best that can be said is that through the course of this Court's decisions it has represented the balance which our Nation, built upon postulates of respect for the liberty of the individual, has struck between that liberty and the demands of organized society. If the supplying of content to this Constitutional concept has of necessity been a rational process, it certainly has not been one where judges have felt free to roam where unguided speculation might take them. The balance of which I speak is the balance struck by this country, having regard to what history teaches are the traditions from which it developed as well as the traditions from which it broke. That tradition is a living thing. A decision of this Court which radically departs from it could not long survive, while a decision which builds on what has survived is likely to be sound. No formula could serve as a substitute, in this area, for judgment and restraint.

It is this outlook which has led the Court continuingly to perceive distinctions in the imperative character of Constitutional provisions, since that character must be discerned from a particular provision's larger context. And inasmuch as this context is one not of words, but of history and purposes, the full scope of the liberty guaranteed by the Due Process Clause cannot be found in or limited by the precise terms of the specific guarantees elsewhere provided in the Constitution. This "liberty" is not a series of isolated points pricked out in terms of the taking of property; the freedom of speech, press, and religion; the right to keep and bear arms; the freedom from unreasonable searches and seizures; and so on. It is a rational continuum which, broadly speaking, includes a freedom from all substantial arbitrary impositions and purposeless restraints, see *Allgeyer v. Louisiana,* 165 U.S. 578; *Holden v. Hardy,* 169 U.S. 366; *Booth v. Illinois,* 184 U.S. 425; *Nebbia v. New York,* 291 U.S. 502; *Skinner v. Oklahoma,* 316 U.S. 535, 544 (concurring opinion); *Schware v. Board of Bar Examiners,* 353 U.S. 232, and which also recognizes, what a reasonable and sensitive judgment must, that certain interests require particularly careful scrutiny of the state needs asserted to justify their abridgment. Cf. *Skinner v. Oklahoma, supra; Bolling v. Sharpe, supra.*

As was said in *Meyer v. Nebraska,* 262 U.S. 390, 399, "this Court has not attempted to define with exactness the liberty thus guaranteed . . . . Without doubt, it denotes not merely freedom from bodily restraint . . . ." Thus, for instance, when in that case and in *Pierce v. Society of Sisters,* 268 U.S. 510, the Court struck down laws which sought not to require what children must learn in schools, but to prescribe, in the first case, what they must *not* learn, and in the second, *where* they must acquire their learning, I do not think it was wrong to put those decisions on "the right of the individual to . . . establish a home and bring up children," *Meyer v. Nebraska, ibid.,* or on the basis that "The fundamental theory of liberty upon which all governments in this Union repose excludes any general power of the State to standardize its children by forcing them to accept instruction from public teachers only," *Pierce v. Society of Sisters,* at 535. I consider this so, even though today those decisions would probably have gone by reference to the concepts of freedom of expression and conscience assured against state action by the Fourteenth Amendment, concepts that are derived from the explicit guarantees of the First Amendment against federal encroachment upon freedom of speech and belief. See *West Virginia State Board of Education v. Barnette,* 319 U.S. 624, and 656 (dissenting opinion); *Prince v. Massachusetts,* 321 U.S. 158, 166. For it is the purposes of those guarantees and not their text, the reasons for their statement by the Framers and not the statement itself, see *Palko v. Connecticut,* 302 U.S. 319,

324–327; *United States v. Carolene Prods.*, 304 U.S. 144, 152–153, which have led to their present status in the compendious notion of "liberty" embraced in the Fourteenth Amendment.

Each new claim to Constitutional protection must be considered against a background of Constitutional purposes, as they have been rationally perceived and historically developed. Though we exercise limited and sharply restrained judgment, yet there is no "mechanical yardstick," no "mechanical answer." The decision of an apparently novel claim must depend on the grounds which follow closely on well-accepted principles and criteria. The new decision must take "its place in relation to what went before and further [cut] a channel for what is to come." *Irvine v. California*, 347 U.S. 128, 147 (dissenting opinion). The matter was well put in *Rochin v. California*, 342 U.S. 165, 170–171:

> "The vague contours of the Due Process Clause do not leave judges at large. We may not draw on our merely personal and private notions and disregard the limits that bind judges in their judicial function. Even though the concept of due process of law is not final and fixed, these limits are derived from considerations that are fused in the whole nature of our judicial process . . . . These are considerations deeply rooted in reason and in the compelling traditions of the legal profession."

On these premises I turn to the particular Constitutional claim in this case.

II.

Appellants contend that the Connecticut statue deprives them, as it unquestionably does, of a substantial measure of liberty in carrying on the most intimate of all personal relationships, and that it does so arbitrarily and without any rational, justifying purpose. The State, on the other hand, asserts that it is acting to protect the moral welfare of its citizenry, both directly, in that it considers the practice of contraception immoral in itself, and instrumentally, in that the availability of contraceptive materials tends to minimize "the disastrous consequence of dissolute action," that is fornication and adultery.

It is argued by appellants that the judgment, implicit in this statute—that the use of contraceptives by married couples is immoral—is an irrational one, that in effect it subjects them in a very important matter to the arbitrary whim of the legislature, and that it does so for no good purpose. Where, as here, we are dealing with what must be considered "a basic liberty," cf. *Skinner v. Oklahoma, supra,* at 541, "There are limits to the extent to which the presumption of constitutionality can be pressed," *id.,* at 544 (concurring opinion), and the mere assertion that the action of the State finds justification in the controversial realm of morals cannot justify alone any and every restriction it imposes. See *Alberts v. California,* 354 U.S. 476.

Yet the very inclusion of the category of morality among state concerns indicates that society is not limited in its objects only to the physical well-being of the community, but has traditionally concerned itself with the moral soundness of its people as well. Indeed to attempt a line between public behavior and what which is purely consensual or solitary would be to withdraw from community concern a range of subjects with which every society in civilized times has found it necessary to deal. The laws regarding marriage which provide both when the sexual powers may be used and the legal and societal context in which children are born and brought up, as well as laws forbidding adultery, fornication and homosexual practices which express the negative of the proposition, confining sexuality to lawful marriage, form a pattern so deeply pressed into the substance of our social life that any Constitutional doctrine in this area must build upon that basis. Compare *McGowan v. Maryland,* 366 U.S. 420.

It is in this area of sexual morality, which contains many proscriptions of consensual behavior having little or no direct impact on others, that the State of Connecticut has expressed its moral judgment that all use of contraceptives is improper. Appellants cite an impressive list of authorities who, from a great variety of points of view, commend the considered use of contraceptives by married couples. What they do not emphasize is that not too long ago the current of opinion was very probably quite the opposite, and that even today the issue is not free of controversy. Certainly, Connecticut's judgment is no more demonstrably correct or incorrect than are the varieties of judgment, expressed in law, on marriage and divorce, on adult consensual homosexuality, abortion, and sterilization, or euthanasia and suicide. If we had a case before us which required us to decide simply, and in abstraction, whether the moral judgment implicit in the application of the present statute to married couples was a sound one, the very controversial nature of these questions would, I think, require us to hesitate long before concluding that the Constitution precluded Connecticut from choosing as it has among these various views. Cf. *Alberts v. California,* 354, U.S. 476, 500–503 (concurring opinion).

But, as might be expected, we are not presented simply with this moral judgment to be passed on as an abstract proposition. The secular state is not an examiner of consciences: it must operate in the realm of behavior, of overt actions, and where it does so operate, not only the underlying, moral purpose of its operations, but also the *choice of means* becomes relevant to any Constitutional judgment on what is done. The moral presupposition on which appellants ask us to pass judgment could form the basis of a variety of legal rules and administrative choices, each presenting a different issue for adjudication. For example, one practical expression of the moral view propounded here might be the rule that a marriage in which only contraceptive relations had taken place had never been consummated and could be annulled. Compare, *e.g.,* 2 Bouscaren, Canon Law Digest, 307–313. Again, the use of contraceptives might be made a ground for divorce, or perhaps tax benefits and subsidies could be provided for large families. Other examples also readily suggest themselves.

III.

Precisely what is involved here is this: the State is asserting the right to enforce its moral judgment by intruding upon the most intimate details of the marital relation with the full power of the criminal law. Potentially, this could allow the deployment of all the incidental machinery of the criminal law, arrests, searches and seizures; inevitably, it must mean at the very least the lodging of criminal charges, a public trial, and testimony as to the *corpus delicti*. Nor could any imaginable elaboration of presumptions, testimonial privileges, or other safeguards, alleviate the necessity for testimony as to the mode and manner of the married couples' sexual relations, or at least the opportunity for the accused to make denial of the charges. In sum, the statute allows the State to enquire into, prove and punish married people for the private use of their martial intimacy.

This, then, is the precise character of the enactment whose Constitutional measure we must take. The statute must pass a more rigorous Constitutional test than that going merely to the plausibility of its underlying rationale. See pp. 542–545, *supra.* This enactment involves what by common understanding throughout the English-speaking world, must be granted to be a most fundamental aspect of "liberty," the privacy of the home in its most basic sense, and it is this which requires that the statute be subjected to "strict scrutiny." *Skinner v. Oklahoma, supra,* at 541.

That aspect of liberty which embraces the concept of the privacy of the home receives explicit Constitutional protection at two places only. These are the Third Amendment, relating to the quartering of soldiers, and the Fourth Amendment, prohibiting unreasonable searches and seizures. While these Amendments reach only the Federal Government, this Court has held in the strongest terms, and today again confirms, that the concept of "privacy" embodied in the Fourth Amendment is part of the "ordered liberty" assured against state action by the Fourteenth Amendment. See *Wolf v. Colorado,* 338 U.S. 25; *Mapp v. Ohio, post,* p. 643.

It is clear, of course, that this Connecticut statute does not invade the privacy of the home in the usual sense, since the invasion involved here may, and doubtless usually would, be accomplished without any physical intrusion whatever into the home. What the statute undertakes to do, however, is to create a crime which is grossly offensive to this privacy, while the Constitution refers only to methods of ferreting out substantive wrongs, and the procedure it requires presupposes that substantive offenses may be committed and sought out in the privacy of the home. But such an analysis forecloses any claim to Constitutional protection against this form of deprivation of privacy, only if due process in this respect is limited to what is explicitly provided in the Constitution, divorced from the rational purposes, historical roots, and subsequent developments of the relevant provisions. Perhaps the most comprehensive statement of the principle of liberty underlying these aspects of the Constitution was given by Mr. Justice Brandeis, dissenting in *Olmstead v. United States,* 277 U.S. 438, at 478:

"The protection guaranteed by the [Fourth and Fifth] Amendments is much broader is scope. The makers of our Constitution undertook to secure conditions favorable to the pursuit of happiness. They recognized the significance of man's spiritual nature, of his feelings and of his intellect. They knew that only a part of the pain, pleasure and satisfactions of life are to be found in material things. They sought to protect Americans in their beliefs, their thoughts, their emotions and their sensations. They conferred, as against the Government, the right to be let alone—the most comprehensive of rights and the right most valued by civilized men. To protect that right, every unjustifiable intrusion by the Government upon the privacy of the individual, whatever the means employed, must be deemed a violation of the Fourth Amendment . . . ."

I think the sweep of the Court's decisions, under both the Fourth and Fourteenth Amendments, amply shows that the Constitution protects the privacy of the home against all unreasonable intrusion of whatever character. "[These] principles . . . affect the very essence of constitutional liberty and security. They reach farther than [a] concrete form of the case . . . before the court, with its adventitious circumstances; they apply to all invasions on the part of the government and its employees of the sanctity of a man's home and the privacies of life. . . ." *Boyd v. United States,* 116 U.S. 616, 630. "The security of one's privacy against arbitrary intrusion by the police—which is at the core of the Fourth Amendment—is basic to a free society." *Wolf v. Colorado, supra,* at 27. In addition, see, *e.g., Davis v. United States,* 328 U.S. 582, 587; *Oklahoma Press Pub. Co. v. Walling,* 327 U.S. 186, 202–203; *Frank v. Maryland,* 359 U.S. 360, 365–366; *Silverman v. United States,* 365 U.S. 505, 511.

It would surely be an extreme instance of sacrificing substance to form were it to be held that the Constitutional principle of privacy against arbitrary official intrusion comprehends only physical invasions by the police. To be sure, the times presented the Framers with two particular threats to that principle, the general warrant, see *Boyd v. United States, supra,* and the quartering of soldiers in private homes. But though "Legislation, both statutory and constitutional, is enacted, . . . from an experience of evils, . . . its general language should not, therefore, be necessarily confined to the form that evil had therefore taken. . . . [A] principle to be vital must be capable of wider application than the mischief which gave birth." *Weems v. United States,* 217 U.S. 349, 373.

Although the form of intrusion here—the enactment of a substantive offense—does not, in my opinion, preclude the making of a claim based on the right of privacy embraced in the "liberty" of the Due Process Clause, it must be acknowledged that there is another sense in which it could be argued that this intrusion on privacy differs from what the Fourth Amendment, and the similar concept of the Fourteenth, were intended to protect: here we have not an intrusion into the home so much as on the life which characteristically has its place in the home. But to my mind such a distinction is so insubstantial as to be captious: if the physical curtilage of the home is protected, it is surely as a result of solicitude to protect the privacies of the life within. Certainly the safeguarding of the home does not follow merely from the sanctity of property rights. The home derives its pre-eminence as the seat of family life. And the integrity of that life is something so fundamental that it has been found to draw to its protection the principles of more than one explicitly granted Constitutional right. Thus, Mr. Justice Brandeis, writing of a statute which made "it punishable to teach [pacifism] in any place [to] a single person . . . no matter what the relation of the parties may be," found such a "statute invades the privacy and freedom of the home. Father and mother may not follow the promptings of religious belief, of conscience or of conviction, and teach son or daughter the doctrine of pacifism. If they do any police officer may summarily arrest them." *Gilbert v. Minnesota,* 254 U.S. 325, 335–336 (dissenting opinion). This same principle is expressed in the *Pierce* and *Meyer* cases, *supra.* These decisions, as was said in *Prince v. Massachusetts,* 321 U.S. 158, at 166, "have respected the private realm of family life which the state cannot enter."

Of this whole "private realm of family life" it is difficult to imagine what is more private or more intimate than a husband and wife's marital relations. We would indeed be straining at a gnat and swallowing a camel were we to show concern for the niceties of property law involved in our recent decision, under the Fourth Amendment, in *Chapman v. United States,* 365 U.S. 610, and yet fail at least to see any substantial claim here.

Of course, just as the requirement of a warrant is not inflexible in carrying out searches and seizures, see *Abel v. United States,* 362 U.S. 217; *United States v. Rabinowitz,* 339 U.S. 56, so there are countervailing considerations at this more fundamental aspect of the right involved. "[T]he family . . . is not beyond regulation," *Prince v. Massachusetts, supra,* and it would be an absurdity to suggest either that offenses may not be committed in the bosom of the family or that the home can be made a sanctuary for crime. The right of privacy most manifestly is not an absolute. Thus, I would not suggest that adultery, homosexuality, fornication and incest are immune from criminal enquiry, however privately practiced. So much has been explicitly recognized in acknowledging the State's rightful concern for its people's moral welfare. See pp. 545–548, *supra.* But not to discriminate between what is involved in this case and either the traditional offenses against good morals or crimes which, though they may be committed anywhere, happen to have been committed or concealed in the home, would entirely misconceive the argument that is being made.

Adultery, homosexuality and the like are sexual intimacies which the State forbids altogether, but the intimacy of husband and wife is necessarily an essential and accepted feature of the institution of marriage, an institution which the State not only must allow, but which always and in every age it has fostered and protected. It is one thing when the State exerts its power either to forbid extra-marital sexuality altogether, or to say who may marry, but it is quite another when, having acknowledged a marriage and the intimacies inherent in it, it undertakes to regulate by means of the criminal law the details of that intimacy.

In sum, even though the State has determined that the use of contraceptives is as iniquitous as any act of extra-marital sexual immorality, the intrusion of the whole machinery of the criminal law into the very heart of marital privacy, requiring husband and wife to render account before a criminal tribunal of their uses of that intimacy, is surely a very different thing indeed from punishing those who establish intimacies which the law has always forbidden and which can have no claim to social protection.

In my view the appellants have presented a very pressing claim for Constitutional protection. Such difficulty as the claim presents lies only in evaluating it against the State's countervailing contention that it be allowed to enforce, by whatever means it deems appropriate, its judgment of the immorality of the practice this law condemns. In resolving this conflict a number of factors compel me to conclude that the decision here must most emphatically be for the appellants. Since, at it appears to me, the statute marks an abridgment of important fundamental liberties protected by the Fourteenth Amendment, it will not do to urge in justification of that abridgment simply that the statute is rationally related to the effectuation of a proper state purpose. A closer scrutiny and stronger justification than that are required.

Though the State has argued the Constitutional permissibility of the moral judgment underlying this statute, neither its brief, nor its argument, nor anything in any of the opinions of its highest court in these or other cases even remotely suggests a justification for the obnoxiously intrusive means it has chosen to effectuate that policy. To me the very circumstance that Connecticut has not chosen to press the enforcement of this statute against individual users, while it nevertheless persists in asserting its right to do so at any time—in effect a right to hold this statute as an imminent threat to the privacy of the households of the State—conduces to the inference either that it does not consider the policy of the statute a very important one, or that it does not regard the means it has chosen for its effectuation as appropriate or necessary.

But conclusive, in my view, is the utter novelty of this enactment. Although the Federal Government and many States have at one time or other had on their books statutes forbidding or regulating the distribution of contraceptives, none, so far as I can find, has made the *use* of contraceptives a crime. Indeed, a diligent search has revealed that no nation, including several which quite evidently share Connecticut's moral policy, has seen fit to effectuate that policy by the means presented here.

Though undoubtedly the States are and should be left free to reflect a wide variety of policies, and should be allowed broad scope in experimenting with various means of promoting those policies, I must agree with Mr. Justice Jackson that "There are limits to the extent to which a legislatively represented majority may conduct . . . experiments at the expense of the dignity and personality" of the individual. *Skinner v. Oklahoma, supra.* In this instance these limits are, in my view, reached and passed.

I would adjudicate these appeals and hold this statute unconstitutional, insofar as it purports to make criminal the conduct contemplated by these married women. It follows that if their conduct cannot be a crime, appellant Buxton cannot be an accomplice thereto. I would reverse the judgment in each of these cases.

Appendix B

GRISWOLD V. CONNECTICUT (1965)

DRAFT OPINION OF JUSTICE DOUGLAS, AND LETTER FROM JUSTICE BRENNAN

I

SUPREME COURT OF THE UNITED STATES

No. 496 — OCTOBER TERM, 1964.

Estelle T. Griswold et al.,
Appellants,
v.
State of Connecticut.

On Appeal From the
Supreme Court of Errors
of Connecticut.

[April —, 1965.]

MR. JUSTICE DOUGLAS delivered the opinion of the Court.

Appellant Griswold is Executive Director of the Planned Parenthood League of Connecticut. Appellant Buxton is a licensed physician and a professor at the Yale Medical School who served as Medical Director for the League at its Center in New Haven — a center open and operating from November 1 to November 10, 1961, when appellants were arrested.

They gave information, instruction, and medical advice to *married persons* as to the means of preventing conception. They examined the wife and prescribed the best contraceptive device or material for her use. Fees were usually charged, although some couples were serviced free.

The statutes whose constitutionality are involved in this appeal are §§ 53–32 and 54–196 of the General Statutes of Connecticut (1938). The former provides:

"Any person who uses any drug, medicinal articles or instruments for the purpose of preventing conception shall be fined not less than fifty dollars or imprisoned not less than sixty days nor more than one year or be both fined and imprisoned."

Section 54–196 provides:

"Any person who assists, abets, counsels, causes, hires, or commands another to commit any offence may be prosecuted and punished as if he were the principal offender."

The appellants were found guilty as accessories and fined $100 each against the claim that the accessory statute as so applied violated the Fourteenth Amendment. The Appellate Division of the Circuit Court affirmed. 3 Conn.Cir. 6. The Court of Errors affirmed that judgment. 151 Conn. 544, 200 A. 2d 479. We noted probable jurisdiction. 378 U.S.—.

We think that appellants have standing to raise the constitutional rights of the married people with whom they had a professional relationship. *Tileston v. Ullman,* 318 U.S. 44. is different, for there the plaintiff seeking to represent others was asked for a declaratory judgment. In that situation we thought that the requirements of standing should be strict lest the standards of "case or controversy" in Article III of the Constitution become blurred. Here those doubts are removed by reason of a criminal conviction for serving married couples in violation of a statute which if invalid makes the conviction unconstitutional. This case is more akin to *Truax v. Raich,* 239 U.S. 33, where an employer was permitted to assert the rights of his employees; to *Pierce v. Society of Sisters,* 268 U.S. 510, where the owners of a private school were entitled to assert the rights of potential pupils and their parents; and to *Barrows v. Jackson,* 346 U.S. 249, where a white defendant, party to a racially restrictive covenant, who was being sued for damages by the covenantor because the defendant had conveyed the property to a Negro, was allowed to raise the issue that enforcement of the covenant violated the rights of Negroes to equal protection, although no Negro was a party to the suit. And see *Meyer v. Nebraska,* 262 U.S. 390; *Adler v. Board of Education,* 342 U.S. 485; *NAACP v. Alabama,* 357 U.S. 449; *NAACP v. Button,* 371 U.S. 415. The rights of husband and wife, pressed here, are likely to be diluted or adversely affected unless those rights are considered in a suit involving those who have a confidential relation to them.

Coming to the merits, we are met with a wide range of questions that implicate the Due Process Clause of the Fourteenth Amendment. Overtones of some arguments suggest that *Lochner v. New York,* 198 U.S. 45, should be our guide. But we decline that invitation as we did in *West Coast Hotel Co. v. Parrish,* 300 U.S. 379; *Lincoln Union v. Northwestern Co.,* 335 U.S. 525; *Williamson v. Lee Optical Co.,* 348 U.S. 483; *Olsen v. Nebraska,* 313 U.S. 236; *Giboney v. Empire Storage Co.,* 336 U.S. 490. We do not sit as a super-legislature to determine the wisdom, need, and propriety of laws that touch economic problems, business affairs, or social conditions. Were this law one that dealt with the manufacture of contraceptives or the sale or marketing of contraceptives in drug stores, we would think no substantial federal question would be presented by this appeal. This case, however, has no commercial aspect nor any marketing aspect. Instead it involves an intimate relation of husband and wife and the physician's role in the maintenance of the aspect of that relation.

The association of husband and wife is not mentioned in the Constitution nor in the Bill of Rights. Neither is any other kind of association. The right to educate a child in a school of the parents' choice—whether public or parochial—is also not mentioned. Nor is the right to study any particular subject or any foreign language. Yet the First Amendment has been construed to include certain of those peripheral rights. By *Pierce v. Society of Sisters, supra,* the right to educate one's children as one chooses is made applicable to the States by the force of the First and Fourteenth Amendments. By *Meyer v. Nebraska, supra,* the same dignity is given the right to study the German language in a public school. In other words, the State may not, consistently with the spirit of the First Amendment, so contract the spectrum of available knowledge. The right to learn, the right to read, the right to know have overtones in freedom of speech and of the press. Without those peripheral rights the specific rights would be less secure. And so we reaffirm the principle of the *Pierce* and the *Meyer* cases.

The family is an instruction unit as much as the school; and husband and wife are both teachers and pupils. To narrow, as does the Connecticut statute, discussion and advice on a problem as important as population and procreation is to introduce a dangerous state influence over First Amendment rights.

Other First Amendment analogies are the ones involving rights of association. In *NAACP v. Alabama,* 357 U.S. 449, 462, we protected the "freedom to associate and privacy in one's association," noting that freedom of association was a First Amendment right. Disclosure of membership lists in a constitutionally valid association, as held, was invalid "as entailing the likelihood of a substantial restraint upon the exercise by petitioner's members of their right to freedom of association." *Id.,* at 462. In like context we have protected forms of "association" that are not political in the customary sense but pertain to the social, legal, and economic benefit of the members. *NAACP v. Button,* 371 U.S. 415, 430–431. In *Schware v. Board of Bar Examiners,* 353 U.S. 232, we held it not permissible to bar a lawyer from practice, because he had once been a member of the Communist Party. The man's "association with that Party" was not shown to be "anything more than a political faith in a political party (*id.,* at 244) and not action of a kind proving bad moral character." *Id.,* at 245–246.

None of those cases involved the "right of assembly"—a right that extends to all irrespective of their race or ideology. *DeJonge v. Oregon,* 299 U.S.353. The right of "association" like the right of belief (*Board of Education v. Barnette,* 319 U.S. 624) is more than the right to attend a meeting; it includes the right to express one's attitudes or philosophies by membership in a group or by affiliation with it or by other lawful means. Association in that context is a form of expression of opinion; and while it is not expressly included in the First Amendment its existence is useful in making the express guarantees fully meaningful.

The foregoing cases do not decide this case. But they place it in the proper frame of reference. Marriage does not fit precisely any of the categories of First Amendment rights. But it is a form of association as vital in life of a man or woman as any other, and perhaps more so. We would, indeed, have difficulty protecting the intimacies of one's relations to NAACP and not the intimacies of one's marriage relation. Marriage is the essence of one form of the expression of love, admiration, and loyalty. To protect other forms of such expression and not this, the central one, would seem to us to be a travesty. We deal with a right of association older than the Bill of Rights—older than our political parties, older than our school system. It is a coming together for better or for worse, hopefully enduring, and intimate to the degree of being sacred. This association promotes a way of life, not a cause; a harmony in living, not a political faith; a bilateral loyalty, not a commercial or social project. Yet it flourishes on the interchange of ideas. It is the main font of the population problem; and education of each spouse in the ramification of that problem, the health of the wife, and the well-being of the family is central to family functioning. Those objects are the end products of free expression and these Acts intrude on them.

If the accessory statute can be enforced as it has been here, so can § 53–32 which also has criminal sanctions. The prospects of police with warrants searching the sacred precincts of marital bedrooms for telltale signs of the use of contraceptives is repulsive to the ideas of privacy and of association that make up a goodly part of the penumbra of the Constitution and Bill of Rights. Cf. *Rochin v. California,* 342 U.S. 165.

Reversed.

Supreme Court of the United States
Washington, D.C. 20543

CHAMBERS OF
JUSTICE WM.J. BRENNAN, JR.

April 24, 1965

Dear Bill:

I have read your draft opinion in *Griswold v. Connecticut,* and, while I agree with a great deal of it, I should like to suggest a substantial change in emphasis for your consideration. It goes without saying, of course, that your rejection of any approach based on *Lochner v. New York* is absolutely right. And I agree that the association of husband and wife is not mentioned in the Bill of Rights, and that that is the obstacle we must hurdle to effect a reversal in this case.

But I hesitate to bring the husband-wife relationship within the right to association we have constructed in the First Amendment context. Any language to the effect that the family unit is a sacred unit, that it is unreachable by the State because it is an instruction unit, may come back to haunt us just as *Lochner* did. If a suitable formulation can be worked out, I would prefer a theory based on privacy, which, as you point out, is the real interest vindicated here. In the First Amendment context, in situations like *NAACP v. Alabama,* privacy is necessary to protect the capacity of an association for fruitful advocacy. In the present context, it seems to me that we are really interested in the privacy of married couples quite apart from any interest in advocacy. Yet if privacy of a group as a group is vindicated by the First Amendment quite apart from lawful advocacy, could not the reasoning of this case be drawn on to resist regulation or investigation of such groups as the Communist Party? In light of what you said in your dissent in the Communist Party registration case (adopted by me in my dissent), I know you do not mean to confer such immunity on associations simply because they are associations. But because we have to strain hard to find a First Amendment interest in advocacy or expression in the marital relationship, where that is not really the primary interest, might not your draft opinion be read to protect any group which can call itself an association?

Your opinion suggests, I think a more fruitful approach, more closely tailored to the real interest at stake. You point out that, in creating a right of association, this Court has invoked the First Amendment to protect something not literally within its terminology of speech and assembly, because the interest protected is so closely related to speech and assembly. Instead of expanding the First Amendment right of association to include marriage, why not say that what has been done for the First Amendment can also be done for some of the other fundamental guarantees of the Bill of Rights? In other words, where fundamentals are concerned, the Bill of Rights guarantees are but expressions or examples of those rights, and do not preclude applications or extensions of those rights to situations unanticipated by the Framers. Whether, in doing for other guarantees what has been done for speech and assembly in the First Amendment, we proceed by an expansive interpretation of those guarantees or by application of the Ninth Amendment admonition that the enumeration of rights is not exhaustive, the result is the same. The guarantees of the Bill of Rights do not necessarily resist expansion to fill in the edges where the same fundamental interests are at stake.

The Connecticut statute would, on this reasoning, run afoul of a right to privacy created out of the Fourth Amendment and the self-incrimination clause of the Fifth, together with the Third, in much the same way as the right to association has been created out of the First. Taken together, those amendments indicate a fundamental concern with the sanctity of the home and the right of the individual to be let alone. We need not say how far it would extend, nor intimate even remotely whether it would encompass "privacy" in the common law sense as expounded by Warren and Brandeis in their article. All that is necessary for the decision of this case is the recognition that, whatever the contours of a constitutional right to privacy, it would preclude application of the statute before us to married couples. For it is plain that, in our civilization, the marital relationship above all else is endowed with privacy.

With this change of emphasis, an opinion resting on the persuasive precedent of the right of association for similar limited expansion of other specific guarantees of the Bill of Rights, would be most attractive to me because it would require less departure from the specific guarantees and because I think there is a better chance it will command a Court.

Sincerely,
Bill

Mr. Justice Douglas.

Appendix C

ROE V. WADE (1973)

(LETTER FROM JUSTICE BRENNAN, DRAFT OPINION OF JUSTICE BLACKMUN, DRAFT DISSENT OF JUSTICE WHITE, MEMORANDUM OF JUSTICE DOUGLAS, AND LETTER FROM JUSTICE MARSHALL)

Supreme Court of the United States
Washington, D. C. 20543

CHAMBERS OF
JUSTICE WM.J. BRENNAN, JR.

December 30, 1971

RE: Abortion Cases

Dear Bill:

I gathered form our conversation yesterday that you too think we might better await Harry Blackmun's circulation in the *Texas* abortion case before circulating one in the *Georgia* case. I appreciate that some time may pass before we hear from Harry and, like you, therefore write down my comments so that I won't forget them.

First, there would seem to be a number of threshold issues that are of varying difficulty. Some, I think, must be expressly addressed, while others perhaps require no discussion or should be simply finessed. None, in my opinion, forecloses decision on the crucial questions here—the existence and nature of a right to an abortion. The threshold issues I see are as follows:

1. Was a three-judge district court improperly convened because the complaint failed to make out a case for an injunction? It would seem that this question must be expressly answered, since we postponed jurisdiction in taking the case. The answer may simply be that the complaint for an injunction was not so frivolous as to warrant refusal to convene a three-judge court.

2. (a) Is it material that Mary Doe was not proved to be a real person who was pregnant and denied an abortion because of application of the Georgia statute? In declining proof on these matters,

the district court presumably found favorably for the plaintiff, a finding that is apparently supported by an affidavit in the record. (b) Since Mary Doe was apparently a resident of Georgia, she seems to lack standing to raise the rights of non-residents vis-a-vis the residency requirement of the Georgia law. Do any other plaintiffs have standing to assert those rights? Although there may well be *Shapiro v. Thompson* difficulties with the residency requirement, it may be best to finesse that question and the related standing issue. (c) Does Mary Doe have standing to assert the equal protection claims of poor and Black persons? On the one hand, the basis for her complaint seems to have been that she was refused an abortion not because of poverty or race, but because the hospital abortion committee passed unfavorably on her application. On the other hand, after filing her complaint, she evidently was granted the right to an abortion at another hospital, but was unable to afford the costs. In any event, I suggest that it may be unnecessary to resolve Mary Doe's standing in this regard, because the equal protection claims need not be reached. The gist of those claims is that the Georgia administrative procedures for obtaining an abortion are overly costly. Since I would strike all of those procedures down except for the requirement that the abortion be performed by a licensed physician, the importance of the equal protection claims would seem diminished. Of course, the question would remain whether there is a *Boddie v. Connecticut*-type right to the cost of the single physician's fee. But that is not the argument pressed here.

3. Is the case moot because Mary Doe is no longer pregnant?

4. Is abstention required?

5. What is the impact of *Younger v. Harris* and *Samuels v. Mackell*? I suggest that we make an express holding, if only in a footnote, to the effect that those cases do not apply where there is no State court proceeding pending. I think it would be helpful to nail this point down while we can.

6. Is it material whether class relief was awarded? If so, what was the class?

As for the merits, I read your memorandum to find the following constitutional defects in the Georgia statute:

(1) The statute infringes the right of privacy by refusing abortions where the mother's mental, but not physical health is in jeopardy.

(2) The statute violates procedural due process requirements by denying the woman notice and hearing when her application for an abortion is refused.

(3) The statute infringes a First Amendment right to seek advice on one's health and rely on the physician of one's choice by subjecting the decision of the doctor and patient to the oversight of other physicians.

(4) The statute possibly denies the poor and the Black equal protection of the laws by requiring administrative procedures to which they may, in effect, lack access.

As indicated, I do not think we need touch upon No. 4. Similarly, if the Georgia scheme for oversight of the individual's abortion decision is struck down (which I would do, for reasons explained below, under the right of privacy rather than under the First Amendment), no need would exist for discussing the procedural due process aspects of the scheme, and your No. 2 could be omitted. The abortion decision would become that of the woman alone, except that the operation could be performed only by a licensed practitioner; if one physician refuses to do it, her recourse would simply be to find another doctor.

With respect to No. 1 and No. 3, I am not sure that we have an authoritative interpretation of "health" within the meaning of the Georgia statute. (Appellees' counsel stated at the oral argument that "not judicially but as a matter of practice— . . . health here includes mental health.") In any case, I believe that the statute infringes the right of privacy not merely because it may restrictively use "health" to mean only the mother's physical well-being, but because it limits abortions to enumerated cases. In other words, I agree with the district court that the state may not limit the number of reasons for which an abortion may be sought, since "such action unduly restricts a decision sheltered by Constitutional right of privacy."

I guess my most significant departure from your approach is in the development of the right-of-privacy argument. I agree with you that the right is a species of "liberty" (although, as I mentioned yesterday, I think the Ninth Amendment (as in your *Papachristou* opinion) should be brought into this problem at greater length), but I would identify three groups of fundamental freedoms that "liberty" encompasses: *first,* freedom from bodily restraint or inspection, freedom to do with one's body as one likes, and freedom to care for one's health and person; *second,* freedom of choice in the basic decisions of life, such as marriage, divorce, procreation, contraception, and the education and upbringing of children; and, *third,* autonomous control over the development and expression of one's intellect and personality.

As to the first group, I would rely on *Terry v. Ohio, Meyer v. Nebraska, Jacobson v. Massachusetts,* and *Union Pacific Ry Co. v. Botsford.* In particular, I would stress the positive aspects of *Jacobson* — that there is "a sphere within which the individual may assert the supremacy of his own will and rightfully dispute the authority of any human government . . . to interfere with the exercise of that will"—rather than the holding that compelling public necessity may justify intrusion into bodily freedom.

I would peg the right to care for one's health and person to the right of privacy rather than directly to the First Amendment partly because (1) it would seem to be broader than the right to consult with, and act on the advice of, the physician of one's choice and include, for example, access to nonprescriptive drugs and (2) it identifies the right squarely as that of the individual, not that of the individual together with his doctor. In addition, *NAACP v. Button,* relied on in the First Amendment analysis of your memorandum, I think was based not on the associational freedom of the lawyer and client, but on the expressional value of litigation and the associational rights of the NAACP and its members. More important, the First Amendment approach may make it difficult to sustain requirements for consultations with other doctors that should be upheld—as, for instance, measures to restrain over-eagerness in performing novel operations for the sake of research (or, worse, publicity) rather than for the sake of the patient's health. Although those measures might be validated under a traditional First Amendment "compelling interest" analysis, the First Amendment approach throws a heavy weight on the scales on the side of associational freedom. The right of privacy approach, in contrast, merely states that there is a fundamental interest in the individual's safeguarding his health. Measures that promote health, then, need not be set off and balanced against that interest, but may merely be judged on whether there is a reasonable basis for believing that they, in fact, promote health.

As to the second group, I'd rely on *Loving v. Virginia, Boddie v. Connecticut, Skinner v. Oklahoma,* my recently circulated *Eisenstadt v. Baird, Griswold v. Connecticut, Prince v. Massachusetts, Pierce v. Society of Sisters,* and *Meyer v. Nebraska.* [Incidentally, *Eisenstadt* in its discussion of *Griswold* is helpful in addressing the abortion question. If you could find it possible to join my proposed Court opinion in *Eisenstadt* in addition to filing a separate opinion, I believe that we would have a four-man majority. As it stands now, Brothers Stewart and Marshall have joined, while Brother Blackmun is yet to be heard from.] Finally, as to the third group, I'd rely on *Stanley v. Georgia* and its quotation from the Brandeis opinion in *Olmstead v. United States.*

The decision whether to abort a pregnancy obviously fits directly within each of the categories of fundamental freedoms I've identified and, therefore, should be held to involve a basic individual right.

Again like you, I would next emphasize that that conclusion is only the beginning of the problem—that the crucial question is whether the State has a compelling interest in regulating abortion that is achieved without unnecessarily intruding upon the individual's right. But here I would deal at length not only with the health concern for the well-being of the mother, but with the material interest in the life of the fetus and the moral interest in sanctifying life in general. This would perhaps be the most difficult part of the opinion. I would come out about where Justice Clark does in his Loyola University Law Review article—that " 'moral predilections must not be allowed to influence our minds in settling legal distinctions' " (quoting Holmes) and that "the law deals in reality, not obscurity—the known rather than the unknown. When sperm meets egg life may eventually form, but quite often it does not. [Indeed, the brief for the appellants in the Texas abortion case quotes an estimate of the rate of "spontaneous wastage" of 50%.] The law does not deal in speculation. The phenomenon of life takes time to develop, and [only after] it is actually present, it cannot be destroyed." The inconsistent position taken by Georgia in allowing destruction of the fetus in some, but not all cases might also be mentioned. Thus, although I would, of course, find a compelling State interest in requiring abortions to be performed by doctors, I would deny any such interest in the life of the fetus in the early stages of pregnancy. On the other hand, I would leave open the question when life "is actually present"—whether there is some point in the term before birth at which the interest in the life of the fetus does become subordinating.

Under the foregoing approach the Georgia provisions for (1) overseeing the individual's abortion decision through the requirement for approval by two additional doctors and the hospital abortion committee, (2) limiting the performance of abortions to accredited hospitals, and (3) restricting abortions to cases where the doctor finds "that an abortion is necessary" must fall together with the limitation on the reasons for abortion that the district court has already declared unconstitutional. First, there is no evidence of any abuse by individual doctors in performing abortions that are unwise from the standpoint of the mother's health. To the contrary, statistics apparently indicate that abortions in the early part of the term are safe, even when performed in clinics rather than hospitals. Secondly, if there is a right to an abortion in the early part of the term, that right cannot be effectively denied through cumbersome and dilatory administrative procedures or requirements. And, finally, the right of privacy in the matter of abortions means that the decision is that of the woman and her alone. The district court was wrong in holding that the State has a legitimate interest in regulating the quality of the decision.

In sum, I would affirm the district court's conclusion that the reasons for an abortion may not be prescribed. I would further hold that the only restraint a State may constitutionally impose upon the woman's individual decision is that the abortion must be performed by a licensed physician. And since the statute, as thus validated, would not limit the right to an abortion by making an early abortion difficult to obtain and since we can presume that Georgia will obey the declaratory judgment of this Court, I would affirm the denial of an injunction.

Sincerely,
Bill

Mr. Justice Douglas.

Supreme Court of the United States
Washington D.C. 20543

CHAMBERS OF
JUSTICE HARRY A. BLACKMUN

May 18, 1972

MEMORANDUM TO THE CONFERENCE
Re: No. 70–18—Roe v. Wade

Herewith is a first and tentative draft for this case.

Due to the presence of multiple parties and the existence of issues of standing and of appellate routes, it may be somewhat difficult to obtain a consensus on all aspects. My notes indicate, however, that we were generally in agreement to affirm on the merits. That is where I come out on the theory that the Texas statute, despite its narrowness, is unconstitutionally vague.

I think that this would be all that is necessary for disposition of the case, and that we need not get into the more complex Ninth Amendment issue. This may or may not appeal to you.

In any event, I am still flexible as to results, and I shall do my best to arrive at something which would command a court. Would it be advisable, rather than having numerous concurring and dissenting opinions immediately written, to have each of you express his general views in order to see if we can come together on something?

The Georgia case, yet to come, is more complex. I am still tentatively of the view, as I have been all along, that the Georgia case merits reargument before a full bench. I shall try to produce something, however, so that we may look at it before any decision as to that is made.

Sincerely,
H.A.B.

1st DRAFT

SUPREME COURT OF THE UNITED STATES

No. 70–18

Jane Roe et al., Appellants, v. Henry Wade.	On Appeal from the United States District Court for the Northern District of Texas.

[May —, 1972]

Memorandum of MR. JUSTICE BLACKMUN.

Under constitutional attack here are abortion laws of the State of Texas.[1] 2A Texas Penal Code, Arts. 1191–1194 and 1196 (1961). These statutes make it a crime to "procure an abortion," as

---

[1] "Article 1191. Abortion.

"If any person shall designedly administer to a pregnant woman or knowingly procure to be administered with her consent any drug or medicine, or shall use towards her any violence or means whatever externally or internally applied, and thereby procure an abortion, he shall be confined in the penitentiary not less than two nor more than five years; if it be done without her consent, the punishment shall be doubled. By 'abortion' is meant that the life of the fetus or embryo shall be destroyed in the woman's womb or that a premature birth thereof be caused.

'Art 1192. Furnishing the means

"Whoever furnishes the means for procuring an abortion knowing the purpose intended is guilty as an accomplice.

"Art. 1193. Attempt at abortion

"If the means used shall fail to produce an abortion, the offender is nevertheless guilty of an attempt to produce abortion, provided it be shown that such means were calculated to produce that result, and shall be fined not less than one hundred nor more than one thousand dollars.

"Art. 1194. Murder in producing abortion

"If the death of the mother is occasioned by an abortion so produced or by an attempt to effect the same it is murder.

"Art. 1196. By medical advice

"Nothing in this chapter applies to an abortion procured or attempted by medical advice for the purpose of saving the life of the mother."

The foregoing Articles, together with Art. 1195. comprise Chapter 9 of Title 15 of the Penal Code. Article 1195, not attacked here reads:

"Art. 1195. Destroying unborn child

"Whoever shall during parturition of the mother destroy the vitality or life in a child in a state of being born and before actual birth, which child would otherwise have been born alive, shall be confined in the penitentiary for life or for not less than five years."

therein defined, or to attempt one, except with respect to "an abortion procured or attempted by medical advice for the purpose of saving the life of the mother."

I

Jane Roe,[2] a single woman residing in Dallas County, Texas, in March 1970 instituted this federal suit against the District Attorney of the county. The plaintiff sought (1) a declaratory judgment that the Texas abortion laws are unconstitutional on their face and (2) an injunction restraining the defendant from enforcing the challenged statutes.

Roe alleged that she was unmarried and pregnant; that she wished to terminate her pregnancy by an abortion "performed by a competent, licensed physician, under safe, clinical conditions"; that her life did not appear to be threatened by the continuation of her pregnancy; and that she could not afford to travel to another jurisdiction in order to secure there a legal abortion under safe conditions. By an amendment to her complaint, Roe purported to sue "on behalf of herself and all other women" similarly situated. She claimed a deprival of rights protected by First, Fourth, Fifth, Eight, Ninth, and Fourteenth Amendments.

James Hubert Hallford, a physician licensed under Texas law, sought, and was granted, leave to intervene in the Roe suit. In his complaint in intervention the doctor specified types of conditions he saw in pregnant women who came to him as patients.

John and Mary Doe,[3] married couple, filed a companion complaint to that of Roe. This also names the District Attorney as defendant, claimed like constitutional deprivations, and sought declaratory and injunctive relief. The Does alleged that they were a childless couple; that Mrs. Doe was suffering from a "neural-chemical" disorder; that her physician had "advised her to avoid pregnancy until such time as her condition was materially improved, although a pregnancy at the present time would not present a serious risk" to her life; that pursuant to medical advice she had discontinued use of birth control pills; and that if she should become pregnant, she would want to terminate the pregnancy by an abortion performed by a competent, licensed physician under safe, clinical conditions. By an amendment to their complaint, the Does purported to sue "on behalf of themselves and all couples similarly situated."

---

[2] The name is a pseudonym.
[3] These names also are pseudonyms.

The two actions were consolidated and heard together by a duly convened three-judge district court. The suits thus presented the situations of the pregnant single woman, the childless and nonpregnant married couple, and the licensed practicing physician, all joining in the attack upon the Texas abortion laws. Upon the filing of affidavits, motions were made to dismiss and for summary judgment. The court found that Roe and Dr. Hallford, and members of their respective classes, had standing, but that the Does had failed to allege facts sufficient to state a present controversy and therefore did not have standing. It concluded that, on the declaratory judgment request, abstention was not warranted; that the "fundamental right of single women and married persons to choose whether to have children is protected by the Ninth Amendment, through the Fourteenth Amendment"; that the Texas abortion laws were void on their face because they were both overbroad and vague; and that abstention was warranted with respect to the request for an injunction. The court then dismissed the Doe complaint, declared the abortion laws void, and dismissed the application for an injunction. 314 F. Supp. 1217 (ND Tex. 1970).

The plaintiffs Roe and Doe and the intervenor, pursuant to 28 U.S.C.§1253, appealed to this Court from that part of the District Court's judgment denying injunctive relief. The defendant District Attorney filed a notice of appeal, pursuant to the same statute, from the District Court's grant of declaratory relief to Roe and Dr. Hallford. Both sides also have taken protective appeals to the United States Court of Appeals for the Fifth Circuit; that court ordered those appeals held in abeyance pending decision here.

We postponed the decision on jurisdiction to the hearing on the merits. 402 U.S.941 (1971).

II

It might have been preferable if the defendant, pursuant to our Rule 20, had presented us a petition for certiorari before judgment in the Court of Appeals with respect to the granting, adverse to him, of declaratory relief. Furthermore, we are aware that, under *Mitchell v. Donovan,* 398 U.S.427 (1970), and *Gunn v. University Committee,* 399 U.S.383 (1970), §1253 does not authorize an appeal to this Court from the grant or the denial of declaratory relief alone. We conclude, nevertheless, that those decisions do not prevent our review of both the injunctive and the declaratory aspects of a case of this kind when it is properly here, as this one is, on appeal under §1253 from specific denial of injunctive relief, and the arguments as to both aspects are necessarily identical. See *Carter v. Jury Commission,* 396 U.S.320 (1970), and *Florida Lime and Avocado Growers, Inc. v. Jacobsen,* 362 U.S. 73, 80–81 (1960). It would be destructive of time and energy for all concerned were we to rule otherwise.

III

We are next confronted with issues of justiciability, standing and abstention. Do Roe and the Does have that "personal stake in the outcome of the controversy," *Baker v. Carr,* 369 U.S. 186, 204 (1962), that insures that "the dispute sought to be adjudicated will be presented in an adversary context and in a form historically viewed as capable of judicial resolution," *Flast v. Cohen,* 392 U.S. 83, 101 (1968), and *Sierra Club v. Morton,* — — U.S. — — (1972)? And what effect does the pendency of criminal charges against Dr. Hallford in state court, for violation the same Texas abortion laws, have upon the propriety of the federal court's granting relief to him as a plaintiff-intervenor?

A. Jane Roe. Despite the use of the pseudonym, it is not suggested that Roe is a fictitious person. For purposes of her case, we accept as true her existence, her pregnant state as of the time of the inception of her suit in March 1970 and as late as May 21 of that year when she filed an alias affidavit with the District Court, and her inability to secure a legal abortion in Texas.

Viewing Roe's case as of the time of its filing and as late as May 21, there can be little dispute that it then presented a case or controversy and that, wholly apart from the class aspects, she, as a pregnant single woman thwarted by the State's abortion laws, had standing to challenge them. Indeed, we do not read the appellee's brief as really asserting anything to the contrary. The "logical nexus between the status asserted and the claim sought to be adjudicated," *Flast v. Cohen,* 392 U.S., at 102, and the necessary degree of contentiousness, *Golden v. Zwickler,* 394 U.S. 103 (1969), are both present.

The appellee notes, however, that the record does not disclose that Roe was pregnant at the time of the District Court hearing on May 22, 1970,[4] or on June 17 when the court's opinion and judgment were filed. He therefore suggests that Roe's case is now moot because

---

[4] The appellee's brief, p. 13 twice states that the hearing before the District Court was held on July 22, 1970. The docket entries, Appendix 2, and the transcript, Appendix 76, disclose this to be an error. The July date apparently is the time of the reporter's transcription. Appendix 77.

she and all others like her are no longer subject to any 1970 pregnancy.

The usual rule in federal cases is that the existence of an actual controversy is necessary at all stages of appellate or certiorari review and not only at the date the action is initiated. *United States v. Munsingwear, Inc.,* 340 U.S. 36, 39–41 (1950); *Golden v. Zwickler,* 394 U.S., at 108; *SEC v. Medical Committee for Human Rights,* 404 U.S. 403, 405 (1972). But if, as here, pregnancy is a significant fact in litigation, the 266-day human gestation period is so short that the pregnancy will have terminated before the usual appellate process is complete. If that termination makes a case moot, pregnancy litigation seldom, if ever, will survive beyond the trial stage, if then, and appellate review will be effectively denied. Our law is not that rigid. Pregnancy often comes more than once to the same woman and in the general population, if man is to survive, it is always with us.

Pregnancy provides almost a classic justification for a conclusion of nonmootness. Otherwise, it is "capable of repetition, yet evading review." See *Southern Pacific Terminal Co. v. Interstate Commerce Commission,* 219 U.S. 498, 515 (1911); *Moore v. Ogilvie,* 394 U.S. 814, 816 (1969); *Carroll v. President and Commissioners,* 393 U.S. 175, 178–179 (1968; *Sibron v. New York,* 392 U.S. 40, 50–53 (1968); *United States v. W.T. Grant Co.,* 345 U.S. 629, 632–633 (1953).

We therefore agree with the District Court that Jane Roe had standing to undertake this litigation and that the termination of her 1970 pregnancy did not render the case moot.

B. Dr. Hallford. The doctor's position is different from that of Roe and from that of the Does. He came into Roe's litigation as a plaintiff-intervenor alleging in his complaint that he:

> "in the past has been arrested for violating the Texas Abortion Laws and at the present time stands charged by indictment with violating said laws in the Criminal District Court of Dallas County, Texas to-wit: (1) The State of Texas vs. James H. Hallford, No. C–69–5307–IH, and (2) The State of Texas vs. James H. Hallford, No. C–69–2524–H. In both cases the defendant is charged with abortion. . . ."

In his immediately preceding application for leave to intervene the doctor made like representations as to the abortion charges pending in the state court. These representations were also repeated in the affidavit he executed and filed in support of his motion for summary judgment.

Dr. Hallford is therefore in the situation of seeking, in a federal court, declaratory and injunctive relief with respect to the same state statutes under which he is charged in criminal prosecutions simultaneously pending in state court. Although he stated that he has been arrested in the past for violating the State's abortion laws, he makes no allegation of any extraordinary circumstance, where the danger of irreparable loss is great and immediate in posing a threat to any federally protected right, that cannot be eliminated by his defense against the state prosecutions. Neither is there any allegation of harassment or bad faith prosecution. He seeks now, for purposes of standing, to draw a distinction between pending prosecutions and possible future ones. We see no merit with that distinction. Under the circumstances, therefore, our decision last Term in *Samuels v. Mackell,* 401 U.S. 66 (1971), compels the conclusion that the District Court erred when it granted declaratory relief to Dr. Hallford and failed to refrain from doing so. The court, of course, was correct in refusing to grand injunctive relief to the doctor; the reasons supportive of that action, however are those expressed in *Samuels v. Mackell, supra,* and in *Younger v. Harris,* 401 U.S. 37 (1971); *Boyle v. Landry,* 401 U.S. 77 (1971); *Perez v. Ledesma,* 401 U.S. 82 (1971): and *Byrne v. Karalexis,* 401 U.S. 216 (1971). See also *Dombrowski v. Pfister,* 380 U.S. 479 (1965). We note, in passing, that *Younger* and its companion cases were declined after the three-judge District Court's decision here.

Dr. Hallford's complaint in intervention, therefore, is to be dismissed.[5] He is remitted to his defenses in the state criminal proceedings against him. We therefore reverse the judgment of the District Court to the extent that it granted Dr. Hallford relief and failed to dismiss his complaint in intervention.

C. The Does. In view of our ruling as to Roe's standing in her case, the issue of the Does' standing in their case has little significance. The claims they assert are essentially the same as those of Roe, and the statutes they attack are the same. Nevertheless, we briefly refer to the Does' posture.

---

[5] We need not consider what different result, if any, would follow if Dr. Hallford's intervention were on behalf of a class. His complaint in intervention does not purport to assert a class suit and makes no reference to any class apart from an allegation that he "and others similarly situated" must necessarily guess at the meaning of Art. 1196. His application for leave to intervene goes a little further for it asserts that plaintiff Roe does not adequately protect the interest of the doctor "and the class of people who are physicians . . . and the class of people who are . . . patients. . . ." The leave application, however, is not the complaint. Despite the District Court's statement to the contrary, 314 F. Supp., at 1225, we fail to perceive the bare essential of a class suit in the Hallford complaint.

Their pleadings present them as a childless married couple, the female not being pregnant, who have no desire to have children at this time because of their having received medical advice that Mrs. Doe should avoid pregnancy, and for "other highly personal reasons." But they "fear . . . they may face the prospect of becoming parents." And if pregnancy ensues, they "would want to terminate" it by an abortion. They then assert the inability to obtain an abortion legally in Texas and, consequently, their facing the alternatives of an illegal abortion there or of going outside Texas to some place where the procedure could be obtained legally and competently.

We thus have a married couple as plaintiffs who have, as their asserted immediate and present injury, only an alleged "detrimental effect upon [their] marital happiness" because they are forced to "the choice of refraining from normal sexual relations or of endangering Mary Doe's health through a possible pregnancy." But they are a couple who, in the future, might develop a condition on Mrs. Doe's part brought about by future intercourse and the future failure of those contraceptive measures they feel they might safely employ, and who thereupon, at that time in the future, might want an abortion that might then be unavailable to them legally under the Texas statute.

This very phrasing of the Doe's position reveals the speculative basis of their alleged injury. It is well settled in Texas that Mrs. Doe may not be a principal or an accomplice under Art. 1191 with respect to any abortion upon her and thus is not herself subject to prosecution under the Texas abortion laws. *Watson v. State,* 9 Tex. App. 237, 244–245 (1880); *Moore v. State,* 37 Tex. Cr. Rep. 552, 561, 40 S.W. 287, 290 (1897): *Shaw v. State,* 73 Tex. Cr. Rep. 337, 339 165 S.W. 930, 931 (1914); *Fondren v. State,* 74 Tex. Cro. Rep. 552, 557, 169 S.W. 411, 414 (1914); *Gray v. State,* 77 Tex. Cr. Rep. 221, 229, 178 S.W. 337, 341 (1915).[6] And their alleged injury rests on possible future contraceptive failure, possible future pregnancy, possible future unpreparedness for parenthood, and possible future impairment of health. Any one or more of these several possibilities may not take place and all may not combine. These possibilities, in the Does' estimation, might have some real or imagined impact upon their

---

[6] There is no immunity in Texas for the father who is not married to the mother. *Hammett v. State,* 84 Tex. Cr. Rep. 635, 209 S.E. 661 (1919). But we have found no case that determines the issue as to the husband of the aborted mother. Since the appellants do not claim or demonstrate that the statute has been used against husbands, and since prosecution is dependent upon the further contingency that Mrs. Doe's husband aid in obtaining abortion, if one becomes necessary or desirable, we conclude that Doe's status in this case is not materially different from his wife's.

marital happiness. But we are not prepared to say that the bare allegation of so indirect an injury is sufficient for their case to present an actual case or controversy. We conclude, as a consequence, that they have no standing to pursue the lawsuit they have initiated. *Golder v. Zwickler, supra,* 394 U.S., at 109–110 (1969); *Younger v. Harris,* 401 U.S., at 41–42. Their purported case falls far short factually of those resolved otherwise in the cases, *Investment Company Institute v. Camp,* 401 U.S. 617 (1971), *Data Processing Service v. Camp,* 397 U.S. 150 (1970), and *Epperson v. Arkansas,* 393 U.S. 97 (1968), that the Does urge upon us.

The Does, therefore, are not appropriate plaintiffs in this litigation. Their complaint was properly dismissed by the District Court and we affirm that dismissal.

IV

We turn to the merits. The Texas abortion laws are not new. They appeared in essentially their present form as Arts. 1071–1076 of Texas Revised Criminal Statutes, 1911. And they read substantially the same as Arts. 536–541 of Revised Statutes of Texas, 1879, and as Arts. 2192–2197 of Paschal's Laws of Texas, 1866. The final article in each of these compilations made reference, as does the present Art. 1196, to "medical advice for the purpose of saving the life of the mother."

A. Long ago a suggestion apparently was made that the Texas statutes were unconstitutionally vague because of definition deficiencies. The Texas Court of Criminal Appeals had little difficulty with that suggestion for it disposed of it peremptorily:

> "It is also insisted in the motion in arrest of judgment that the statute is unconstitutional and void in that it does not sufficiently define or describe the offense of abortion. We do not concur [with counsel] in respect to this question." *Jackson v. State,* 55 Tex. Cr. Rep. 79, 89; 115 S.W. 262, 268 (1908).

We are advised, however, that the same court, on November 2, 1971 in *Thompson v. State,* No. 44,071, an opinion apparently not yet published, held, against constitutional challenge, that the Texas abortion laws are not vague or overbroad. The copy of the opinion with which we have been furnished indicates that the court held "that the State of Texas has a compelling interest to protect fetal life"; that Art. 1191 "is designed to protect fetal life," citing *Mayberry v. State,* 271 S.W. 2d 635 (Tex. Crim. App. 1954); that the Texas homicide statutes, particularly 2A Texas Penal Code Art. 1205, are intended to protect a person "in existence by actual birth" and thereby implicitly recognize other human life that is not "in existence by actual birth"; that the definition of human life is for the legislature and not the courts; that Art. 1196 "is more definite than the District of Columbia statute upheld in *Vuitch*"; and that the statute "is not vague and indefinite or overbroad." A physician's abortion conviction was therefore affirmed.[7] The *Thompson* case thus appears to be a flat and recent holding by the Texas court that the State's abortion laws are not unconstitutional for vagueness.

Elsewhere, decisions on constitutional challenges, on various grounds, to other state abortion statutes do not appear to be fully consistent. See *Babbitz v. McCann,* 310 F. Supp. 293, 297–298 (ED Wis. 1970) appeal dismissed, 400 U.S. 1 (1970); *Rosen v. Louisiana State Board of Medical Examiners,* 318 F. Supp. 1217 (ED La. 1970), appeal pending; *Steinberg v. Brown,* 321 F. Supp. 741 (ND Ohio 1970); *Doe v. Scott,* 321 F. Supp. 1385 (ND Ill. 1971), appeal pending; *Corkey v. Edwards,* 322 F. Supp. 1248 (WDNC 1971), appeal pending; *Doe v. Rampton,* — — F. Supp. — — (Utah 1971), appeal pending: *People v. Belous,* 71 Cal. 2d 954, 458 P. 2d 194 (1969), cert. denied, 397 U.S. 915 (1970).

B. Last Term, in *United States v. Vuitch,* 402 U.S. 62 (1971), decided after the District Court's ruling in the present cases was handed down, we had under consideration a District of Columbia statute that made the procuring of an abortion a crime unless it "were done as necessary for the preservation of the mother's life or health and under the direction of a competent licensed practitioner of medicine." The District Court had dismissed a physician's indictment under that statute on the ground that it was unconstitutionally vague. This Court reversed that dismissal and remanded the case. MR. JUSTICE DOUGLAS was of the view that the statute failed to meet the requirements of procedural due process, 402 U.S., at 74, and dissented in part. MR. JUSTICE STEWART, also dissenting in part, 402 U.S., at 96, was of the opinion that a "competent licensed practitioner of medicine" was wholly immune from being charged with the commission of a criminal offense under the District of Columbia statute.

The vagueness claim in *Vuitch* focused only on the word "health" in the District statute and on its application to mental as well as to physical well-being. The Texas statute, Art. 1196, with

---

[7] In a footnote the Texas court observed that any issue as to the burden of proof under the exemption of Art. 1196 "is not before us." See *Veevers v. State,* 354 S.W. 2d 161, 166 (Tex. Cr. App. 1962). Cf. *United States v. Vuitch,* 402 U.S. 62, 69–71 (1971).

which we are here concerned, exempts from criminal abortion, described in Art. 1191, only an abortion procured "by medical advice for the purpose of saving the life of the mother." No reference whatsoever is made to health. Saving the mother's life is the sole standard. *Vuitch's* analysis was that the word "health" in the statute was employed in accord with general usage and modern understanding and included psychological as well as physical well-being, and thus presented no problem of vagueness, because this "is a judgment that physicians are obviously called upon to make routinely," 402 U.S., at 72, and is of little assistance here. Certainly it provides no answer to the constitutional challenge to the Texas statute.

C. We are not here concerned with broad areas of medical judgment as to health generally. We are concerned, in contrast, with a procedure that is exempt from criminality only if it is "for the purpose of saving the life of the mother." So viewed, we encounter difficulties of great consequence under the vagueness challenge.

The exempting Art. 1196, of course, has application only to one rendering "medical advice." Although even this is by no means certain or clear, we assume, for purposes of simplifying the issue, that this protective provision is available only to the licensed physician, and is not available to the unlicensed physician or particularly to the nonphysician who would procure the abortion under the guise of rendering "medical advice," whatever that may mean as applied to him. But what does the statute say even for the licensed physician? Does it mean that he may procure an abortion only when, without it, the patient will surely die? Or when there is a mere possibility that she will not survive? So far as we can determine, the Texas courts have not limited the statute and have only repeated its phrasing. See *Ex parte Vick,* 292 S.W. 889, 890 (Tex. Crim. App. 1927). Further, who is to exercise that judgment—the physician alone in the light of his training and experience, or a group or committee of his peers, or a medical association, or a hospital review committee? And when is the saving of a life to be measured in the time scale? Must death be imminent? Or is it enough if life is prolonged for a year, a month, a few days, overnight? Is a mother's life "saved" if a post-rape or post-incest or "fourteenth-child" abortion preserves, or tends to preserve, her mental health? If the procedure is generally favorable to the mother's health, is her life thereby "saved" within the meaning of the statute? One's well-being and the very continuance of life depends sometimes on slender differences in medical treatment, in body chemistry, in exposure to infection, and in medical knowledge.

The applicable standard is whether the statute is "so vague that men of common intelligence must necessarily guess at its meaning and differ as to its application," *Connally v. General Construction Co.,* 269 U.S. 385, 391 (1926); *Cameron v. Johnson,* 390 U.S. 611, 616 (1968), or phrased another way:

> "It is established that a law fails to meet the requirements of the Due Process Clause if it is so vague and standardless that it leaves the public uncertain as to the conduct it prohibits or leaves judges and jurors free to decide, without any legally fixed standards, what is prohibited and what is not in each particular case." *Giaccio v. Pennsylvania,* 382 U.S. 399, 402–403 (1966).

We conclude that Art. 1196, with its sole criterion for exemption as "saving the life of the mother," is insufficiently informative to the physician to whom it purports to afford a measure of professional protection but who must measure its indefinite meaning at the risk of his liberty, and that the statute cannot withstand constitutional challenge on vagueness grounds.

V

This conclusion that Art. 1196 is unconstitutionally vague means, of course, that the Texas abortion laws, as a unit must fall. The medical exception of Art. 1196 does not go out alone for then the State would be left with a statute proscribing all abortion procedures no matter how medically urgent the cause. Then, too, the physician's professional obligation and duty would be improperly thwarted.

Our holding today does not imply that a State has no legitimate interest in the subject of abortions or that abortion procedures may not be subjected to control by the State. The nub of the matter is the appropriateness of the control when criminal sanctions are imposed. We do not accept the argument of the appellants and of some of the *amici* that a pregnant woman has unlimited right to do with her body as she pleases. The long acceptance of statutes regulating the possession of certain drugs and other harmful substances, and making criminal indecent exposure in public, or an attempt at suicide, clearly indicate the contrary.

There is no need in Roe's case to pass upon her contention that under the Ninth Amendment a pregnant woman has an absolute right to an abortion, or even to consider the opposing rights of the embryo or fetus during the respective prenatal trimesters. We are literally showered with briefs—with physicians and paramedical and other knowledgeable people on both sides—but this case, as it comes to us, does not require the resolution of those issues.

VI

Although the District Court granted plaintiff Roe and intervenor Hallford declaratory relief, it stopped short of issuing an injunction against enforcement of the Texas abortion laws. The Court has recognized that different considerations enter into a federal court's determination of declaratory relief, on the one hand, and injunctive relief, on the other. *Zwickler v. Koota,* 389 U.S. 241, 252–255 (1967); *Dombrowski v. Pfister,* 380 U.S. 479 (1965). We are not dealing here with a statute that, on its face, appears to abridge free expression, an area of particular concern under *Dombrowski* and refined in *Younger v. Harris,* 401 U.S., at 50.

We find it unnecessary to decide whether the District Court erred in withholding injunctive relief for we assume that the Texas prosecutorial authorities will give full credence to the decision of this Court relative to the constitutional invalidity of the Texas abortion laws.

The judgment of the District Court as to intervenor Hallford is reversed and Dr. Hallford's complaint in intervention is dismissed. In all other respects, the judgment of the District Court is affirmed. Costs are allowed to the appellee.

MR. JUSTICE POWELL and MR. JUSTICE REHNQUIST took no part in the consideration or decision of this case.

★ ★ ★

1st DRAFT

SUPREME COURT OF THE UNITED STATES

No. 70–18

Jane Roe et al., Appellants, v. Henry Wade.	On Appeal from the United States District Court for the Northern District of Texas.

[May —, 1972]

MR. JUSTICE WHITE, dissenting.

I dissent from the Court's decision that the Texas abortion statute, which allows abortions only when they are "procured or attempted by medical advice for the purpose of saving the life of the mother," 2A Texas Penal Code Art. 1196, is unconstitutionally vague.

This decision necessarily overrules *United States v. Vuitch,* 402 U.S. 62 (1971), decided only last Term, which upheld against vagueness attack D.C. Code Ann. § 22–201 which allowed abortion only when "necessary for the preservation of the mother's life or health and under the direction of a competent licensed practitioner of medicine." In that case, a district court had dismissed an indictment on the ground that the statutory standard was unconstitutionally vague, 305 F. Supp. 1032, and the Government appealed directly to this Court, which reversed the District Court's decision. The vagueness discussion in *Vuitch* did not, as the majority asserts, "focus . . . only on the word 'health,' " although the greater part of the discussion in this Court's opinion and in that of the District Court was devoted to parsing that phrase. The lower court had treated the statutory standard as the "preservation-of-life-or-health standard," 305 F. Supp., at 1035, as did this Court, 402 U.S., at 70, 71. Furthermore, the decision that the "preservation-of-life" standard is not impermissibly vague was a necessary part of the Court's holding, since it would otherwise have been forced to affirm the District Court's decision voiding the statute, despite the fact that it had overruled that court's decision regarding the vagueness of the "preservation-of-health" standard. Instead, the Court upheld the D.C. statute in its entirety.

If called upon to reconsider this Court's decision in *Vuitch,* I would reaffirm it and would not, therefore, void the Texas statute on vagueness grounds. If a standard which refers to the "health" of the mother, a referent which necessarily entails the resolution of perplexing questions about the interrelationship of physical, emotional, and mental well-being, is not impermissibly vague, a statutory standard which focuses only on "saving the life" of the mother would appear to be *a fortiori* acceptable. The Court's observation that "whether a particular operation is necessary for a patient's physical or mental health is a judgment that physicians are obviously called upon to make routinely whenever surgery is considered," 402 U.S., at 72 (footnote omitted), is particularly applicable to medical decisions as to when the life of a mother is endangered, since the relevant factors in the latter situation are less numerous and are primarily physiological.

Finally, the vagueness claim is not properly presented in appellant Roe's attack on the Texas statute. There is no question that Art. 1196 does not authorize abortions-by-request and that it instead articulates a standard which a woman seeking an abortion would recognize as relevant to her case. Any Texas doctor would similarly realize that an abortion could not be performed unless the requirements of Art. 1196, whatever they might be, were met. On its face, therefore, the statute divides women seeking abortions into two classes: those who make some claim that an abortion is necessary to save their life and those who do not. Assuming that the statutory standard is impermissibly vague, confusion and uncertainty will be created among women in the former group. Appellant Roe, however, falls into the latter group, since her complaint asserts that she desires an abortion "[b]ecause of the economic hardships and social stigmas involved in bearing an illegitimate child." and admits that her "life does not appear to be threatened by the continuation of her pregnancy." (R., at 11.) Indeed, appellant Roe argues at length that the right to terminate an unwanted pregnancy, for whatever reason, is an integral part of constitutionally protected rights of privacy. (Brief of Appellants, at 99–109.) For such women, who make no claim that an abortion is necessary for the purpose of saving their life, the possible vagueness of the statutory standard is irrelevant, since, however, the class of women is defined who qualify for an abortion because their life is somehow endangered, they are *ipso facto* outside of this class. "The underlying principle [of the void for vagueness doctrine] is that no man shall be held criminally responsible for conduct which he could not reasonably understand to be proscribed." *United States v. Harriss,* 347 U.S. 612, 617 (1954). See also: *United States v. National Dairy Corp.,* 372 U.S. 29, 32–33 (1963); *Jordan v. De George,* 341 U.S. 223, 231 (1951); *United States v. Petrillo,* 332 U.S. 1, 7 (1947). Whatever merit appellant's Ninth Amendment and related claims may have, it cannot be rationally contended that it is not perfectly apparent that the abortion she desires is clearly prohibited by the Texas statute. This is not a case involving "the transcendent value to all society of constitutionally protected expression," *Gooding v. Wilson,* 405 U.S. — —, — — (1972), in which appellant might have standing to attack the possible infirmity of the statute as applied to members of another class. Cf. *Baggett v. Bullitt,* 377 U.S. 360, 366 (1964); *NAACP v. Button,* 371 U.S. 415, 433 (1963).

★ ★ ★

6th DRAFT

SUPREME COURT OF THE UNITED STATES

NOS. 70–18 AND 70–40

Jane Roe et al., Appellants, 70-18 v. Henry Wade.	On Appeal from the United States District Court for the Northern District of Texas.
Mary Doe at al., Appellants, 70-40 v. Arthur K. Bolton, as Attorney General of the State of Georgia, et al.	On Appeal from the United States District Court for the Northern District of Georgia.

[June —, 1972]

MR. JUSTICE DOUGLAS.

I dissent from the order putting these cases down for reargument.

The problem involving state abortion legislation is not a brand new one to the Court. *United States v. Vuitch,* 402 U.S. 62, involved the District of Columbia statute. It was argued January 12, 1971, and decided April 21, 1971. The case presented a troublesome question of the jurisdiction of this Court as well as a substantial constitutional question. Yet it was disposed of in shortly over three months after oral argument, Mr. Justice Black writing for the majority.

The present abortion cases involve the statute of Texas and the statute of Georgia. They were put down for argument last Term and were heard December 13, 1971. The Conference on the two cases was held on December 16, 1971.

THE CHIEF JUSTICE represented the minority view in the Conference and forcefully urged his viewpoint on the issues. It was a seven-man Court that heard these cases and voted on them. Out of that seven there were four who initially took a majority view. Hence traditionally the senior Justice in the majority—who in this case was not myself—should have made the assignment of the opinion. For the tradition is a longstanding one that the senior Justice in the majority makes the assignment.[1] The cases were, however, assigned by THE CHIEF JUSTICE.

The matter of assignment is not merely a matter of protocol. The main function of the Conference is to find the consensus.[2] When that is known, it is only logical that the majority decide who their spokesman should be; and traditionally the selection has been made after a very informal discussion among the majority.

When that procedure is followed, the majority view is promptly written out and circulated, after which dissents or concurrences may be prepared.

When, however, the minority seeks to control the assignment, there is a destructive force at work in the Court.

Perhaps the purpose of the minority in the *Abortion Cases* is to try to keep control of the merits. If that is the aim, the plan has been unsuccessful Opinions in these two cases have been circulated and each commands the votes of five members of the Court. The decisions should therefore be announced.[3]

The plea that the cases be reargued is merely another strategy by a minority somehow to suppress the majority view with the hope that exigencies of time will change the result. That might be

---

[1] Chief Justice Hughes described the opinion assignment process as follows: "After a decision has been reached, the Chief Justice assigns the case for opinion to one of the members of the Court, that is, of course, to one of the majority if there is a division and the Chief Justice is a member of the majority. If he is in a minority, the senior Associate Justice in the majority assigns the case for opinion." C. Hughes, The Supreme Court of the United States 58-59 (1966). See also W. Brennan, "Inside View of the High Court," *The New York Times Magazine*, October 6, 1963, at 35, 102; F. Frankfurter, "Chief Justices I Have Known," in A. Westin, *An Autobiography of The Supreme Court*, 211, 231 (1963); J. Harlan, "Some Aspects of the Judicial Process in the Supreme Court of the United States," 33 Aust. L.J. 108, 116 (1959); T. Clark, "Internal Operation of the United States Supreme Court," 43 J. Am. Jud. Soc. 45, 50-51 (1959).

[2] Chief Justice Hughes said of the Conference: "In the Supreme Court every judge comes to the conference to express his views and to vote, not knowing but that he may have the responsibility of writing the opinion which will accord with the vote. He is thus keenly aware of his responsibility in voting. It is not the practice in Supreme Court to postpone voting until an opinion has been brought in by one of the judges which may be plausible enough to win the adherence of another judge who has not studied the case carefully." Op. cit., 59.

[3] Last Fall we all agreed to deny a motion for additional oral argument in spite of counsel's admonition that the issues warranted more extended airing. 404 U.S. 813. And, though we again were advised that the cases were of paramount significance, we nonetheless denied a request by Texas to postpone argument until it could be heard by a full bench. 404 U.S. 981. That should have settled it.

achieved of course by death or conceivably retirement. But that kind of strategy dilutes the integrity of the Court.

Historically this institution has been composed of fiercely independent men with fiercely opposed views. There have been—and will always be—clashes of views. The Conference, though deeply disagreeing on legal and constitutional issues, has traditionally been a group marked by good-will. A majority view, no matter how unacceptable to the minority, has been honored as such. The incumbents have honored and revered the institution more than their own view of the public good.

The *Abortion Cases* are symptomatic. This is an election year. Both political parties have made abortion an issue. What the political parties say or do is none of our business. We sit here not to make the path of any candidate easier or more difficult. We decide questions only on their constitutional merits. To prolong these *Abortion Cases* into the next election would in the eyes of many be a political gesture unworthy of the Court.

Five members of the Court have agreed on a disposition of the Texas and Georgia *Abortion Cases*. One dissent has already been written. Those opinions should come down forthwith.

A number of abortion cases are being held[4] for the present two cases. The log jam should be broken.

I dissent with the deepest regret that we are allowing the consensus of the Court to be frustrated.

---

[4] The cases now being held for the Texas and Georgia *Abortion Cases* are:
Rosen v. Louisiana State Bd. of Medical Examiners, 70–42 (La.)
Rodgers v. Danforth, 70–89 (Missouri)
Hanrahan v. Doe, 70–105 (Illinois)
Heffernan v. Doe, 70–106 (Illinois)
Corkey v. Edwards, 71–92 (North Carolina)
Thompson v. Texas, 71–1200 (Texas)
Doe v. Rampton, 71–5666 (Utah)
The State in parenthesis indicates the statute involved.

Supreme Court of the United States
Washington D.C. 20543

CHAMBERS OF
JUSTICE THURGOOD MARSHALL

December 12, 1972

Re: Abortion Cases

Dear Harry:

I am inclined to agree that drawing a line at viability accommodates the interests at stake better than drawing it at the end of the first trimester. Given the difficulties which many woman may have in believing that they are pregnant and in deciding to seek an abortion, I fear that the earlier date may not in practice serve the interests of those women, which your opinion does seek to serve.

At the same time, however, I share your concern for recognizing the State's interest in insuring that abortions be done under safe conditions. If the opinion stated explicitly that, between the end of the first trimester and viability, state regulations directed at health and safety alone were permissible, I believe that those concerns would be adequately met.

It is implicit in your opinion that at some point the State's interest in preserving the potential life of the unborn child overrides any individual interests of the women. I would be disturbed if that point were set before viability, and I am afraid that the opinion's present focus on the end of the first trimester would lead states to prohibit abortions completely at any later date.

In short, I believe that, as the opinion now stands, viability is a better accommodation of the interests involved, but that the end of the first trimester would be acceptable if additions along the lines I have suggested were made.

Sincerely,
T.M.

Mr. Justice Blackmun
cc: Conference

Appendix D

HARRIS V. McRAE

448 U.S. (EXCERPTS) 297 (1980)

It is well settled that, quite apart from the guarantee of equal protection, if a law "impinges upon a fundamental right explicitly or implicitly secured by the Constitution [it] is presumptively unconstitutional." *Mobile v. Bolden,* 446 U.S. 55, 76 (plurality opinion). Accordingly, before turning to the equal protection issue in this case, we examine whether the Hyde Amendment violates any substantive rights secured by the Constitution.

A

We address first the appellees' argument that the Hyde Amendment, by restricting the availability of certain medically necessary abortions under Medicaid, impinges on the "liberty" protected by the Due Process Clause as recognized in *Roe v. Wade,* 410 U.S. 113, and its progeny.

In the *Wade* case, this Court held unconstitutional a Texas statute making it a crime to procure or attempt an abortion except on medical advice for the purpose of saving the mother's life. The constitutional underpinning of *Wade* was a recognition that the "liberty" protected by the Due Process Clause of the Fourteenth Amendment includes not only the freedoms explicitly mentioned in the Bill of Rights, but also a freedom of personal choice in certain matters of marriage and family life. This implicit constitutional liberty, the Court in *Wade* held, includes the freedom of a woman to decide whether to terminate a pregnancy.

But the Court in *Wade* also recognized that a State has legitimate interests during a pregnancy in both ensuring the health of the mother and protecting potential human life. These state interests, which were found to be "separate and distinct" and to "gro[w] in substantiality as the woman approaches term," *id.,* at 162–163, pose a conflict with a woman's untrammeled freedom of choice. In resolving this conflict, the Court held that before the end of the first trimester of pregnancy, neither state interest is sufficiently substantial to justify any instrusion on the woman's freedom of choice. In the second trimester, the state interest in maternal health was found to be sufficiently substantial to justify regulation reasonably related to that concern. And at viability, usually in the third trimester, the state interest in protecting the potential life of the fetus was found to justify a criminal prohibition against abortions, except where necessary for the preservation of the life or health of the mother. Thus, inasmuch as the Texas criminal statute allowed abortions only where necessary to save the life of the mother and without regard to the stage of the pregnancy, the Court held in *Wade* that the statute violated the Due Process Clause of the Fourteenth Amendment.

In *Maher v. Roe,* 432 U.S. 464, the Court was presented with the question whether the scope of personal constitutional freedom recognized in *Roe v. Wade* included an entitlement to Medicaid payments for abortions that are not medically necessary. At issue in *Maher* was a Connecticut welfare regulation under which Medicaid recipients received payments for medical services incident to childbirth, but not for medical services incident to nontherapeutic abortions. The District Court held that the regulation violated the Equal Protection Clause of the Fourteenth Amendment because the unequal subsidization of childbirth and abortion impinged on the "fundamental right to abortion" recognized in *Wade* and its progeny.

It was the view of this Court that "the District misconceived the nature and scope of the fundamental right recognized in *Roe.*" 432 U.S., at 471. The doctrine of *Roe v. Wade,* the Court held in *Maher,* "protects the woman from unduly burdensome interference with her freedom to decide whether to terminate her pregnancy," *id.,* at 473–474, such as the severe criminal sanctions at issue in *Roe v. Wade, supra,* or the absolute requirement of spousal consent for an abortion challenged in *Planned Parenthood of Central Missouri v. Danforth,* 428 U.S. 52.

But the constitutional freedom recognized in *Wade* and its progeny, the *Maher* Court explained, did not prevent Connecticut from making "a value judgment favoring childbirth over abortion, and . . . implement[ing] that judgment by the allocation of public funds." 432 U.S., at 474. As the Court elaborated:

> "The Connecticut regulation before us is different in kind from the laws invalidated in our previous abortion decisions. The Connecticut regulation places no obstacles—absolute or otherwise—in the pregnant woman's path to an abortion. An indigent woman who desires an abortion suffers no disadvantage as a consequence of Connecticut's decision to fund childbirth; she continues as before to be

dependent on private sources for the service she desires. The State may have made childbirth a more attractive alternative, thereby influencing the woman's decision, but it has imposed no restriction on access to abortions that was not already there. The indigency that may make it difficult—and in some cases, perhaps, impossible for some women to have abortions is neither created nor in any way affected by the Connecticut regulation." *Ibid.*

The Court in *Maher* noted that its description of the doctrine recognized in *Wade* and its progeny signaled "no retreat" from those decisions. In explaining why the constitutional principle recognized in *Wade* and later cases—protecting a woman's freedom of choice—did not translate into a constitutional obligation of Connecticut to subsidize abortions, the Court cited the "basic difference between direct state interference with a protected activity and state encouragement of an alternative activity consonant with legislative policy. Constitutional concerns are greatest when the State attempts to impose its will by force of law; the State's power to encourage actions deemed to be in the public interest is necessarily far broader." 432 U.S., at 475–476 (footnote omitted). Thus, even though the Connecticut regulation favored childbirth over abortion by means of subsidization of one and not the other, the Court in *Maher* concluded that the regulation did not impinge on the constitutional freedom recognized in *Wade* because it imposed no governmental restriction on access to abortions.

The Hyde Amendment, like the Connecticut welfare regulation at issue in *Maher,* places no governmental obstacle in the path of a woman who chooses to terminate her pregnancy, but rather, by means of unequal subsidization of abortion and other medical services, encourages alternative activity deemed in public interest. The present case does differ factually from *Maher* insofar as that case involved a failure to fund nontherapeutic abortions, whereas the Hyde Amendment withholds funding of certain medically necessary abortions. Accordingly, the appellees argue that because the Hyde Amendment affects a significant interest not present or asserted in *Maher*—the interest of a woman in protecting her health during pregnancy—and because that interest lies at the core of the personal constitutional freedom recognized in *Wade,* the present case is constitutionally different from *Maher*. It is the appellees' view that to the extent that the Hyde Amendment withholds funding for certain medically necessary abortions, it clearly impinges on the constitutional principle recognized in *Wade.*

It is evident that a woman's interest in protecting her health was an important theme in *Wade*. In concluding that the freedom of a woman to decide whether to terminate her pregnancy falls within the personal liberty protected by the Due Process Clause, the Court in *Wade* emphasized the fact that the woman's decision carries with it significant personal health implications—both physical and psychological. 410 U.S., at 153. In fact, although the Court in *Wade* recognized that the state interest in protecting potential life becomes sufficiently compelling in the period after fetal viability to justify an absolute criminal prohibition of nontherapeutic abortions, the Court held that even after fetal viability a State may not prohibit abortions "necessary to preserve the life or health of the mother." *Id.*, at 164. Because even the compelling interest of the State in protecting potential life after fetal viability was held to be insufficient to outweigh a woman's decision to protect her life or health, it could be argued that the freedom of a woman to decide whether to terminate her pregnancy for health reasons does in fact lie at the core of the constitutional liberty identified in *Wade*.

But, regardless of whether the freedom of a woman to choose to terminate her pregnancy for health reasons lies at the core or the periphery of the due process liberty recognized in *Wade*, it simply does not follow that a woman's freedom of choice carries with it a constitutional entitlement to the financial resources to avail herself of the full range of protected choices. The reason why was explained in *Maher:* although government may not place obstacles in the path of a woman's exercise of her freedom of choice, it need not remove those not of its own creation. Indigency falls in the latter category. The financial constraints that restrict an indigent woman's ability to enjoy the full range of constitutionally protected freedom of choice are the product not of governmental restrictions on access to abortions, but rather of her indigency. Although Congress has opted to subsidize medically necessary services generally, but not certain medically necessary abortions, the fact remains that the Hyde Amendment leaves an indigent woman with at least the same range of choice in deciding whether to obtain a medically necessary abortion as she would have had if Congress had chosen to subsidize no health care costs at all. We are thus not persuaded that the Hyde Amendment impinges on the constitutionally protected freedom of choice recognized in *Wade*.[19]

---

[19] The appellees argue that the Hyde Amendment is unconstitutional because it "penalizes" the exercise of a woman's choice to terminate a pregnancy by abortion. See *Memorial Hospital v. Maricopa County,* 415 U.S. 250; *Shapiro v. Thompson,* 394 U.S.

Although the liberty protected by the Due Process Clause affords protection against unwarranted government interference with freedom of choice in the context of certain personal decisions, it does not confer an entitlement to such funds as may be necessary to realize all the advantages of that freedom. To hold otherwise would mark a drastic change in our understanding of the Constitution. It cannot be that because government may not prohibit the use of contraceptives, *Griswold v. Connecticut*, 381 U.S. 479, or prevent parents from sending their child to a private school, *Pierce v. Society of Sisters*, 268 U.S. 510, government, therefore, has an affirmative constitutional obligation to ensure that all persons have the financial resources to obtain contraceptives or send their children to private schools. To translate the limitation on governmental power implicit in the Due Process Clause into an affirmative funding obligation would require Congress to subsidize the medically necessary abortion of an indigent woman even if Congress had not enacted a Medicaid program to subsidize other medically necessary services. Nothing in the Due Process Clause supports such an extraordinary result. Whether freedom of choice that is constitutionally protected warrants federal subsidization is a question for Congress to answer, not a matter of constitutional entitlement. Accordingly, we conclude that the Hyde Amendment does not impinge on the due process liberty recognized in *Wade*.

---

618. This argument falls short of the mark. In *Maher,* the Court found only a "semantic difference" between the argument that Connecticut's refusal to subsidize non-therapeutic abortions "unduly interfere[d]" with the exercise of the constitutional liberty recognized in *Wade* and the argument that it "penalized" the exercise of that liberty. 432 U.S., at 474, n. 8. And, regardless of how the claim was characterized, the *Maher* Court rejected the argument that Connecticut's refusal to subsidize protected conduct, without more, impinged on the constitutional freedom of choice. This reasoning is equally applicable in the present case. A substantial constitutional question would arise if Congress had attempted to withhold all Medicaid benefits from an otherwise eligible candidate simply because that candidate had exercised her constitutionally protected freedom to terminate her pregnancy by abortion. This would be analogous to *Sherbert v. Verner,* 374 U.S. 398, where this Court held that a State may not, consistent with the First and Fourteenth Amendments, withhold *all* unemployment compensation benefits from a claimant who would otherwise be eligible for such benefits but for the fact that she is unwilling to work one day per week on her Sabbath. But the Hyde Amendment, unlike the statute at issue in *Sherbert,* does not provide for such a broad disqualification from receipt of public benefits. Rather, the Hyde Amendment, like the Connecticut welfare provision at issue in *Maher,* represents simply a refusal to subsidize certain protected conduct. A refusal to fund protected activity, without more, cannot be equated with the imposition of a "penalty" on that activity.

B

The appellees also argue that the Hyde Amendment contravenes rights secured by the Religion Clauses of the First Amendment. It is the appellees' view that the Hyde Amendment violates the Establishment Clause because it incorporates into law the doctrines of the Roman Catholic Church concerning the sinfulness of abortion and the time at which life commences. . . .

1

It is well settled that "a legislative enactment does not contravene the Establishment Clause if it has a secular legislative purpose, if its principal or primary effect neither advances nor inhibits religion, and if it does not foster an excessive governmental entanglement with religion." *Committee for Public Education v. Regan*, 444 U.S. 646, 653. Applying this standard, the District Court properly concluded that the Hyde Amendment does not run afoul of the Establishment Clause. Although neither a State nor the Federal Government can contitutionally "pass laws which aid one religion, aid all religions, or prefer one religion over another," *Everson v. Board of Education*, 330 U.S. 1, 15, it does not follow that a statute violates the Establishment Clause because it "happens to coincide or harmonize with the tenets of some or all religions." *McGowan v. Maryland*, 366 U.S. 420, 442. That the Judaeo-Christian religions oppose stealing does not mean that a State or the Federal Government may not, consistent with the Establishment Clause, enact laws prohibiting larceny. The Hyde Amendment, as the District Court noted, is as much a reflection of "traditionalist" values towards abortion, as it is an embodiment of the views of any particular religion. In sum, we are convinced that the fact that the funding restrictions in the Hyde Amendment may coincide with the religious tenets of the Roman Catholic Church does not, without more, contravene the Establishment Clause.

Appendix E

PLANNED PARENTHOOD OF SOUTHEASTERN PENNSYLVANIA V. CASEY

*505 U.S. 833 (1992)
(JOINT OPINION OF JUSTICES O'CONNOR,
KENNEDY, AND SOUTER – EXCERPTS, AND
DISSENT OF JUSTICE SCALIA – EXCERPTS)*

Justice O'CONNOR, Justice KENNEDY, and Justice SOUTER announced to the Court and delivered the opinion of the Court with respect to Parts I, II, III, V-A, V-C, and VI, an opinion with respect to Part V-E, in which Justice STEVENS joins, and an opinion with respect to Parts IV, V-B, and V-D.

I

Liberty finds no refuge in a jurisprudence of doubt. Yet 19 years after our holding that the Constitution protects a woman's right to terminate her pregnancy in its early stages, *Roe v. Wade*, 410 U.S. 113 (1973), that definition of liberty is still questioned. Joining the respondents as amicus curiae, the United States, as it has done in five other cases in the last decade, again asks us to overrule *Roe*. . . . After considering the fundamental constitutional questions resolved by *Roe*, principles of institutional integrity, and the rule of stare decisis, we are led to conclude this: the essential holding of *Roe v. Wade* should be retained and once again reaffirmed.

It must be stated at the outset and with clarity that *Roe's* essential holding, the holding we reaffirm, has three parts. First is a recognition of the right of the woman to choose to have an abortion before viability and to obtain it without undue interference from the State. Before viability, the State's interests are not strong enough to support a prohibition of abortion or the imposition of a substantial obstacle to the woman's effective right to elect the procedure. Second is a confirmation of the State's power to restrict abortions after fetal viability, if the law contains exceptions for pregnancies which endanger a woman's life or health. And third is the principle that the State

176

has legitimate interests from the outset of the pregnancy in protecting the health of the woman and the life of the fetus that may become a child. These principles do not contradict one another; and we adhere to each.

II

Constitutional protection of the woman's decision to terminate her pregnancy derives from the Due Process Clause of the Fourteenth Amendment. It declares that no State shall "deprive any person of life, liberty, or property, without due process of law." The controlling word in the case before us is "liberty." Although a literal reading of the Clause might suggest that it governs only the procedures by which a State may deprive persons of liberty, for a least 105 years, at least since *Mugler v. Kansas,* 123 U.S. 623, 660–661 (1887), the Clause has been understood to contain a substantive component as well, one "barring certain government actions regardless of the fairness of the procedures used to implement them." *Daniels v. Williams,* 474 U.S. 327, 331 (1986). As Justice BRANDEIS (joined by Justice HOLMES) observed, "[d]espite arguments to the contrary which had seemed to me persuasive, it is settled that the due process clause of the Fourteenth Amendment applies to matters of substantive law as well as to matters of procedure. Thus all fundamental rights comprised within the term liberty are protected by the Federal Constitution from invasion by the States." *Whitney v. California,* 274 U.S. 357, 373 (1927) (BRANDEIS, J., concurring). "[T]he guaranties of due process, though having their roots in Magna Carta's 'per legem terrae' and considered as procedural safeguards 'against executive usurpation and tyranny,' have in this country 'become bulwarks also against arbitrary legislation.'" *Poe v. Ullman,* 367 U.S. 497, 541 (1961) (HARLAN, J., dissenting from dismissal on jurisdictional grounds) . . .

It is also tempting, for the same reason, to suppose that the Due Process Clause protects only those practices, defined at the most specific level, that were protected against government interference by other rules of law when the Fourteenth Amendment was ratified. See *Michael H. v. Gerald D.,* 491 U.S. 110, 127–128, n 6 (1989) (opinion of SCALIA, J.). But such a view would be inconsistent with our law. It is a promise of the Constitution that there is a realm of personal liberty which the government may not enter. We have vindicated this principle before. Marriage is mentioned nowhere in the Bill of Rights and interracial marriage was illegal in most States in the 19th century, but the Court was no doubt correct in finding it to be an aspect of liberty protected against state interference by the substantive component of the Due Process Clause in *Loving v. Virginia,* 388 U.S. 1, 12 (1967) (relying, in an opinion for eight Justices, on the Due Process Clause).

Neither the Bill of Rights nor the specific practices of States at the time of the adoption of the Fourteenth Amendment marks the outer limits of the substantive sphere of liberty which the Fourteenth Amendment protects. See U.S. Const., Amend. 9.

The inescapable fact is that adjudication of substantive due process claims may call upon the Court in interpreting the Constitution to exercise that same capacity which by tradition courts always have exercised: reasoned judgment. Its boundaries are not susceptible of expression as a simple rule. That does not mean we are free to invalidate state policy choices with which we disagree; yet neither does it permit us to shrink from the duties of our office . . .

Men and women of good conscience can disagree, and we suppose some always shall disagree, about the profound moral and spiritual implications of terminating a pregnancy, even in its earliest stage. Some of us as individuals find abortion offensive to our most basic principles of morality, but that cannot control our decision. Our obligation is to define the liberty of all, not to mandate our own moral code. The underlying constitutional issue is whether the State can resolve these philosophic questions in such a definitive way that a woman lacks all choice in the matter, except perhaps in those rare circumstances in which the pregnancy is itself a danger to her own life or health, or is the result of rape or incest.

It is conventional constitutional doctrine that where reasonable people disagree the government can adopt one position or the other. See, e.g., *Ferguson v. Skrupa,* 373 U.S. 726 (1963); *Williamson v. Lee Optical of Oklahoma, Inc.,* 348 U.S. 483 (1955). That theorem, however, assumes a state of affairs in which the choice does not intrude upon a protected liberty. Thus, while some people might disagree about whether or not the flag should be saluted, or disagree about the proposition that it may not be defiled, we have ruled that a State may not compel or enforce one view or the other. See *West Virginia State Bd. of Education v. Barnette,* 319 U.S. 624 (1943); *Texas v. Johnson,* 491 U.S. 397 (1989).

Our law affords constitutional protection to personal decisions relating to marriage, procreation, contraception, family relationships, child rearing, and education. *Carey v. Population Services International,* 431 U.S. at 685. Our cases recognize "the right of the *individual,* married or single, to be free from unwarranted governmental intrusion into matters so fundamentally affecting a person as the decision whether to bear or beget a child." *Eisenstadt v. Baird,* (emphasis in original). Our precedents "have respected the private realm of family life which the state cannot enter." *Prince v. Massachusetts,* 321 U.S. 158, 166 (1944). These matters, involving the most intimate and personal choices a person may make in a lifetime, choices central to personal dignity and autonomy, are central to the liberty protected by the Fourteenth Amendment. At the heart of liberty is the right to define one's own concept of existence, of meaning, of the universe, and of the mystery of human life. Beliefs about these matters could not define the attributes of personhood were they formed under compulsion of the State.

These considerations begin our analysis of the woman's interest in terminating her pregnancy but cannot end it, for this reason: though the abortion decision may originate within the zone of conscience and belief, it is more than a philosophic exercise. Abortion is a unique act. It is an act fraught with consequences for others: for the woman who must live with the implications of her decision; for the persons who perform and assist in the procedure; for the spouse, family, and society which must confront the knowledge that these procedures exist, procedures some deem nothing short of an act of violence against innocent human life; and, depending on one's beliefs, for the life or potential life that is aborted. Though abortion is conduct, it does not follow that the State is entitled to proscribe it in all instances. That is because the liberty of the woman is at stake in a sense unique to the human condition so unique to the law. The mother who carries a child to full term is subject to anxieties, to physical constraints, to pain that only she must bear. That these sacrifices have from the beginning of the human race been endured by woman with a pride that ennobles her in the eyes of others and gives to the infant a bond of love cannot alone be grounds for the State to insist she make the sacrifice. Her suffering is too intimate and personal for the State to insist, without more, upon its own vision of the woman's role, however dominant that vision has been in the course of our history and our culture. The destiny of the woman must be shaped to a large extent on her own conception of her spiritual imperatives and her place in society.

It should be recognized, moreover, that in some critical respects the abortion decision is of the same character as the decision to use contraception, to which *Griswold v. Connecticut, Eisenstadt v. Baird,* and *Carey v. Populations Services International,* afford constitutional protection. We have no doubt as to the correctness of those decisions. They support the reasoning in *Roe* relating to the woman's liberty because they involve personal decisions concerning not only the meaning of procreation but also human responsibility and respect for it. As with abortion, reasonable people will have differences of opinion about these matters. One view is based on such reverence for the wonder of creation that any pregnancy ought to be welcomed and carried to full term no matter how difficult it will be to provide for the child and ensure its well-being. Another is that the inability to provide for the nurture and care of the infant is a cruelty to the child and an anguish to the parent. These are intimate views with infinite variations, and their deep, personal character underlay our decisions in *Griswold, Eisenstadt,* and *Carey.* The same concerns are present when the woman confronts the reality that, perhaps despite her attempts to avoid it, she has become pregnant.

It was this dimension of personal liberty that *Roe* sought to protect, and its holding invoked the reasoning and the tradition of the precedents we have discussed, granting protection to substantive liberties of the person. *Roe* was, of course, an extension of those cases and, as the decision itself indicated, the separate States could act in some degree to further their own legitimate interests in protecting prenatal life. The extent to which the legislatures of the States might act to outweigh the interests of the woman in choosing to terminate her pregnancy was a subject of debate both in *Roe* itself and in decisions following it.

While we appreciate the weight of the arguments made on behalf of the State in the case before us, arguments which in their ultimate formulation conclude that *Roe* should be overruled, the reservations any of us may have in reaffirming the central holding of *Roe* are outweighed by the explication of individual liberty we have given combined with the force of stare decisis. We turn now to that doctrine.

III

A

The obligation to follow precedent begins with necessity, and a contrary necessity marks its outer limit. With Cardozo, we recognize that no judicial system could do society's work if it eyed each issue afresh in every case that raised it. See B. Cardozo, *The Nature of the Judicial Process* 149 (1921). Indeed, the very concept of the rule of law underlying our own Constitution requires such continuity over time that a respect for precedent is, by definition, indispensable. See Powell, "Stare Decisis and Judicial Restraint," 1991 *Journal of Supreme Court History* 13, 16. At the other extreme, a different necessity would make itself felt if a prior judicial ruling should come to be seen so clearly as error that its enforcement was for that very reason doomed.

Even when the decision to overrule a prior case is not, as in the rare, latter instance, virtually foreordained, it is common wisdom that the rule of stare decisis is not an "inexorable command," and certainly it is not such in every constitutional case, see *Burnet v. Coronado Oil Gas Co.,* 285 U.S. 393, 405–411 (1932) (BRANDEIS, J., dissenting).

Rather, when this Court reexamines a prior holding, its judgment is customarily informed by a series of prudential and pragmatic considerations designed to test the consistency of overruling a prior decision with the ideal of the rule of law, and to gauge the respective costs of reaffirming and overruling a prior case. Thus, for example, we may ask whether the rule has proved to be intolerable simply in defying practical workability, *Swift & Co. v. Wickham,* 382 U.S. 111, 116 (1965); whether the rule is subject to a kind of reliance that would lend a special hardship to the consequences of overruling and add inequity to the cost of repudiation, e.g., *United States v. Title Ins. & Trust Co.,* 265 U.S. 472, 486 (1924); whether related principles of law have so far developed as to have left the old rule no more than a remnant of abandoned doctrine, see *Patterson v. McLean Credit Union,* 491 U.S. 164, 173–174 (1989); or whether facts have so changed or come to be seen so differently, as to have robbed the old rule of significant application or justification, e.g., *Burnet, supra,* at 412 (BRANDEIS, J., dissenting).

So in this case we may inquire whether *Roe's* central rule has been found unworkable; whether the rule's limitation on state power could be removed without serious inequity to those who have relied upon it or significant damage to the stability of the society governed by the rule in question; whether the law's growth in the intervening years has left *Roe's* central rule a doctrinal anachronism discounted by society; and whether *Roe's* premises of fact have so far changed in the ensuing two decades as to render its central holding somehow irrelevant or unjustifiable in dealing with the issue it addressed.

1

Although *Roe* has engendered opposition, it has in no sense proven "unworkable," see *Garcia v. San Antonio Metropolitan Transit Authority,* 469 U.S. 528, 546 (1985), representing as it does a simple limitation beyond which a state law is unenforceable. While *Roe* has, of course, required judicial assessment of state laws affecting the exercise of the choice guaranteed against government infringement, and although the need for such review will remain as a consequence of today's decision, the required determinations fall within judicial competence.

2

The inquiry into reliance counts the cost of a rule's repudiation as it would fall on those who have relied reasonably on the rule's continued application. Since the classic case for weighing reliance heavily in favor of following the earlier rule occurs in the commercial context where advance planning of great precision is most obviously a necessity, it is no cause for surprise that some would find no reliance worthy of consideration in support of *Roe*.

While neither respondents nor their amici in so many words deny that the abortion right invites some reliance prior to its actual exercise, one can readily imagine an argument stressing the dissimilarity of this case to one involving property or contract. Abortion is customarily chosen as an unplanned response to the consequence of unplanned activity or to the failure of conventional birth control, and except on the assumption that no intercourse would have occurred but for *Roe's* holding, such behavior may appear to justify no reliance claim. Even if reliance could be claimed on that unrealistic assumption, the argument might run, any reliance interest would be de minimis. This argument would be premised on the hypothesis that reproductive planning could take virtually immediate account of any sudden restoration of state authority to ban abortions.

To eliminate the issue of reliance that easily, however, one would need to limit cognizable reliance to specific instances of sexual activity. But to do this would be simply to refuse to face the fact that for two decades of economic and social developments, people have organized intimate relationships and made choices that define their views of themselves and their places in society, in reliance on the availability of abortion in the event that contraception should fail. The ability of women to participate equally in the economic and social life of the Nation has been facilitated by their ability to control their reproductive lives. See, e.g., R. Petchesky, *Abortion and Woman's Choice* 109, 133, n 7 (rev. ed. 1990). The Constitution serves human values, and while the effect of reliance on *Roe* cannot be exactly measured, neither can the certain cost of overruling *Roe* for people who have ordered their thinking and living around that case be dismissed.

No evolution of legal principle has left *Roe's* doctrinal footings weaker than they were in 1973. No development of constitutional law since the case was decided has implicitly or explicitly left *Roe* behind as a mere survivor of obsolete constitutional thinking.

It will be recognized, of course, that *Roe* stands at an intersection of two lines of decisions, but in whichever doctrinal category one reads the case, the result for present purposes will be the same. The *Roe* Court itself placed its holding in the succession of cases most prominently exemplified by *Griswold v. Connecticut,* 381 U.S. 479 (1965), see *Roe,* 410 U.S., at 152–153. When it is so seen, *Roe* is clearly in no jeopardy, since subsequent constitutional developments have neither disturbed, nor do they threaten to diminish, the scope of recognized protection accorded to the liberty relating to intimate relationships, the family, and decisions about whether or not to beget or bear a child. See, e.g., *Carey v. Population Services International,* 431 U.S. 678 (1977); *Moore v. East Cleveland,* 431 U.S. 494 (1977).

Roe, however, may be seen not only as an exemplar of *Griswold* liberty but as a rule (whether or not mistaken) of personal autonomy and bodily integrity, with doctrinal affinity to cases recognizing limits on governmental power to mandate medical treatment or to bar its rejection. If so, our cases since *Roe* accord with *Roe's* view that a State's interest in the protection of life falls short of justifying any plenary override of individual liberty claims. *Cruzan v. Director, Missouri Dept. of Health,* 497 U.S. 261, 278 (1990).

Finally, one could classify *Roe* as sui generis. If the case is so viewed, then there clearly has been no erosion of its central determination. The original holding resting on the concurrence of seven Members of the Court in 1973 was expressly affirmed by a majority of six in 1983, see *Akron v. Akron Center for Reproductive Health, Inc.,* 462 U.S. 416 (1983) (Akron I), and by a majority of five in 1986, see *Thornburgh v. American College of Obstetricians and Gynecologists,* 476 U.S. 747 (1986), expressing adherence to the constitutional ruling despite legislative efforts in some States to test its limits. More recently, in *Webster v. Reproductive Health Services,* 492 U.S. 490 (1989), although two of the present authors questioned the trimester framework in a way consistent with our judgment today. . .

Nor will courts building upon *Roe* be likely to hand down erroneous decisions as a consequence. Even on the assumption that the central holding of *Roe* was in error, that error would go only to the strength of the state interest in fetal protection, not to the recognition afforded by the Constitution to the woman's liberty. The latter aspect of the decision fits comfortably within the framework of the Court's prior decisions including *Skinner v. Oklahoma ex rel. Williamson,* 316 U.S. 535 (1942), *Griswold, supra, Loving v. Virginia,* 388 U.S. 1 (1967), and *Eisenstadt v. Baird,* 405 U.S. 438, 1029 (1972), the holdings of which are "not a series of isolated points," but mark a "rational continuum." *Poe v. Ullman,* 367 U.S., at 543 (1961) (HARLAN, J., dissenting). As we described in *Carey v. Population Services International, supra,* the liberty which encompasses those decisions

> "includes 'the interest in independence in making certain kinds of important decisions.' While the outer limits of this aspect of [protected liberty] have not been marked by the Court, it is clear that among the decisions that an individual may make without unjustified government interference are personal decisions 'relating to marriage, procreation, contraception, family relationships, and child rearing and education.'" *Id.,* at 684–685 (citations omitted).

The soundness of this prong of the *Roe* analysis is apparent from a consideration of the alternative. If indeed the woman's interest in deciding whether to bear and beget a child had not been recognized as in *Roe,* the State might as readily restrict a woman's right to choose to carry a pregnancy to term as to terminate it, to further asserted state interests in population control, or eugenics, for example. Yet *Roe* has been sensibly relied upon to counter any such suggestions. *E.g., Arnold v. Board of Education of Escambia County, Ala.,* 880 F.2d. 305, 311 (CA11 1989) (relying upon *Roe* and concluding that government officials violate the Constitution by coercing a minor to have an abortion); *Avery v. County of Burke,* 660 F.2d. 111, 115 (CA4 1981) (county agency inducing teenage girl to undergo unwanted sterilization on the basis of misrepresentation that she had sickle cell trait); see also *In re Quinlan,* 70 N.J. 10, 355 A.2d. 647, cert. denied sub nom *Garger v. New Jersey,* 429 U.S. 922, 50 L. Ed. 2d. 289, 97 S. Ct. 319 (1976) (relying on *Roe* in finding a right to terminate medical treatment). In any event, because *Roe's* scope is confined with post-conception potential life, a concern otherwise likely to be implicated only by some forms of contraception protected independently under *Griswold* and later cases, any error in *Roe* is unlikely to have serious ramifications in future cases.

4

We have seen how time has overtaken some of *Roe's* factual assumptions: advances in maternal health care allow for abortions safe to the mother later in pregnancy that was true in 1973, see *Akron I, supra,* at 429, n 11, and advances in neonatal care have advanced viability to a point somewhat earlier. But these facts go only to the scheme of time limits on the realization of competing interests, and the divergences from the factual premises of 1973 have no bearing on the validity of *Roe's* central holding, that viability marks the earliest point at which the State's interest in fetal life is constitutionally adequate to justify a legislative ban on nontherapeutic abortions. The soundness or unsoundness of that constitutional judgment in no sense turns on whether viability occurs at approximately 28 weeks, as was usual at the time of *Roe,* at 23 to 24 weeks, as it sometimes does today, or at some moment even slightly earlier in pregnancy, as it may if fetal respiratory capacity can somehow be enhanced in the future. Whenever it may occur, the attainment of viability may continue to serve as the critical fact, just as it has done since *Roe* was decided; which is to say that no change in *Roe's* factual underpinning has left its central holding obsolete, and none supports an argument for overruling it.

5

The sum of the precedential inquiry to this point shows *Roe's* underpinnings unweakened in any way affecting its central holding. While it has engendered disapproval, it has not been unworkable. An entire generation has come of age free to assume *Roe's* concept of liberty in defining the capacity of women to act in society, and to make reproductive decisions; no erosion of principle going to liberty or personal autonomy has left *Roe's* central holding a doctrinal remnant; *Roe* portends no developments at odds with other precedent for the analysis of personal liberty; and no changes of fact have rendered viability more or less appropriate as the point at which the balance of interests tips. Within the bounds of normal stare decisis analysis, then, and subject to the considerations on which it customarily turns, the stronger argument is for affirming *Roe's* central holding, with whatever degree of personal reluctance any of us may have, not for overruling it.

B

In a less significant case, stare decisis analysis could, and would, stop at the point we have reached. But the sustained and widespread debate *Roe* has provoked calls for some comparison between that case and others of comparable dimension that have responded to national controversies and taken on the impress of the controversies addressed. Only two such decisional lines lines from the past century present themselves for examination, and in each instance the result reached by the Court accorded with the principles we apply today.

The first example is that line of cases identified with *Lochner v. New York,* 198 U.S. 45 (1905), which imposed substantive limitations on legislation limiting economic autonomy in favor of health and welfare regulation, adopting, in Justice HOLMES', view the theory of laissez-faire. *Id.,* at 75 (HOLMES, J., dissenting). The *Lochner* decisions were exemplified by *Adkins v. Children's Hospital of D.C.,* 261 U.S. 525 (1923), in which this Court held it to be an infringement of constitutionally protected liberty of contract to require the employers of adult women to satisfy minimum wage standards. Fourteen years later, *West Coast Hotel Co. v. Parrish,* 300 U.S. 379 (1937), signalled the demise of *Lochner* by overruling *Adkins.* In the meantime, the Depression had come and, with it, the lesson that seemed unmistakable to most people by 1937, that the interpretation of contractual freedom in *Adkins* rested on fundamentally false factual assumptions about the capacity of a relatively unregulated market to satisfy minimal levels of human welfare. See *West Coast Hotel Co., supra,* at 399. As Justice JACKSON wrote of the constitutional crisis of 1937 shortly before he came on the bench, "The older world of laissez-faire was recognized everywhere outside the Court to be dead." R. Jackson, *The Struggle for Judicial Supremacy* 85 (1941). The facts upon which the earlier case had premised a constitutional resolution of social controversy had proved to be untrue, and history's demonstration of their untruth not only justified but required the new choice of constitutional principle that *West Coast Hotel* announced. Of course, it was true that the Court lost something by its misperception, or its lack of prescience, and the Court-packing crisis only magnified the loss; but the clear demonstration that the facts of economic life were different from those previously assumed warranted the repudiation of the old law.

The second comparison that 20th century history invites is with the cases employing the separate-but-equal rule for applying the Fourteenth Amendment's equal protection guarantee. They began with *Plessy v. Ferguson,* 163 U.S. 537 (1896), holding that legislatively mandated racial segregation in public transportation works no denial of equal protection, rejecting the argument that racial separation enforced by the legal machinery of American society treats the black race as inferior. The *Plessy* Court considered "the underlying fallacy of the plaintiff's argument to consist in the assumption that the enforced separation of the two races stamps the colored race with a badge of inferiority. If this be so, it is not by reason of anything found in the act, but solely because the colored race chooses to put that construction upon it." *Id.,* at 551. Whether, as a matter of historical fact, the Justices in the *Plessy* majority believed this or not, see *id.,* at 557, 562 (HARLAN, J., dissenting), this understanding of the implication of segregation was the stated justification for the Court's opinion. But this understanding of the facts and the rule it was stated to justify were repudiated in *Brown v. Board of Education,* 347 U.S. 483 (1954). As one commentator observed, the question before the Court in *Brown* was "whether discrimination inheres in that segregation which is imposed by law in the twentieth century in certain specific states in the American Union. And that question has meaning and can find an answer only on the ground of history and of common knowledge about the facts of life in the times and places aforesaid." Black, The Lawfulness of the Segregation Decisions, 69 Yale LJ 421, 427 (1960).

The Court in *Brown* addressed these facts of life by observing that whatever may have been the understanding in *Plessy's* time of the power of segregation to stigmatize those who were segregated with a "badge of inferiority," it was clear by 1954 that legally sanctioned segregation had just such an effect, to the point that racially separate public educational facilities were deemed inherently unequal. 347 U.S., at 494–495. Society's understanding of the facts upon which a constitutional ruling was sought in 1954 was thus fundamentally different from the basis claimed for the decision in 1896. While we think *Plessy* was wrong the day it was decided, see *Plessy, supra,* at 552–564 (HARLAN, J., dissenting), we must also recognize that the *Plessy* Court's explanation for its decision was so clearly at odds with the facts apparent to the Court in 1954 that the decision to reexamine *Plessy* was on this ground alone not only justified but required.

West Coast Hotel and *Brown* each rested on facts, or an understanding of facts, changed from those which furnished the claimed justifications for the earlier constitutional resolutions. Each case was comprehensible as the Court's response to facts that the country could understand, or had come to understand already, but which the Court of an earlier day, as its own declarations disclosed, had not been able to perceive. As the decisions were thus comprehensible they were also defensible, not merely as the victories of one doctrinal school over another by dint of numbers (victories though they were), but as applications of constitutional principle to facts as they had not been seen by the Court before. In constitutional adjudication as elsewhere in life, changed circumstances may impose new obligations, and the thoughtful part of the Nation could accept each decision to overrule a prior case as a response to the Court's constitutional duty.

Because the case before us presents no such occasion it could be seen as no such response. Because neither the factual underpinnings of *Roe's* central holding nor our understanding of it has changed (and because no other indication of weakened precedent has been shown) the Court could not pretend to be reexamining the prior law with any justification beyond a present doctrinal disposition to come out differently from the Court of 1973. To overrule prior law for no other reason than that would run counter to the view repeated in our cases, that a decision to overrule should rest on some special reason over and above the belief that a prior case was wrongly decided.

C

The examination of the conditions justifying the repudiation of *Adkins* by *West Coast Hotel* and *Plessy* by *Brown* is enough to suggest the terrible price that would have been paid if the Court had not overruled as it did. In the present case, however, as our analysis to this point makes clear, the terrible price would be paid for overruling. Our analysis would not be complete, however, without explaining why overruling *Roe's* central holding would not only reach an unjustifiable result under principles of stare decisis, but would seriously weaken the Court's capacity to exercise the judicial power and to function as the Supreme Court of a Nation dedicated to the rule of law. To understand why this would be so it is necessary to understand the source of this Court's authority, the conditions necessary for its preservation, and its relationship to the country's understanding of itself a constitutional Republic.

The root of American governmental power is revealed most clearly in the instance of the power conferred by the Constitution upon the Judiciary of the United States and specifically upon this Court. As Americans of each succeeding generation are rightly told, the Court cannot buy support for its decisions by spending money and, except to a minor degree, it cannot independently coerce obedience to its decrees. The Court's power lies, rather, in its legitimacy, a product of substance and perception that shows itself in the people's acceptance of the Judiciary as fit to determine what the Nation's law means and to declare what it demands.

The underlying substance of this legitimacy is of course the warrant for the Court's decisions in the Constitution and the lesser sources of legal principle on which the Court draws. That substance is expressed in the Court's opinions, and our contemporary understanding is such that a decision without principled justification would be no judicial act at all. But even when justification is furnished by apposite legal principle, something more is required. Because not every conscientious claim of principled justification will be accepted as such, the justification claimed must be beyond dispute. The Court must take care to speak and act in ways that allow people to accept its decisions on the terms the Court claims for them, as grounded truly in principle, not as compromises with social and political pressures having, as such, no bearing on the principled choices that the Court is obliged to make. Thus, the Court's legitimacy depends on making legally principled decisions under circumstances in which their principled character is sufficiently plausible to be accepted by the Nation.

The need for principled action to be perceived as such is implicated to some degree whenever this, or any other appellate court, overrules a prior case. This is not to say, of course, that this Court cannot give a perfectly satisfactory explanation in most cases. People understand that some of the Constitution's language is hard to fathom and that the Court's Justices are sometimes able to perceive significant facts or to understand principles of law that eluded their predecessors and that justify departures from existing decisions. However upsetting it may be to those most directly affected when one judicially derived rule replaces another, the country can accept some correction of error without necessarily questioning the legitimacy of the Court.

In two circumstances, however, the Court would almost certainly fail to receive the benefit of the doubt in overruling prior cases. There is, first, a point beyond which frequent overruling would overtax the country's belief in the Court's good faith. Despite the variety of reasons that may inform and justify a decision to overrule, we cannot forget that such a decision is usually perceived (and perceived correctly) as, at the least, a statement that a prior decision was wrong. There is a limit to the amount of error that can plausibly be imputed to prior courts. If that limit should be exceeded, disturbance of prior rulings would be taken as evidence that justifiable reexamination of principle had given way to drives for particular results in the short term. The legitimacy of the Court would fade with the frequency of its vacillation.

That first circumstance can be described as hypothetical; the second is to the point here and now. Where, in the performance of its judicial duties, the Court decides a case in such a way as to resolve the sort of intensely divisive controversy reflected in *Roe* and those rare, comparable cases, its decision has a dimension that the resolution of the normal case does not carry. It is the dimension present whenever the Court's interpretation of the Constitution calls the contending sides of a national controversy to end their national division by accepting a common mandate rooted in the Constitution.

The Court is not asked to do this very often, having thus addressed the Nation only twice in our lifetime, in the decisions of *Brown* and *Roe*. But when the Court does act in this way, its decision requires an equally rare precedential force to counter the inevitable efforts to overturn it and to thwart its implementation. Some of those efforts may be mere unprincipled emotional reactions; others may proceed from principles worthy of profound respect. But whatever the premises of opposition may be, only the most convincing justification under accepted standards of precedent could suffice to demonstrate that a later decision overruling the first was anything but a surrender to political pressure, and an unjustified repudiation of the principle on which the Court staked its authority in the first instance. So to overrule under fire in the absence of the most compelling reason to reexamine a watershed decision would subvert the Court's legitimacy beyond any serious question. Cf. *Brown v. Board of Education,* 349 U.S. 294, 300 (1955) (*Brown II*) ("[I]t should go without saying that the vitality of th[e] constitutional principles [announced in *Brown v. Board of Education,* 347 U.S. 483 (1954),] cannot be allowed to yield simply because of disagreement with them.")

The country's loss of confidence in the judiciary would be underscored by an equally certain and equally reasonable condemnation for another failing in overruling unnecessarily and under pressure. Some cost will be paid by anyone who approves or implements a constitutional decision where it is unpopular, or who refuses to work to undermine the decision or to force its reversal. The price may be criticism or ostracism, or it may be violence. An extra price will be paid by those who themselves disapprove of the decision's results when viewed outside of constitutional terms, but who nevertheless struggle to accept it, because they respect the rule of the law. To all those who will be so tested by following, the Court implicitly undertakes to remain steadfast, lest in the end a price be paid for nothing. the promise of constancy, once given, binds its maker for as long as the power to stand by the decision survives and the understanding of the issue has not changed so fundamentally as to render the commitment obsolete. From the obligation of this promise this Court cannot and should not assume any exemption when duty requires it to decide a case in conformance with the Constitution. A willing breach of it would be nothing less than a breach of faith, and no Court that broke its faith with the people could sensibly expect credit for principle in the decision by which it did that.

It is true that diminished legitimacy may be restored, but only slowly. Unlike the political branches, a Court thus weakened could not seek to regain its position with a new mandate from the voters, and even if the Court could somehow go to the polls, the loss of its principled character could not be retrieved by the casting of so many votes. Like the character of an individual, the legitimacy of the Court must be earned over time. So, indeed, must be the character of a Nation of people who aspire to live according to the rule of law. Their belief in themselves as such a people is not readily separable from their understanding of the Court invested with the authority to decide their constitutional cases and speak before all others for their constitutional ideas. If the Court's legitimacy should be undermined, then, so would the country be in its very ability to see itself through its constitutional ideals. The Court's concern with legitimacy is not for the sake of the Court but for the sake of the Nation to which it is responsible.

The Court's duty in the present case is clear. In 1973, it confronted the already-divisive issue of governmental power to limit personal choice to undergo abortion, for which it provided a new resolution based on the due process guaranteed by the Fourteenth Amendment. Whether or not a new social consensus is developing on that issue, its divisiveness is no less today than in 1973, and pressure to overrule the decision, like pressure to retain it, has grown only more intense. A decision to overrule *Roe's* essential holding under the existing circumstances would address error, if error there was, at the cost of both profound and unnecessary damage to the Court's legitimacy, and to the Nation's commitment to the rule of law. It is therefore imperative to adhere to the essence of *Roe's* original decision, and we do so today . . .

Justice SCALIA, with whom The CHIEF JUSTICE, Justice WHITE, and Justice THOMAS join, concurring in the judgment in part and dissenting in part.

My views on this matter are unchanged from those I set forth in my separate opinions in *Webster v. Reproductive Health Services,* 492 U.S. 490, 532 (1989) (SCALIA, J., concurring in part and concurring in judgment). The States may, if they wish, permit abortion-on-demand, but the Constitution does not *require* them to do so. The permissibility of abortion, and the limitations upon it, are to be resolved like most important questions in our democracy: by citizens trying to persuade one another and then voting. As the Court acknowledges, "where reasonable people disagree the government can adopt one position or the other." The Court is correct in adding the qualification that this "assumes a state of affairs in which the choice does not intrude upon a protected liberty,"—but the crucial part of that qualification is the penultimate word. A State's choice between two positions on which reasonable people can disagree is constitutional even when (as is often the case) it intrudes upon a "liberty" in the absolute sense. Laws against bigamy, for example—which entire societies of reasonable people disagree with—intrude upon men and women's liberty to marry and live with one another. But bigamy happens not to be a liberty specially "protected" by the Constitution.

That is, quite simply, the issue in this case: not whether the power of a woman to abort her unborn child is a "liberty" in the absolute sense; or even whether it is a liberty of great importance to many women. Of course it is both. The issue is whether it is a liberty protected by the Constitution of the United States. I am sure it is not. I reach that conclusion not because of anything so exalted as my views concerning the "concept of existence, of meaning, of the universe, and of the mystery of human life." *Ibid.* Rather, I reach it for the same reason I reach the conclusion that bigamy is not constitutionally protected—because of two simple facts: (1) the Constitution says absolutely nothing about it, and (2) the longstanding traditions of American society have permitted it to be legally proscribed.[1]

The Court destroys the proposition, evidently meant to represent my position, that "liberty" includes "only those practices, defined at the most specific level, that were protected against governmental interference by other rules of law when the Fourteenth

---

[1] The Court's suggestion that adherence to tradition would require us to uphold laws against interracial marriage is entirely wrong. Any tradition in that case was contradicted *by a text* — an Equal Protection Clause that explicitly establishes racial equality as a constitutional value. See *Loving v. Virginia,* 388 U.S. 1 (1967) ("In the case at bar, . . . we deal with statutes containing racial classifications, and the fact of equal application does not immunize the statute from the very heavy burden of justification which the Fourteenth Amendment has traditionally required of state statutes drawn according to race"); see also *id.,* at 13 (STEWART, J., concurring in judgment). The enterprise launched in *Roe,* by contrast, sought to *establish* — in the teeth of a clear, contrary tradition—a value found nowhere in the constitutional text.

There is, of course, no comparable tradition barring recognition of a "liberty interest" in carrying one's child to term free from state efforts to kill it. For that reason, it does not follow that the Constitution does not protect childbirth simply because it does not protect abortion. The Court's contention that the only way to protect childbirth is to protect abortion shows the utter bankruptcy of constitutional analysis deprived of tradition as a validating factor. It drives one to say that the only way to protect the right to eat is to acknowledge the constitutional right to starve oneself to death.

Amendment was ratified," (citing *Michael H. v. Gerald D.*, 491 U.S. 110, 127, n 6 (1989) (opinion of SCALIA, J.). That is not, however, what *Michael H.* says; it merely observes that, in defining "liberty," we may not disregard a specific, "relevant tradition protecting, or denying protection to, the asserted right," 491 U.S. at 127 n 6. But the Court does not wish to be fettered by any such limitations on its preferences. The Court's statement that it is "tempting" to acknowledge the authoritativeness of tradition in order to "cur[b] the discretion of federal judges" is of course rhetoric rather than reality; no government official is "tempted" to place restraints upon his own freedom of action, which is why Lord Acton did not say "Power tends to purify." The Court's temptation is in the quite opposite and more natural direction—towards systematically eliminating checks upon its own power; and it succumbs.

Beyond that brief summary of the essence of my position, I will not swell the United States Reports with repetition of what I have said before; and applying the rational basis test, I would uphold the Pennsylvania statute in its entirety. I must, however, respond to a few of the more outrageous arguments in today's opinion, which it is beyond human nature to leave unanswered. I shall discuss each of them under quotation from the Court's opinion to which they pertain.

> "The inescapable fact is that adjudication of substantive due process claims may call upon the Court in interpreting the Constitution to exercise that same capacity which by tradition courts always have exercised: reasoned judgment."

Assuming that the question before us it to be resolved at such a level of philosophical abstraction, in such isolation from the traditions of American society, as by simply applying "reasoned judgment," I do not see how that could possibly have produced the answer the Court arrived at in *Roe v. Wade*, 410 U.S. 113 (1973). Today's opinion describes the methodology of *Roe*, quite accurately, as weighing against the woman's interest the State's " 'important and legitimate interest in protecting the potentiality of human life.' " But "reasoned judgment" does not begin by begging the question, as *Roe* and subsequent cases unquestionably did by assuming that what the State is protecting is the mere "potentiality of human life."

The whole argument of abortion opponents is that what the Court calls the fetus and what others call the unborn child *is a human life*. Thus, whatever answer *Roe* came up with after conducting its "balancing" is bound to be wrong, unless it is correct that the human fetus is in some critical sense merely potentially human. There is of course no way to determine that as a legal matter; it is in fact a value judgment. Some societies have considered newborn children not yet human, or the incompetent elderly no longer so.

The authors of the joint opinion, of course, do not squarely contend that *Roe v. Wade* was a *correct* application of "reasoned judgment"; merely that it must be followed, because of stare decisis. But in their exhaustive discussion of all the factors that go into the determination of when stare decisis should be observed and when disregarded, they never mention "how wrong was the decision on its face?" Surely, if "[t]he Court's power lies . . . in its legitimacy, a product of substance and perception," the "substance" part of the equation demands that plain error be acknowledged and eliminated. *Roe* was plainly wrong—even on the Court's methodology of "reasoned judgment," and even more so (of course) if the proper criteria of text and tradition are applied.

The emptiness of the "reasoned judgment" that produced *Roe* is displayed in plain view by the fact that, after more that 19 years of effort by some of the brightest (and most determined) legal minds in the country after more than 10 cases upholding abortion rights in this Court, and after dozens upon dozens of amicus briefs submitted in this and other cases, the best the Court can do to explain how it is that the word "liberty" *must* be thought to include the right to destroy human fetuses is to rattle off a collection of adjectives that simply decorate a value judgment and conceal political choice. The right to abort, we are told, inheres in "liberty" because it is among "a person's most basic decisions," it involves a "most intimate and personal choic[e]," it is "central to personal dignity and autonomy," it "originate[s] within the zone of conscience and belief," it is "too intimate and personal" for state interference, it reflects "intimate views" of "deep, personal character," it involves "intimate relationships," and notions of "personal autonomy and bodily integrity," and it concerns a particularly "'important decision'" (citation omitted). But it is obvious to anyone applying "reasoned judgment" that the same adjectives can be applied to many forms of conduct that this Court (including one of the Justices in today's majority, see *Bowers v. Hardwick,* 478 U.S. 186 (1986)) has held are *not* entitled to constitutional protection—because, like abortion, they are forms of conduct that have long been criminalized in American society. Those adjectives might be applied, for example, to homosexual sodomy, polygamy, adult incest, and suicide, all of which are equally "intimate" and "deep[ly] personal" decisions involving "personal autonomy and bodily integrity," and all of which can constitutionally be proscribed because it is our unquestionable constitutional tradition that they are proscribable. It is not reasoned judgment that supports the Court's decision; only personal predilection. Justice CURTIS'S warning is as timely today as it was 135 years ago:

> "[W]hen a strict interpretation of the Constitution, according to the fixed rules which govern the interpretation of laws, is abandoned, and the theoretical opinions of individuals are allowed to control its meaning, we have no longer a Constitution; we are under the government of individual men, who for the time being have power to declare what the Constitution is, according to their own views of what it ought to mean." *Dred Scott v. Sandford,* 19 How. 393, 621 (1857) (CURTIS, J., dissenting).

"Liberty finds no refuge in a jurisprudence of doubt."

One might have feared to encounter this august and sonorous phrase in an opinion defending the real *Roe v. Wade,* rather than the revised version fabricated today by the authors of the joint opinion. The shortcomings of *Roe* did not include lack of clarity: Virtually all regulation of abortion before the third trimester was invalid. But to come across this phrase in the joint opinion—which calls upon federal district judges to apply an "undue burden" standard as doubtful in application as it is unprincipled in origin—is really more than one should have to bear.

The joint opinion frankly concedes that the amorphous concept of "undue burden" has been inconsistently applied by the Members of this Court in the few brief years since that "test" was first explicitly propounded by Justice O'Connor in her dissent in *Akron I, supra.* . . .

To the extent I can discern *any* meaningful content in the "undue burden" standard as applied in the joint opinion, it appears to be that a State may not regulate abortion in such a way as to reduce significantly its incidence. The joint opinion repeatedly emphasizes that an important factor in the "undue burden" analysis is whether the regulation "prevent[s] a significant number of women from obtaining an abortion," whether a "significant number of women . . . are likely to be deterred from procuring an abortion," *ibid.;* and whether the regulation often "deters" women from seeking abortions. We are not told, however, what forms of "deterrence" are impermissible or what degree of success in deterrence is too much to be tolerated. If, for example, a State required a woman to read a pamphlet describing, with illustrations, the facts of fetal development before she could obtain an abortion, the effect of such legislation might be to "deter" a "significant number of women" from procuring abortions, thereby seemingly allowing a district judge to invalidate it as an undue burden. Thus, despite flowery rhetoric about the State's "substantial" and "profound" interest in "potential human life," and criticism of *Roe* for undervaluing that interest, the joint opinion permits the State to pursue that interest only so long as it is not too successful. As Justice BLACKMUN recognizes (with evident hope), the "undue burden" standard may ultimately require the invalidation of each provision upheld today if it can be shown, on a better record, that the State is too effectively "express[ing] a preference for childbirth over abortion." Reason finds no refuge in this jurisprudence of confusion.

> "While we appreciate the weight of the arguments . . . that *Roe* should be overruled, the reservations any of us may have in reaffirming the central holding of *Roe* are outweighed by the explication of individual liberty we have given combined with the force of stare decisis."

The Court's reliance upon stare decisis can best be described as contrived. It insists upon the necessity of adhering not to all of *Roe*, but only to what it calls the "central holding." It seems to me that stare decisis ought to be applied even to the doctrine of stare decisis, and I confess never to have heard of this new, keep-what-you-want-and-throw-away-the-rest version. I wonder whether, as applied to *Marbury v. Madison,* 1 Cranch 137 (1803), for example, the new version of stare decisis would be satisfied if we allowed courts to review the constitutionality of only those statutes that (like the one in *Marbury*) pertain to the jurisdiction of the courts.

I am certainly not in a good position to dispute that the Court *has saved* the "central holding" of *Roe,* since to do that effectively I would have to know what the Court has saved, which in turn would require me to understand (as I do not) what the "undue burden" test means. I must confess, however, that I have always thought, and I think a lot of other people have always thought, that the arbitrary trimester framework, which the Court today discards, was quite as central to *Roe* as the arbitrary viability test, which the Court today retains. It seem particularly ungrateful to carve the trimester framework out of the core of *Roe*, since its very rigidity (in sharp contrast to the utter indeterminability of the "undue burden" test) is probably the only reason the Court is able to say, in urging stare decisis, that *Roe* "has in no sense proven 'unworkable.' " I suppose the Court is entitled to call a "central holding" whatever it wants to call a "central holding"—which is, come think of it, perhaps one of the difficulties with this modified version of stare decisis. I thought I might note, however, that the following portions of *Roe* have not been saved:

- Under *Roe,* requiring that a woman seeking an abortion be provided truthful information about abortion before giving informed written consent is unconstitutional, if the information is designed to influence her choice. Under the joint opinion's "undue burden" regime (as applied today, at least) such a requirement is constitutional.

- Under *Roe,* requiring that information be provided by a doctor, rather than a nonphysician counselors, is unconstitutional. Under the "undue burden" regime (as applied today, at least) it is not.

- Under *Roe,* requiring a 24-hour waiting period between the time the woman gives her informed consent and the time of the abortion is unconstitutional. Under the "undue burden" regime (as applied today, at least) it is not.

- Under *Roe,* requiring detailed reports that include demographic data about each woman who seeks an abortion and various information about each abortion is unconstitutional. Under the "undue burden" regime (as applied today, at least) it generally is not.

"Where, in the performance of its judicial duties, the Court decides a case in such a way as to resolve the sort of intensely divisive controversy reflected in Roe . . . , its decision has a dimension that the resolution of the normal case does not carry. It is the dimension present whenever the Court's interpretation of the Constitution calls the contending sides of a national controversy to end their national division by accepting a common mandate rooted in the Constitution."

The Court's description of the place of *Roe* in social history of the United States in unrecognizable. Not only did *Roe* not, as the Court suggests, *resolve* the deeply divisive issue of abortion; it did more than anything else to nourish it, by elevating it to the national level where it is infinitely more difficult to resolve. National politics were not plagued by abortion protests, national abortion lobbying, or abortion marches on Congress, before *Roe v. Wade* was decided. Profound disagreement existed among our citizens over the issue—as it does over other issues, such as the death penalty—but that disagreement was being worked out at the state level. As with many other issues, the division of sentiment within each State was not as closely balanced as it was among the population of the Nation as a whole, meaning not only that more people would be satisfied with the results of state-by-state resolution, but also that those results would be more stable. Pre-*Roe,* moreover, political compromise was possible.

Roe's mandate for abortion-on-demand destroyed the compromises of the past, rendered compromise impossible for the future, and required the entire issue to be resolved uniformly, at the national level. At the same time, *Roe* created a vast new class of abortion consumers and abortion proponents by eliminating the moral opprobrium that had attached to the act. ("If the Constitution "guarantees" abortion, how can it be bad?"—not an accurate line of thought, but a natural one.) Many favor all of those developments, and it is not for me to say that they are wrong. But to portray *Roe* as the statesmanlike "settlement" of a divisive issue, a jurisprudential Peace of Westphalia that is worth preserving is nothing less than Orwellian. *Roe* fanned into life an issue that has inflamed our national politics in general, and has obscured with its smoke the selection of Justices to this Court in particular, ever since. And by keeping us in the abortion umpiring business, it is the perpetuation of that disruption, rather than of any pax Roeana, that the Court's new majority decrees.

> "[T]o overrule under fire . . . would subvert the Court's legitimacy . . .

> "To all those who will be . . . tested by following, the Court implicitly undertakes to remain steadfast. . . The promise of constancy, once given, binds its maker for as long as the power to stand by the decision survives and . . . the commitment [is not] obsolete . . .

> "[The American people's] belief in themselves as . . . a people [who aspire to live according to the rule of the law] is not readily separable from their understanding of the Court invested with the authority to decide their constitutional cases and speak before all others for their constitutional ideals. If the Court's legitimacy should be undermined, then, so would the country be in its very ability to see itself through its constitutional ideals."

The Imperial Judiciary lives. It is instructive to compare this Nietzschean vision of us unelected, lifetenured judges—leading a Volk who will be "tested by following," is mystically bound up in their "understanding" of a Court that "speak[s] before all others for their constitutional ideals"—with the somewhat more modest role envisioned for these lawyers by the Founders.

> "The judiciary . . . has . . . no direction either of the strength or of the wealth of the society, and can take no active resolution whatever. It may truly be said to have

neither FORCE nor WILL but merely judgment . . ." *The Federalist* No. 78, pp 393–394 (G. Wills ed 1982).

Or, again, to compare this ecstasy of a Supreme Court in which there is, especially on controversial matters, no shadow of change or hint of alteration ("There is a limit to the amount of error that can plausibly be imputed to prior courts," with the more democratic views of a more humble man:

> "[T]he candid citizen must confess that if the policy of the Government upon vital questions affecting the whole people is to be irrevocably fixed by decisions of the Supreme Court, . . . the people will have ceased to be their own rulers, having to that extent practically resigned their Government into the hands of that eminent tribunal." A. Lincoln, First Inaugural Address (Mar. 4, 1861), reprinted in *Inaugural Addresses of the Presidents of the United States*, S. Doc. No. 101–10, p. 139 (1989). . . .

I cannot agree with, indeed I am appalled by, the Court's suggestion that the decision whether to stand by an erroneous constitutional decision must be strongly influenced—*against* overruling, no less—by the substantial and continuing public opposition the decision has generated. The Court's judgment that any other course would "subvert the Court's legitimacy" must be another consequence of reading the error-filled history book that described the deeply divided country brought together by *Roe*. In my history book, the Court was covered with dishonor and deprived of legitimacy by *Dred Scott v. Sandford,* 19 How. 393 (1857), an erroneous (and widely opposed) opinion that it did not abandon, rather than by *West Coast Hotel Co. v. Parrish,* 300 U.S. 379 (1937), which produced the famous "switch in time" from the Court's erroneous (and widely opposed) constitutional opposition to the social measures of the New Deal. (Both *Dred Scott* and one line of the cases resisting the New Deal rested upon the concept of "substantive due process" that the Court praises and employs today. Indeed, *Dred Scott* was "very possibly the first application of substantive due process in the Supreme Court, the original precedent for *Lochner v. New York* and *Roe v. Wade*." D. Currie, The Constitution in the Supreme Court 271 (1985) (footnotes omitted).)

But whether it would "subvert the Court's legitimacy" or not, the notion that we would decide a case differently from the way we otherwise would have in order to show that we can stand firm against public disapproval is frightening. It is a bad enough idea, even in the head of someone like me, who believes that the text of the Constitution, and our traditions, say what they say and there is no fiddling with them. But when it is in the mind of a Court that believes the Constitution has an evolving meaning, that the Ninth Amendment's reference to "othe[r]" rights is not a disclaimer, but a charter for action, and that the function of this Court is to "speak before all others for [the people's] constitutional ideals" unrestrained by meaningful text or tradition—then the notion that the Court must adhere to a decision for as long as the decision faces "great opposition" and the Court is "under fire" acquires a character of almost czarist arrogance. We are offended by these marchers who descend upon us, every year on the anniversary of *Roe,* to protest our saying the Constitution requires what our society has never thought the Constitution requires. These people who refuse to be "tested by following" must be taught a lesson. We have no Cossacks, but at least we can stubbornly refuse to abandon an erroneous opinion that we might otherwise change—to show how little they intimidate us.

Of course, as THE CHIEF JUSTICE points out, we have been subjected to what the Court calls "political pressure" by *both* sides of this issue. Maybe today's decision *not* to overrule *Roe* will be seen as buckling to pressure from *that* direction. Instead of engaging in the hopeless task of predicting public perception—a job not for lawyers but for political campaign managers—the Justices should do what is *legally* right by asking two questions: (1) Was *Roe* correctly decided? (2) Has *Roe* succeeded in producing a settled body of law? If the answer to both questions is no, *Roe* should undoubtedly be overruled.

In truth, I am as distressed as the Court is—and expressed my distress several years ago, see *Webster,* 492 U.S., at 535—about the "political pressure" directed to the Court: the marches, the mail, the protests aimed at inducing us to change our opinions. How upsetting it is, that so many of our citizens (good people, not lawless ones, on both sides of this abortion issue, and on various sides of other issues as well) think that we Justices should properly take into account their views, as though we were engaged not in ascertaining an objective law but in determining some kind of social consensus. The Court would profit, I think, from giving less attention to the *fact* of this distressing phenomenon, and more attention to the *cause* of it. That cause permeates today's opinion: a new mode of constitutional adjudication that relies not upon text and traditional practice to determine the law, but upon what the Court calls "reasoned judgment," which turns out to be nothing but philosophical predilection and moral intuition. All manner of "liberties," the Court tells us, inhere in the Constitution and are enforceable by this Court—not just those mentioned in the text or established in the traditions of our society. Why even the Ninth Amendment—which says only that "[t]he enumeration in the Constitution of certain rights shall not be construed to deny or disparage others retained by the people"—is, despite our contrary understanding for almost 200 years, a literally boundless source of additional, unnamed, unhinted-at "rights," definable and enforceable by us, through "reasoned judgment."

What makes all this relevant to the bothersome application of "political pressure" against the Court are the twin facts that the American people love democracy and the American people are not fools. As long as this Court thought (and the people thought) that we Justices were doing essentially lawyers' work up here—reading text and discerning our society's traditional understanding of that text—the public pretty much left us alone. Texts and traditions are facts to study, not convictions to demonstrate about. But if in reality our process of constitutional adjudication consists primarily of making *value judgments;* if we can ignore a long and clear tradition clarifying an ambiguous text, as we did, for example, five days ago in declaring unconstitutional invocations and benedictions at public-high-school graduation ceremonies, *Lee v. Weisman,* 505 U.S.— —, (1992); if, as I say, our pronouncement of constitutional law rests primarily on value judgments, then a free and intelligent people's attitude towards us can be expected to be (*ought* to be) quite different. The people know that their value judgments are quite as good as those taught in any law school—maybe better. If, indeed, the "liberties" protected by the Constitution are, as the Court says, undefined and unbounded, then the people *should* demonstrate, to protest that we do not implement *their* values instead of *ours.* Not only that, but confirmation hearings for new Justices *should* deteriorate into question-and-answer sessions in which Senators go through a list of their constituents' most favored and most disfavored alleged constitutional rights, and seek the nominee's commitment to support or oppose them. Value judgments, after all, should be voted on, not dictated; and if our Constitution has somehow accidently committed them to the Supreme Court, at least we can have a sort of plebiscite each time a new nominee to that body is put forward."

There is a poignant aspect to today's opinion. Its length, and what might be called its epic tone, suggest that its authors believe they are bringing to an end a troublesome era in the history of our Nation and of our Court. "It is the dimension" of authority, they say, to "cal[l] the contending sides of national controversy to end their national division by accepting a common mandate rooted in the Constitution."

201

There comes vividly to mind a portrait by Emanuel Leutze that hangs in the Harvard Law School: Roger Brooke Taney, painted in 1859, the 82d year of his life, the 24th of his Chief Justiceship, the second after his opinion in *Dred Scott*. He is all in black, sitting in a shadowed red armchair, left hand resting upon a pad of paper in his lap, right hand hanging limply, almost lifelessly, beside the inner arm of the chair. He sits facing the viewer, and staring straight out. There seems to be on his face, and in his deep-set eyes, an expression of profound sadness and disillusionment. Perhaps he always looked that way, even when dwelling upon the happiest of thoughts. But those of us who know how the lustre of his great Chief Justiceship came to be eclipsed by *Dred Scott* cannot help believing that he had that case—its already apparent consequences for the Court, and its soon-to-be-played-out consequences for the Nation—burning on his mind. I expect that two years earlier he, too, had thought himself "call[ing] the contending sides of national controversy to end their national division by accepting a common mandate rooted in the Constitution."

It is no more realistic for us in this case, than it was for him in that, to think that an issue of the sort they both involved—an issue involving life and death, freedom and subjugation—can be "speedily and finally settled" by the Supreme Court, as President James Buchanan in his inaugural address said the issue of slavery in the territories would be. See *Inaugural Addresses of the Presidents of the United States*, S. Doc. No. 101–10, p. 126 (1989). Quite to the contrary, by foreclosing all democratic outlet for the deep passions this issue arouses, by banishing the issue from the political forum that gives all participants, even the losers, the satisfaction of a fair hearing and an honest fight, by continuing the imposition of allowing for regional differences, the Court merely prolongs and intensifies the anguish.

We should get out of this area, where we have no right to be, and where we do neither ourselves nor the country any good by remaining.

Bibliography

The literature on abortion as a constitutional issue is quite large. Because the constitutional law of abortion has changed, as have the politics associated with that law, much of the legal literature in particular has been rapidly outdated. In addition, the literature tends to be highly partisan. Two studies explaining why are by a sociologist and an anthropologist, who examine the cultural significance of the abortion controversy: Kristin Luker, *Abortion and the Politics of Motherhood* (Berkeley: University of California Press, 1984); Faye D. Ginsburg, *Contested Lives: The Abortion Debate in an American Community* (Berkeley: University of California Press, 1989). A useful overview from a generally pro-choice perspective is Laurence H. Tribe, *Abortion: The Clash of Absolutes* (New York: W. W. Norton, 1990). An important resource is the series edited by J. Douglas Butler and David F. Walbert, *Abortion, Medicine, and the Law* (New York: Facts on File). The current edition, published in 1992, is the fourth, but articles in earlier editions remain useful.

The articles in Randy E. Barnett, ed., *The Rights Retained by the People* (vols. 1 and 2, Fairfax, Virginia: George Mason University Press, 1989, 1993), provide a full treatment of the questions associated with judicial enforcement on unenumerated constitutional rights. Judith Jarvis Thompson's article, "A Defense of Abortion," is widely reprinted in collections that provide additional philosophical perspectives on abortion. Joel Feinberg. ed., *The Problem of Abortion* (2nd ed., Belmont, California: Wadsworth Publishing Co., 1984), includes most of the important articles, and has a good short bibliography. A sophisticated and difficult recent elaboration of a position related to Thompson's is F. M. Kamm, *Creation and Abortion: A Study in Moral and Legal Philosophy* (New York: Oxford University Press, 1992). Another useful collection is Jay L. Garfield and Patricia Hennessey, *Abortion: Moral and Legal Perspectives* (Amherst: University of Massachusetts Press, 1984), although its articles about law are dated. A pre-*Roe* collection from a generally antiabortion perspective is John J. Noonan, Jr., ed., *The Morality of Abortion: Legal and Historical Perspectives* (Cambridge: Harvard University Press, 1970). Noonan's post-*Roe* contribution is *A Private Choice: Abortion in America in the Seventies* (New York: Free Press, 1979).

David J. Garrow, *Liberty and Sexuality: The Right to Privacy and the Making of* Roe v. Wade (New York: Macmillan, 1994), is the most important study of the twentieth-century campaigns against Connecticut's anti-contraceptive law and for abortion law reform. Garrow's massively researched work displaces all previous historical accounts. It includes detailed accounts of the Supreme Court's deliberations in *Griswold* and the abortion cases. Additional details are provided in John C. Jeffries, Jr., *Justice Lewis F. Powell, Jr.: A Biography* (New York: Charles Scribner's Sons, 1994), which was not available to Garrow. Two of the leading participants in the litigation have written about their involvement: Sarah Weddington, *A Question of Choice* (New York: G.P. Putnam's Sons, 1992); Norma McCorvey, *I am Roe: My Life,* Roe v. Wade, *and Freedom of Choice* (New York: HarperCollins, 1994). Interviews with activists on both sides provide the basis for Fred M. Frohock, *Abortion: A Case Study in Law and Morals* (Westport, Connecticut.: Greenwood Press, 1983).

The politics of abortion during the 1970s and 1980s are treated in Eva R. Rubin, *Abortion, Politics, and the Courts:* Roe v. Wade *and Its Aftermath* (Westport, Connecticut: Greenwood Press, 1982); Carl E. Schneider and Maris Vinovskis, eds., *The Law and Politics of Abortion* (Lexington, Massachusetts.: Lexington Books, 1980), in part 2; Raymond, Tatalovich and Byron W. Daynes, *The Politics of Abortion: A Study of Community Conflict in Public Policymaking* (New York: Praeger, 1981). A journalistic account is Catherine Whitney, *Whose Life?* (New York: William Morrow, 1991). Edward Keynes, with Randall K. Miller, *The Court vs. Congress: Prayer, Busing, and Abortion* (Durham: Duke University Press, 1989), discusses the constitutionality of congressional efforts to overturn *Roe v. Wade* by restricting judicial review.

The leading comparative study of abortion is Mary Ann Glendon, *Abortion and Divorce in Western Law: American Failures, European Challenges* (Cambridge: Harvard University Press, 1987). Reviews include Leslie Pickering Francis, *Harvard Law Review* 102 (1988): 469; Jane Maslow Cohen, *Yale Law Journal* 98 (1989): 1235; Lauren Robel, *Constitutional Commentary* 6 (1989): 131; and Katharine T. Bartlett, *Duke Law Journal* 1987 (1987): 760.

J. M. Kelly, *The Irish Constitution* (3rd ed., Gerard Hogan and Gerry White eds., Dublin: Butterworths, 1994), pp. 790–810, is the standard exposition of Irish constitutional law. For additional perspectives on the Irish experience, see Gerard Hogan, "Law, Liberty and the Abortion Controversy," in *Law and Liberty in Ireland* (Anthony Whelan, ed., Dublin: Oak Tree Press, 1993), pp. 113–19; Peter Charleton, "Judicial Discretion in Abortion: The Irish Perspective," *International Journal of Law and the Family* 6 (1992): 349; Brian Wilkinson, "Abortion, the Irish Constitution and the EEC,"

Public Law 1992 (1992): 10; and Marie Fox and Therese Murphy, "Irish Abortion: Seeking Refuge in a Jurisprudence of Doubt and Delegation," *Journal of Law and Society* 19 (1992): 454.

The Canadian experience is described in F. L. Morton, *Pro-Choice vs. Pro-Life: Abortion and the Courts in Canada* (Norman: University of Oklahoma Press, 1993), and analyzed from a feminist perspective in Janine Brodie, Shelley A. M. Gavigan, and Jane Jenson, *The Politics of Abortion* (Toronto: Oxford University Press, 1992). Glendon's views on *Morgentaler* are in "*A Beau Mentir Qui Vient de Loin*: The 1988 Canadian Abortion Decision in Comparative Perspective," *Northwestern University Law Review* 83 (1989): 569.

For Germany, Donald Kommers, "The Constitutional Law of Abortion in Germany: Should Americans Pay Attention?", *Journal of Contemporary Health Law and Policy* 10 (1994): 1, describes the events. An earlier analysis is Donald Kommers, "Liberty and Community in Constitutional Law: The Abortion Cases in Comparative Perspective," *Brigham Young University Law Review* 1985 (1985): 371. Gabriele Czarnowski, "Abortion as Political Conflict in the Unified Germany," *Parliamentary Affairs* 47 (1994): 252, provides details on the post-unification events. Albin Eser, "Abortion law reform in Germany in international comparative perspective," *European Journal of Health Law* 1 (1994): 15, places the events in a larger framework. Additional essays on abortion law and politics outside the United States are in a special issue of *Parliamentary Affairs* 47 (April 1994).

A short summary of the "critique of rights" is Mark Tushnet, "The Critique of Rights," *SMU Law Review* 47 (1993): 23. A more extensive presentation, describing and addressing some criticisms of that position, is Mark Tushnet, "Rights: An Essay in Informal Political Theory," *Politics & Society* 17 (1989): 403.

The *Cruzan* case is discussed in Melvin Urofsky, *Letting Go: Death, Dying, and the Law* (New York: Charles Scribner's Sons, 1993). A legal analysis, on which the discussion in Chapter 4 relies, is Louis Michael Seidman, "Confusion at the Border: *Cruzan*, the 'Right to Die,' and the Public/Private Distinction," *Supreme Court Review* 1992 (1992): 47.

Index